GIDLEIGH

GIDLEIGH

A DARTMOOR VILLAGE
PAST AND PRESENT

TONY GRUMLEY-GRENNAN
AND
MICHAEL HARDY

GLEBE PUBLISHING

First published in the United Kingdom in 2000 by
Glebe Publishing
Glebe Farm, Gidleigh, Devon, TQ13 8HT

British Library Cataloguing in Publication Data
A catalogue record for this book is available from the British Library.

ISBN 0-9538922-0-4

Designed by A&L Design
Printed in the UK by Butler & Tanner, Frome, Somerset

CONTENTS

INTRODUCTION   1

MAP OF GIDLEIGH   4

CHAPTER I. GENERAL HISTORY   7

CHAPTER 2. THE BUILDINGS AND THE PEOPLE   21

CHAPTER 3. FARMING AND LAND USE   161

APPENDIX 1. RECTORS OF GIDLEIGH   179

APPENDIX 2. THE LETTERS PATENT OF HENRY VIII   183

BIBLIOGRAPHY   195

INDEX   197

INTRODUCTION

To put things into perspective straight away, Gidleigh is not a big place - it covers about 3,500 acres, has a population of just over 100, around 40 houses and an awful lot of sheep. There is a church, a ruined castle, a village hall, a world-famous hotel and a postman, but no pub or shop. It is situated in the middle of Devon on the north-east slopes of Dartmoor, 24 miles from Exeter and midway between Bideford in the north and Torbay to the south.

Visitors leave before realising they have arrived. The road signs are designed for farm deliveries and ignore the fact that people may wish to go elsewhere. The lanes, created in another age, meander through the countryside as though built by workmen keen to keep their backs to the sun. It has been described as 'scattered', a village with no centre, lost in time, a haven and 'a rough poor place' - but we love it.

We hope it is accurate but beg forgiveness if we have failed to mention all that could be mentioned, or have included stories that are not totally correct. We have invited contributions from everyone and have tried to relate faithfully the facts as they were presented to us.

Many people have helped with this venture. In particular we would like to thank Alice Wells for her exhaustive research on our behalf at the Devon Record Office, Felicity Capper for the excellent drawings of many of the houses and William Hannaford and Chris Chapman for the photographs old and new. Louise Cole brought a skilled hand to the design and layout of the book and without her professional help and advice the book would never have been published. We wish to thank the Ordnance Survey for permission to reproduce the map of Gidleigh and the Trustees of the British Museum for permission to reproduce the photograph of the Gidley medal. We are also grateful to Mr

John Somers Cocks for permission to reproduce the map of Dartmoor and the border parishes and we would like to thank the staff of the West Country Studies Library in Exeter for their assistance.

We should like in addition to thank all those who have kindly lent photographs from their own collections for inclusion in the book.

Our chief debt of gratitude, however, is owed to our fellow residents of Gidleigh who have so patiently dealt with much badgering and questions.

The profits from sales of the book will be contributed to the future maintenance and upkeep of the Village Hall.

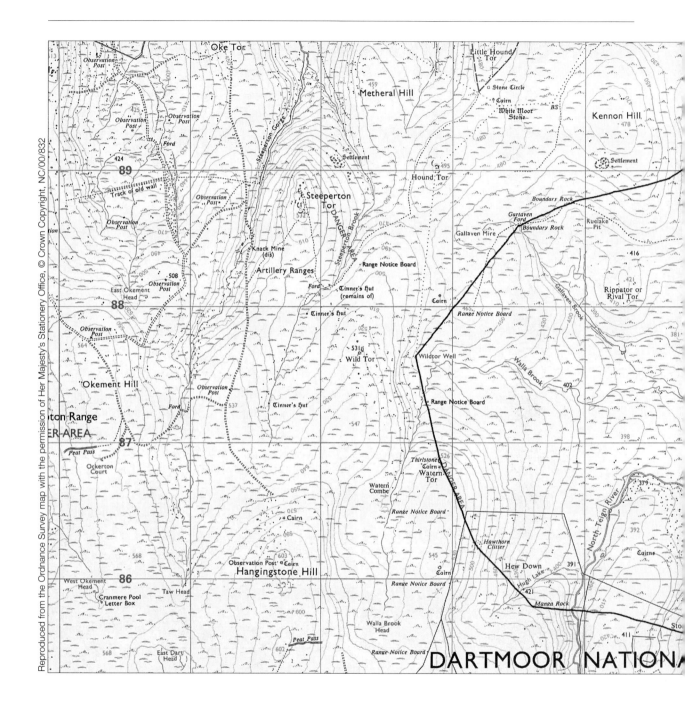

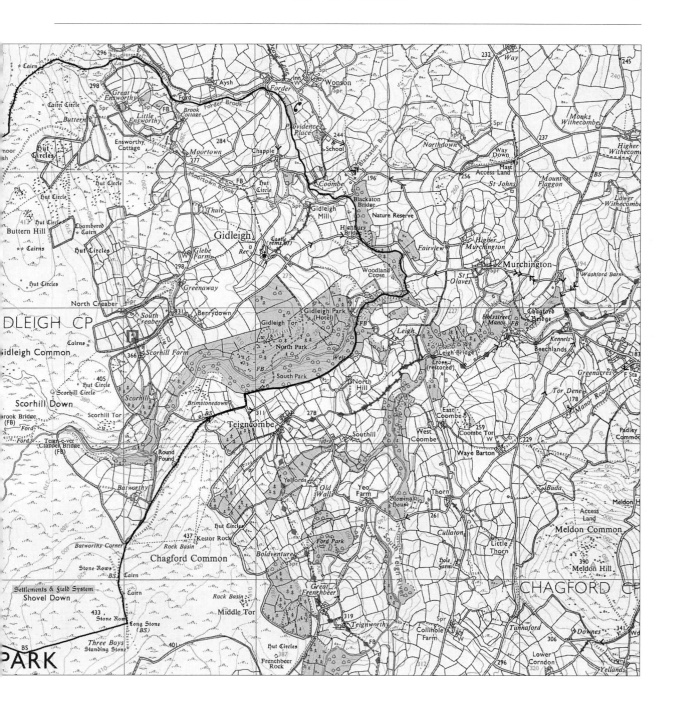

CHAPTER ONE

GENERAL HISTORY

The first evidence of human life on Dartmoor dates from the late Mesolithic period around 5000 BC. Quantities of worked flints of this period have been found on Gidleigh Common and other sites on the north-east foothills of the Moor. Hunter-gatherers who occupied the Moor seasonally were active at this stage. By the time of the New Stone Age, around 3,500 BC, there may have been settlers on the Moor but the size of the population or how much of Dartmoor was occupied at this period is unknown.[1]

The ceremonial monuments such as Scorhill Circle and the stone rows at Shovel Down are believed to have been constructed by the indigenous population around 2000 BC, during the late Neolithic or early Bronze Age. The settlement sites (hut circles, enclosures and fields) are probably a little later, say around the middle of the Second Millennium BC. Good examples of hut circles and reaves (Bronze Age field boundaries) are to be seen on Buttern Hill. Settlements were gradually abandoned in late prehistoric times, however, perhaps because of climatic changes. Occupation in the Kestor area, for example, seems to have extended into the Iron Age before petering out. Pottery from around 1000-500 BC was found in excavations at the Round Pound near Batworthy.

Gidleigh and the surrounding area thus have an array of prehistoric remains, ranging from the ceremonial to the domestic. The field boundaries in use today around Scorhill and Creaber, for example, are prehistoric in origin, 3,500 years old, while Scorhill Circle (circa 2000 BC) is one of the best preserved of the major monuments, still mysterious when you come across it on a rainy day.

There is no trace of Roman tin workings, coins or pottery and little evidence can be found of

---

[1] For further information on the early prehistory, see S Gerrard, *Dartmoor,* and the excellent National Park publications, *A Guide to the Archaeology of Dartmoor,* and *The Archaeology of Dartmoor from the Air.* J Butler, *Dartmoor Atlas of Archaeology, Vol Two - The North,* contains maps, plans and detailed descriptions of the archaeology on the Moor, including Gidleigh.

intensive farming or permanent dwellings during the Celtic period, still recorded, it is said, in the name of the Wallabrook (Walla or Welsh). As the Saxons under Cenwealh pushed their way west-ward in the mid 7th century AD larger settlements and more systematic farming began around the Moor. There appears to have been an improvement in the climate towards the end of the First Millennium AD which led to a growth in population and the start of colonisation of the moorland fringes which had been abandoned in prehistoric times. The story of Gidleigh as a distinct settle-ment really begins a thousand years ago, during the 11th century.

The name Gidleigh derives from the Saxon word "leah" or "leigh", meaning a clearing, and pos-sibly that of Gydda or Gytha, the name of a Danish princess and the sister-in-law of King Canute (Cnut), who ruled Denmark, Norway and England between 1017 and 1035. In 1019 she married Earl Godwine of Wessex, a principal Saxon nobleman who governed most of southern England. Gytha had extensive lands in Devon, including the large manor of Tawton of which Gidleigh may have originally formed part. [2] The name was spelt "Ghiderleia" in the Domesday Book, which is the first written evidence we have, "Giddeleia" in the 12th century, with other variations over the years ("Gydleghe" etc) until settling down to "Gidley" or "Gidleigh".

Gytha, who must have been a remarkable woman, had a large number of children (nine by all accounts), including Edith (AEdgytha) who married King Edward the Confessor (reigned 1042-1066) and the famous King Harold (Godwineson), who was killed at the Battle of Hastings in 1066. After the Battle she retreated to Exeter and helped organise the defence of the city until its surren-der to William's forces in 1068. The Anglo-Saxon Chronicle records that Gytha escaped "with the

---

[2] While there is no direct documentary tie there is considerable circumstantial evidence linking Gytha with Gidleigh, besides the isimilarity of the name. She held Tawton and the notion that Gidleigh was an offshoot of that manor has the support of Reichel, who remains an accepted authority O Reichel, 'The Hundred of South Tawton in Early Times', *Trans. Dev. Assoc.,* vol 44, (1912), p. 343. East Ash, only a few miles from Gidleigh, was a separate holding within South Tawton (and remains part of that parish). Gytha was a keen supporter of the Church and the founding of a church at the settlement at Gidleigh might have appealed when the new diocese was being established at Exeter in 1050 in which her daughter, Queen Edith (AEdgytha) played a leading part and where her husband participated. Lastly, as Reichel points out, the Exeter scribe was not a native of Devon and spelt the name Gytha in various ways in the Domesday Book, perhaps because of the local pronunciation (*Victoria History of Devon*, Part 2, 1906, p. 79). On the background generally, see I Walker, *Harold: the Last Anglo-Saxon King,* A Williams, *The English and the Norman Conquest,* and P Stafford, *Queen Emma and Queen Edith.*

wives of many good men" to an island in the Bristol Channel named Flatholme. From there she fled, with Harold's sister and his daughter, also called Gytha, taking with her "a good part of treasure", to St Omer in Flanders. She is thought to have died in Bruges a few years later. Her granddaughter Gytha went on to Denmark, where the King was a distant cousin, and from there to Russia where in 1074 she married one of the Grand Princes of Kiev. [3]

The wealth of the Godwine family prior to the Conquest can be gauged by the fact that of the land held by the 350 women mentioned in the Domesday Book about half was in the possession of three women: Queen Edith (Harold's sister), Gytha (his mother, the widow of Earl Godwine) and Edith, Harold's wife by Danish Law.

Under the Norman settlement William the Conqueror's half brother, Robert, Earl of Mortain, was granted the manor of Gidleigh amongst almost 800 estates he received in the south-west as a reward for his services. The entry in the Domesday Book, which was compiled in 1086, is short:

> "*Godwin the Priest holds Gidleigh from the Count. He held it himself before 1066. It paid tax for 3 furlongs. Land for 1 plough…Value 5sh.*" [4]

The land was only about 100 acres, enough for one oxen driven plough. By way of comparison, Throwleigh had 8 ploughs (value £4), Chagford 6 ploughs and South Tawton 50 ploughs (£48). The original clearing was thus small, situated in the midst of virtually untamed country.

The period immediately after the Norman settlement is largely blank so far as direct evidence goes. Dartmoor itself is not mentioned in the Domesday Book. Godwin the Priest is one of only

---

[3] Walker gives details and lists the Scandinavian and Russian sources (pp. 192-195 and p. 234). To round off the story, her great-granddaughter married King Valdemar of Denmark, a distant ancestor of the present Queens of Denmark and Great Britain.

[4] This is a modernised version of the original, folio 104, chapter 15,7. The reference to "the Priest" is contained in the Exeter Domesday Book (still in the Cathedral Library) and was not retained in the Exchequer version. When the Domesday Book was compiled the Saxons and Normans gave evidence in their own language and the language of record was Latin. This was put down in an abbreviated form, almost like shorthand. The manorial value was the net value, after costs and subsistence were deducted. For the text and further information see Thorn (eds) *Domesday Book, Devon* and Loyn (intro) *Domesday Book Studies*. On the size of Dartmoor furlongs ("ferlongs") as approximately 30 acres, see Gill (ed) *Dartmoor: A New Study*, p. 150.

two cases in the Domesday Book where a cleric who held land before 1066 was permitted to remain in possession after the Norman Conquest. The Earl of Mortain retained only four manors under his direct control and granted out the rest to be managed on his behalf.

A document issued in 1516 by Henry VIII confirms a charter by which it appears that Martin, Earl of Mortain, granted the manor of Gidleigh to his nephew, Giles de Gydleghe in the 12th century. There is abundant evidence, however, that no such grant could have been issued at this early date, or certainly not in the terms used in the document most of which are 13th or 14th century legal expressions. The most likely explanation is that the purpose of Henry VIII's Letters Patent was to ensure the grazing rights of Gidleigh farmers on the Moor. In Westcote's *View of Devonshire,* completed in 1630, the author introduces the document with the comment:

> *"I shall by some be thought to lead you a Pixy path by telling you an old tale (and yet perchance new to you) of one Martin, Duke and Erle of Cornwall, who granted to his nephew Giles de Gydleghe the manor of Gydleghe. Of the truth of which donation albeit some make doubt and some question and some utterly denye."*

For him therefore the matter was already "an old tale". The text and the issues surrounding the Letters Patent are considered further in Appendix 2.

It seems reasonably established at all events that the Prouz family were in possession of the manor of Gidleigh by the late 12th century. Of the early authorities, Risdon and Polwhele speak of the Prouzs having been at Gidleigh "from the first Normans time" and Pole and Lysons refer to them having been in possession "as early as the reign of Henry II", which brings us to the period 1154-1189.[5] How the manor passed from the Earl of Mortain and, under him, Godwin the Priest, in 1086, to the Prouzs is uncertain. The lands of the Earls of Mortain were, however, forfeited to the Crown several times and there were a number of occasions when the King could have acted so that the manor passed to the Prouzs.[6]

---

[5] Risdon, *Choreographical Description or Survey of the County of Devon.* This was begun in 1605 and finished in 1630, but not published until 1811. The phrase cited is from the 1811 edition, p. 124. Polwhele, *History of Devonshire,* 1793. Pole (1561-1635) left a large manuscript part of which was published in 1791 as *Collections towards a Description of the County of Devon.* Lysons, *Magna Britannia,* 1832, vol 6, p. 245, drawing on Pole. Lysons was the first to deal on a parish as opposed to family basis. In this he was followed by subsequent writers, notably Hoskins and Pevsner.

The Prouz family claim descent from Eudo de Prouz who came to England at the time of the Conquest and whose son, Osbert, settled in Devon. His grandson, Walter le Prouz, is thought to have married Isabella, daughter of Lord Dinham, who had extensive lands in Devon. It is not known if Walter le Prouz was given Gidleigh by Dinham on his marriage or if he received it by some other means, but he was in possession by the time of Henry II, the first of the Prouz family to own it The estate passed to his son John le Prouz in 1192 (2nd generation) and then to his son, the first Sir William Prouz (3rd) in 1224.

William was Steward to Richard, Earl of Poitou and Cornwall, who was granted the manor of Lydford, its Castle and the Forest of Dartmoor by Henry III in 1239. Sir William is mentioned, together with three other knights, in a writ ordering the first perambulation of the Forest of Dartmoor in 1240. He married Margaret Helion, the daughter of Sir Alan de Helion of Gatcombe, Widecombe and Whiteleagh. In 1256 the Gidleigh estate passed to his son, another Sir William (4th), who married Alice Ferrers, the daughter and heiress of Fulk de Ferrers of Throwleigh. Alice, with her husband, owned a considerable number of estates including Gidleigh, Throwleigh, Aveton Gifford, Gatcombe, Whiteleagh and Widecombe. Sir William became Sheriff of Devon in 1269.

Their son, Sir William (5th), who was born in 1245 and died in 1316, was the last of the Prouz family to own the estate which he inherited in 1280. He married Alicia, heiress of Sir Hugh de Widworthy, who is buried at Lustleigh. It was this Sir William who was responsible for building the Castle at Gidleigh in about 1295 as a stone manor house or "hall house". He died without male heir and his estates passed to his daughter Alice, who was a substantial heiress when she married Sir Roger Moeles of North Cadbury in 1323. Her daughter and heiress, also called Alice, was abducted "from her home in Lustleigh" by John D'Aumale or Damarell of Flete Damarell, who married her in 1347. There are several versions of this kidnapping story and it may be that young Alice, then 15, had fallen in love with John but her father would not give his consent to the marriage. Her mother, who approved of the match, arranged to have Alice 'abducted' by John. In order to lessen the scandal of going against her husband's wishes she made sure she was abducted as well.

John Damarell died in 1392, leaving his property to his son William. He in turn had a daughter, yet another Alice, who married Walter Coade (born 1360) of Morval in Cornwall. The manor remained

---

[6] Rawson, 'The Earls of Mortain', *Devon and Cornwall Notes and Queries*, (1921, p. 1). The Rev J Rawson was Rector of Gidleigh in the 1920s. Mortain land was eventually settled on the Prince of Wales in 1337, leading to the estates of the Duchy of Cornwall which include the Forest of Dartmoor. See further Chapter Three, Farming and Land Use.

with the Coades for 220 years and it was during their period that the main fabric of the Church was built in the 15th century. In 1628 the estate was bought by an Exeter merchant named Henry Battishill.

In what must have been of more immediate concern to the inhabitants of Gidleigh, over the three hundred years between 1100 and 1400 the land was progressively cleared from the initial 100 acres in 1066 to at least four times that size and the original farm hamlets established. The main farms, Berrydown, Scorhill, Creaber, Greenaway, Thule, Moortown, Ensworthy, Chapple and Forder have their origin in this period. A description of Gidleigh in the late 13th century was given in the proceedings of an After-Death Inquest held in 1280 following the death of the fourth Sir William Prouz. Gidleigh manor is summarised as follows:

> "A certain capital messsuage worth 4s per annum, 60 acres of arable land worth 10s and 30 acres of scrub and pasture worth 40d, and a certain waste, the proceeds of which are worth 6s 8d, and 2 mills worth 26s 8d, and 60 free tenants who pay £4 3s and 40 villagers (nativi), each of whom holds _ ferling of land, who pay 60s at Michaelmas; pleas and perquisites are worth 1 mark" [7]

This indicates a total of 300 acres or more and a population of three or four hundred when women and children are included. At the Inquest held 30 years later, after the death of the next William Prouz in 1316, it was recorded that "in his manor of Gyddelgh the arable land was valued at twopence an acre" and that he paid 72s to the Exchequer. This shows an increase to over 400 acres of arable land alone.

Up to 1450 or so developments remained formally within the scope of the manor. Though vestiges remained for centuries afterwards (in the Gidleigh sale in 1819 reference is still made to the manor court), the feudal system evolved towards a pattern of individual land ownership and tenancies from which the present day system derived. Separate rights of ownership became steadily established through the shifts in the legal system. By the early 16th century at the latest the main farms were under individual owners, well aware of their independent status.

At that time the population was small, less than had been recorded in the 13th century. The Black Death in the 1340s greatly reduced the population; in Gidleigh there were three priests in succession, in 1347, 1348 and 1349. The size of the Parish remained small for many years and indeed never regained the

---

[7] Cited in Reichel, 'Extracts from the Pipe Rolls of Henry II relating to Devon', *Trans Dev Assoc.*, vol 29, 1897, p. 453 & p. 459, note 14. The 1316 Inquest is from the Exchequer Red Book, cited by Whale, *Trans Dev Assoc,* vol 33, p. 393 – p. 394

former scale. The 1525 Subsidy Roll listed 35 men in Gidleigh and in 1641 it was still only 34. Names that appear over this 100 year span are Tincombe or Tencombe, Risdon or Rysedon, Ash, Roo (presumably Rowe), Thewyll or Thewill (presumably Thule), Denninge or Dunnyng, Parlebyn, Knapman, and Vogwell.

The impact in Gidleigh of the Reformation and the establishment of the Anglican Church under the Tudors must have been substantial. [8] The men of the Parish (the "brethren" of Gidleigh) had long been amongst the main participants in the religious guilds (the store of St Michael, St Katharine, St Mary, the Holy Cross) administered at Chagford. All this ended in the 1540s and 1550s. The "Prayer Book Rebellion" of 1549 that began in Sampford Courtney nearby may have had an echo here. In Chagford in 1551, during the reign of Edward VI, the wall paintings were defaced and the altar replaced by a table. In 1554, when Queen Mary was on the throne, the altar was restored and the rood screen put up again. Then in 1560, under Elizabeth, all the images were removed and a communion table replaced the altar. Similar developments must have occurred in Gidleigh, where the Church had recently been largely rebuilt. The rood screen appears to have been taken down at this time and the cross above it removed. In 1580 the Crown took over responsibility for the Living and appointed the Rector.

The Elizabethan settlement strengthened the parish system as a form of local government. The 16th century Poor Law was administered through the Parish Churchwardens. Nevertheless Westcote describes the Parish in 1630 as remaining "remote and difficult to access". "Passing from Chagford", he wrote, "we are travelling to the moor to find Gidleigh, where if we take not great heed, we may wander and stray, and so make longer stay in this coarse place than we willingly would". [9]

The Civil War came close with the skirmish at Chagford in which Godolphin was shot and an encounter on 8th February 1643 between a party of Parliamentary troops under Sir John Northcote and a band of Royalists under Sir John Berkley. This occurred along what became known as "War Cleave", a steep valley between Chagford and Throwleigh. The fight raged along Blackaton brook, where there is a field still called "Bloody Meadow", said to have been used after the battle as a burial ground.

The Reverend John Scott, a retired naval officer who became Rector of Gidleigh in the 1950s, recounted that he used to walk to Throwleigh to replenish his supply of gin. On one occasion when returning via Blackaton in a swirling evening mist he heard the thundering hooves of horses behind

---

[8] The Chagford records give details, see Osborne, *Chagford Churchwardens Accounts, 1480-1600* and *Parish Magazine*, December 1999. The earliest Gidleigh Church records that have survived are from 1599.

[9] Westcote, *View of Devonshire,* 1845 edition, p. 433.

him. He was quick to add that he had not had a drink since the night before, but the sound of charging horses convinced him of the truth of the local belief that noise of the skirmish could be heard in Bloody Meadow at night on the anniversary of the battle. As he peered through the mist "the charging horses" suddenly materialised - a group of ponies in the field who had heard his step in the lane had galloped over in anticipation of an early evening feed. Alas! But do not despair; others passing along that way have also heard, and sometimes seen, charging horses and 17th century riders.

To return to the 17th century, Bartholomew Gidley (1st) bought the estate in 1638, having married Johanna Northleigh of Peamore near Exeter the previous year. He came originally from Hollacombe Paramour near Winkleigh and was an energetic and thrustful character, described by a contemporary as "a man of great designs and contrivancies" [10] He raised and became captain of the Tinners Regiment, composed of Devon tin miners and the best in the King's Western Army in the Civil War. In the 1660s he received a coat of arms and in 1683 a silver medal, now in the British Museum, from Charles II.

> *Or, a castle within a bordure sable bezantee. Crest a gryphons head couped, or, between two wings tinctured as the bordure on the arms.*

He became a Justice of the Stannaries and, dying in 1686, was buried at Winkleigh in the Gidley chapel. His widow and his heir, also called Bartholomew Gidley (2nd), the eldest son of his brother John Gidley, a court surgeon in London, became engaged in the extended law suit known as the Bradford Pool case. In the 16th century a leat was constructed to bring water from Watern Coombe on Dartmoor to Bradford Pool, situated above Shilston in Drewsteignton, a distance of some 12 miles. The water was required to leach the tin being mined there. The means did not exist at that time to pump water from the river nearby. Accordingly the water was brought, by force of gravity, from the Moor to Drewsteignton using a combination of leats and timber built aquaducts (called launders) to get over the valleys and streams. This was a substantial undertaking requiring a good knowledge of the terrain in order to make the best use of the downward slope and a considerable

---

[10] Cited in L Costello, 'The Bradford Pool Case'. *Trans Dev Assoc,* (vol 113, 1981, p. 59), where a full account is given of the law suit. The contemporary map is of interest. *The Archaeology of Dartmoor from the Air* contains photos showing the course of the leat at Buttern and Throwleigh, plates 6 and 9. On the Civil War aspect, see M Stoyle, *Loyalty and Locality.*

*The Gidleigh Medal awarded in
1683 by Charles II*

investment. Some £1,500 was spent in the 16th century, easily equivalent to many millions today. Devon and Cornwall were at this time the principal source of tin in Europe. The leat fell into disuse for tin mining and in 1653 Bartholomew Gidley (1st) diverted the leat at a spot between Scorhill and Creaber and channeled it through Berrydown to his own lands. He used it for a mill in Gidleigh village, possibly Gidleigh Mill. A contemporary map shows the main sites.

The matter dragged on through various stages. In the 1690s the owners of the tin-working project (the "Adventurers", the venture capitalists of the day) brought a case against Bartholomew Gidley (2nd) in the Stannary Court in Chagford, which dealt with tin mining disputes. They were successful in their action for "trespass upon the case in nuisance" and Gidley was threatened with imprisonment and a claim for damages of £2,000 (probably more than the value of his estate).

Gidley counterattacked by obtaining a writ of habeas corpus which meant that the action was transferred from Chagford to the common law Court of King's Bench at Westminster. There he was upheld, the common law judges claimed jurisdiction, and the case was sent back to the Devon

Assizes where judgement was given against the tinners. With the collapse of the tinners' case, parts of the leat from Watern Coombe to Bradford Pool fell into further disuse or were absorbed into the course of streams (including a branch of the Wallabrook). The wooden aquaducts soon collapsed. The sections of the leat which became filled in, or partly so, may have contributed to the anecdotes reported over the years of ploughs and carts falling into tunnels.

In the 18th century a succession of Gidleys lived in the house built by the original Bartholomew where Castle House now stands. The nephew died in 1702, aged 34, leaving a son, also called Bartholomew (3rd) (b 1689 d 1776), whose Godfather is thought to have been King William III. He married Ann, the sister of Robert Avery of Crewys Morchard in 1707 and had seven children, including yet another Bartholomew (4th). Some of these died at a young age and their tombstones are amongst those outside the Church

Bartholomew (3rd) was a spendthrift who suffered a recovery of his estates and left his family almost penniless. His third son, Gustavus, moved with his wife Mary (née Knapman) and family to Wonson Manor in 1772. In 1773 the sister, Ann, married Dr Henry Rattray who took over the estate after the last Bartholomew Gidley died. By this time it was so deeply in debt through a series of mortgages that a Chancery suit was started to determine who should have possession. This lasted 20 years, from the 1790s to 1819 when the estate was sold by an Order in Chancery. (This was the period of notorious legal delays in the Chancery court - remember the lawsuit in Dickens' *Bleak House*). Even then it took a further two years to complete the conveyance. The estate still remained the largest part of the Parish, with two to three thousand acres of common and wastelands and nearly 400 acres of enclosed land. A notice published in 1817 gives the flavour:

DEVONSHIRE

TO be SOLD by PUBLIC AUCTION, at the Seven Stars Inn, in Saint Thomas the Apostle, near Exeter, on Tuesday the 5th day of August next, at Four o'clock in the afternoon, (unless previously disposed of by Private Contract,) either altogether, or in two or more Lots, as the Vendor or his Agent may hereafter determine, all that the FEE-SIMPLE and INHERITANCE of the extensive

MANOR and LORDSHIP of GIDLEY

in the county of Devon, with its Courts Leets and Baron, quit and chief rents (amounting to £4, 11s, 11d, yearly, extensive common and waste Lands, containing between Three and Four Thousand Acres, with all its privileges, immunities, deodands, waters, fishery, etc, in the river Teign.

Also the MESSUAGE, OUTHOUSES, BARTON and FARM,

Called GIDLEY BARTON ;

comprising, by admeasurement, about Five Hundred Acres of rich watered Pasture, Meadow, and Arable Land, including Gardens, Orchards, a Rabbit-warren, and large Park.

Also, the RECTORY, GLEBE LANDS, and TITHES, of and the RIGHT of PATRON-AGE and PERPETUAL PRESENTATION to the Parish Church of Gidley aforesaid, the present incumbent of which is aged about 60, - There are two Estates (in Trustees names) belonging to the Rectory, called SOUTH FORD and NORTH FORD ; consisting of two small Farmhouses, and about Twenty-five Acres of Arable, Meadow, and Pasture Land, now let on Lease at £30 per annum, for keeping the Church in good and substantial repair, (not included in the before-mentioned Five Hundred Acres) on which acount there are no Church-rates in the parish.

The Proprietor reserves to himself Lords Place and Ainsworthy, two detached parts of the Barton, but which are now included in the above Five Hundred Acres, and the Oak and other Timber Trees, Saplings, and Underwood, of which there are a considerable quantity on the Premises, must be taken at a fair valuation.

The Premises are situate within 18 miles of the city of Exeter, 3 of Chagford, 7 of Moretonhampstead, 9 of Okehampton, 10 of the New prison on Dartmoor, and 19 of Plymouth ; and the Manor affords abundance of Game, which renders the property a most desirable situation for any Gentleman fond of Farming and the Field Sports.

The Proprietor or his Agent will be at the Seven Srars Inn aforesaid, six days previous to the Sale, to receive proposals, and treat with those who may be inclined to become purchasers by Private Contract.

For viewing the Premises, (possession of a part whereof may be had immediately, or on the purchaser or purchasers making good his or their purchase, and the residue at Lady-day next), apply to Mr JOHN ROWE, Berry-Down, in Gidley; and printed particulars may be had (gratis,) at the office of Mr JOHN RAPHAEL, solicitor for the Proprietor, No 6, John-street, Bedford-row, London; and of Mr JOHN CHUBB, solicitor, Exeter. N. B. All Letter must be post-paid. (Dated 9th July, 1817).

In 1991, Paul and Kay Henderson discovered an Australian connection to the Gidley story. Philip Gidley King from Launceston was Second Lieutenant on the Sirius, the flagship of the First Fleet which arrived in Botany Bay in 1788. He rose to become Governor of New South Wales when it is said that to show his dignity he refused to shake hands in the street. His mother was the daughter of John Gidley, a lawyer in Exeter related to the Gidleys of Gidleigh. He eventually returned to England, became an Admiral and died in Tooting. His son, Philip Parker King, also joined the Navy and was especially proud of the voyage he made on the Beagle with Charles Darwin. He too became an Admiral in due course and in 1834 was granted 25,000 acres in recognition of his services surveying the coast of New South Wales. He built two homesteads on the property, named Gidley after his ancestors. By a coincidence, a Captain William Prouse, a descendant of the family that had lived at Gidleigh, commanded the Sirius at Trafalgar. He was a naval hero who fought more single ship actions than any other man in the Royal Navy.

Samuel Landick and Henry Stanbury held the estate in trust from 1795 to 1819 when it was bought out of Chancery by the Reverend Thomas Whipham from Kingston, Surrey, who was Vicar of Kingsteignton. He ran the estate through tenants, rebuilt or remodelled the house at Gidleigh Barton, and nominated the rectors (including his relation, the Reverend Arthur Whipham). There is no evidence that he spent any great time in Gidleigh. His nephew, the Reverend Arthur Whipham, who lived at one time at Holystreet in Chagford and who built a house at Gidleigh Park in the 1850s, succeeded him. His son, Alfred Guy Whipham, who lived at Gidleigh Park, died in 1916, the last of the Whiphams. There is a memorial window in the Church showing an angel with a sword "erected by parishioners and friends". By the time he died the estate was encumbered with debts; the agricultural crisis from the 1870s on meant that he had no means of restoring his capital and overcoming his losses.

The estate was sold in 1918 to an Australian shipping magnate and wool farmer named Mr Charles McIlwraith. He was responsible for the rebuilding of Gidleigh Park after the fire there in 1925 and providing the Village Hall, as well as constructing other houses in the village. The great slump in 1929 and the resulting depression reduced his fortune and he himself died fairly soon afterwards of TB. The estate, consisting of 2,000 acres of moorland and over 300 acres of cultivated land was broken up and sold by his heirs in 1933. The sale marked the end of the remains of the medieval estate and the start of the modern history of Gidleigh. The enclosed land was mostly bought by existing farmers and a number of houses were sold separately.

By this time there had already been major changes in occupations and land use. The 19th century statistics show an agricultural community with its roots in the locality. The 1861 Census recorded 25 families, the heads of households being twelve farmers, ten agricultural workers, one thatcher, one blacksmith and the rector. Nineteen of the heads of households were born in Gidleigh, Throwleigh or Chagford, five in parishes nearby, and only one, the rector, from further away. The main family names in the 18th and 19th centuries (most from much further back) were Endacott, Aggett. Dunning, Rowe, Perryman, Webber, Brock and Gidley, who were joined by Hill, Osborne, Sampson. Bowden and Vallance amongst others. People bearing these names are still living in the neighbourhood. According to Kelly's Directory in 1878 the Endacott family seem to have taken over much of the village, occupying Little Ensworthy, Gidleigh Barton, Gidleigh Mill, Greenaway, Forder and Brimstone Down.

The 19th century was marked, as the detailed account of the houses shows, by a rapid turnover of tenancies as farmers sought desperately to keep afloat. No security of tenure then! With limited work opportunities the children left increasingly for the towns. The population figures show an increase up to the middle of the 19th century and then a decline.

1801	1851	1901	1931	1961	2000[11]
125	166	121	143	117	120

The figure for the population in 2000 includes 17 children of school age. This is by far the largest number of children living in Gidleigh for well over 50 years. An encouraging sign!

The farm boundaries have changed substantially over the past hundred years, as farms were consolidated or divided into small holdings around individual houses. This process, which got underway in the 1900s continued throughout the 20th century. The 1930s to 1950s saw an influx of retired officers from the services, and many others, mostly from London and the home counties, have followed in their train, so as to produce the range of present inhabitants. The Dartmoor National Park Authority, set up in 1951, casts a benevolent eye over Gidleigh and the surrounding countryside. While voices are raised over its decisions from time to time, there is no doubt that it has done much to safeguard the pattern of life in the area.

---

[11] The figures from 1801 to 1961 are from Hoskins *Devon*, p. 527. The 2000 figure is based on the Electoral Roll to which the number of children have been added.

The more detailed breakdown of the 19th century census figures shows that the number of households remained steady but that the number of children fell from the middle of the century on

	Houses	Males	Females	Total	Heads	Children	(under ten)
1841	28	98	84	182	29	85	(58)
1851	28	93	73	166	28	71	(58)
1861	25	73	61	134	25	48	(32)
1871	29	77	77	154	31	59	(44)

See R Rankin, *Gidleigh Parish, A Rough Guide,* where further data are given.

CHAPTER TWO

THE BUILDINGS AND THE PEOPLE

This Chapter deals with the buildings in the village, describing their origins and occupants over the years. The information has been provided by those living here and in conversations with people who grew up in Gidleigh or are connected with it, as well as by a large range of records. This does not purport to be an architectural history of the individual houses or a collection of detailed family histories but an account of the village, and of where and how people have lived from past centuries up to the present day. The survey made covers every house in the Parish. The exact origins of many houses are hard to determine, lost or overlain by subsequent rebuilding and the period of the main existing building has been taken as the chief point of reference.

So far as the growth of Gidleigh is concerned, the area round the Church and Castle was the centre of the original settlement dating back to the Saxon period. The enclosed land was small, around 100 acres initially. As fields were cleared, the village expanded in a series of isolated farmsteads or small hamlets, like the spokes of a wheel - a pattern found in most of the Dartmoor uplands.

The result is a scattered village with a small centre and half-a-dozen hamlets, as well as a number of houses in between. What is remarkable about Gidleigh is that the landscape is much the same as it was 600 years ago, there has been little change; the layout of the village is still that of a dispersed community following the pattern established many years ago. This contrasts with the more closely grouped houses to be found in, say, the villages of East Anglia or the Midlands. Whether because of its relative isolation or its dispersed nature Gidleigh has had the good fortune to retain virtually all of the houses built before 1700. When reading Emmie Varwell's book on Throwleigh one can sense her regret at Father Lowe's activities in pulling down what must have been a very fine medieval house in order to provide building material for a new house.

For most of its recorded history, the Church played a leading part in the life of the village and it was here that rites of passage such as christenings, confirmation, marriage and death were celebrated.

The manorial system dominated existence from the 11th to 14th centuries, after which the distinction between the estate and the land owned individually became fully established. Rights on the Moor, however, remained matters of economic significance and general interest to all, as indeed they are today.

The Parish Church, **HOLY TRINITY, GIDLEIGH**, is on the site where the original Saxon chapel is believed to have stood. The presence of "Godwin the priest" before the Norman Conquest indicates that a church was already here at that time, though nothing now remains of what must have been a simple building.

We do not know when the Saxon church was founded but there was considerable church activity in Devon at this stage, notably the transfer of the diocese from Crediton to Exeter and the establishment of the Cathedral there in 1050.

This was done on the authority of King Edward the Confessor and his Queen, Edith, Gytha's daughter. The opening words of the Cathedral Charter recall the event.

"I, Edward, King, with my hand do place this charter upon the altar of St Peter; and leading the prelate Leofric by his right arm, and my Queen EAdgytha leading him by the left, I do place him on the episcopal throne."

Earl Godwine, Gytha's husband, was among those who signed the Cathedral Charter. It may be therefore that support for the Church at the settlement came from Gytha at this time though this can be no more than a conjecture. There are no distinct portions from this early period in the present building, which dates largely from the 15th century. A thatched oratory is believed to have stood where the chancel is now; the south wall of the chancel, some six inches thicker than the aisle wall, may be the oldest part that remains. The new building was constructed of tooled freestone granite from the Moor in the Perpendicular style, with a thatched roof which records show was re-thatched in 1753. An extra course of stone, put on when the roof was slated in the late 18th century, can be seen outside on the side of the tower. There was some rebuilding in the 17th century but the main fabric - "all granite, all ashlar" in Pevsner's phrase - remains little changed since the 1400s.

The Church consists of a nave continuous with the chancel, with a waggon shaped roof of Devon oak, and a side aisle on the south side. The two are separated by a three-bay arcade, supported by monolithic granite columns, which gives the Church a feeling of light and space. The tower at the west end almost forms part of the nave It is a solid, simple Church, reflecting the inability of a Parish of this size to afford anything more elaborate.

The simplicity of the building is offset by the 15th century rood screen, with its colourful decoration. This appears to have been taken down and then reassembled during the 16th century, and the large cross which would have been above the screen removed, as part of the changes brought about by the Reformation. As noted in the previous Chapter, this period saw a marked change in beliefs and practices. The carving running along the top of the screen includes a pomegranate, the emblem of Catherine of Aragon, Henry VIII's first wife (the one he divorced in order to marry Anne Boleyn). Each of the uprights is carved in a different manner, providing a highly rustic image. The main part was repainted in 1853, altering the original colour scheme of gold, white, red and green to the present red, gold and blue. The lower panels have transfers of saints, added in the 19th century restoration. On the north side of the screen there is a small doorway in the wall, with the remains of steps leading to an opening above the screen. The steps would have led to the vaulted rood loft, where a cross would originally have stood. The priest's door (now closed) in the north wall of the chancel was used until the 19th century, when the vestry was built in the corner of the side aisle.

The windows are simple, that in the tower having fine tracery. A large window was inserted in the north wall in the 17th century. The glass is plain, mostly Victorian or early 20th century with the exception of some 15th century fragments in the east window. These show parts of a blue clad Mary and a fair headed St John; they may have been part of a Crucifixion destroyed in the 16th century. On the south wall of the side aisle is a memorial window to Alfred Guy Whipham.

The font is 15th century. The wooden cover was made by Charles Finch, the Parish Clerk, in 1843. The granite pulpit and lectern were made in 1853 by John Aggett, a local mason, who also carved the reredos. The small cross on the altar, made of yew wood from a tree that once stood in the churchyard, was carved by Michael Gaillard-Bundy, who lived at Scorhill. A large pewter alms dish, marked "Gidleigh Parish Bason 1672", is still in use. After being discovered in the garden at Berrydown in 1896 it was returned to the Church by a Mr N Noel. A silver chalice and patten, made by Jon Jons (John Jones) of Exeter in 1576, is used at the Eucharist on feast days. No other plate or similar utensils have survived.

The tower has five bells, three of them from the 15th century. Two were cast in the churchyard by a follower of a bell founder named Robert Norton. The fourth, made by Thomas Pennington of Exeter, was given in 1671 by a Churchwarden, Alexander Vogwell. In 1553 the Church Goods Commissioners reported that at Gidleigh there were

"iiij belles yn the towre their - and bell in the chapel there."

This would have been a relatively large number for so small a place, suggesting that funds had come from beyond the Parish. The 1671 bell must have replaced an earlier one. The third old bell might have been moved from the chapel at Chapple Farm. The fifth bell was hung in the 1920s as a thank offering for the end of the First World War.

The order and inscriptions of the bells are as follows:

1. Tenor. A. Early 15th c. Est mihi collatum ihc istud nomen amatum *(To me is given Jesus that beloved name).*
2. Fourth. B. Early 15th c. St Thoma ora pro nobis *(St Thomas [à Becket] pray for us).*
3. Third. C. 1671. Alexander Vogwell. Churchwarden. (Evidently a man of few words).
4. Second. D. Peace Bell.
5. Treble. E. Circa 1450. Plebs o's plaudit ut me tam sepius audit *(The people all rejoice the more often they hear me).*

In the 1970s the bell frame became unsafe and ringing was discontinued. By the aid of a widespread community effort and a grant from the Millennium Commission, the bells and frame were restored in 1998. [1] The work was done by Peter Bazley of Tavistock. A bell team has been formed under Julia Endacott, the tower captain at Chagford, whose family have a long connection with the bells at Gidleigh. The bells were rung on the first of January, 2000, to celebrate the Millennium. Some time before 2066 it will be possible to mark a thousand years since the first bell was rung at Gidleigh.

The inside of the tower was cleaned in 1998 in order to remove the peeling plaster and a bitumen lining which had been used in the 1920s to keep out the damp (it only kept the moisture in). With the stones now revealed, the line of the Church from the west door to the altar is a fine sight. The tower has an iron band round it on the outside, put there by Tom Hill, the Throwleigh blacksmith, in the 19th century. Originally the tower had pinnacles at the top. Two have been found. One serves as a gatepost on the right hand side of the Mariners Way footpath (at the junction of the road from the Church and that leading to Chapple). It is a dressed stone, square, with an interrupted chamfer at each angle. There is a drilled hole at the top, showing where a finial was attached. The other is now a gatepost in a field on the Aggetts farm at Forder, near Wonson in Throwleigh. The question is, where are the other two? A drink or two for the first person who can provide any information.

As was noted in the Rural Dean's Visitation Book in the 1820s, "Damp remains a problem". J L Page visiting in the 1870s noted ferns growing inside the Church tower. It was no doubt with these considerations in mind that when the heating was installed and the pews removed in 1903, the tombstones were taken from the floor of the Church and placed along the wall outside. These memorials of late 17th and 18th century Gidleys, Vogwells and others make remarkable reading. The division of words suggests a local stonemason copying dutifully from a book. They bring the remoteness of Gidleigh then sharply to life, and contrast with the more elegant copper plate style of the 19th century gravestones. The long tombstone marked with a cross or sword which lies at the Church entrance dates from the 13th or 14th century.

Perhaps as a result of the disturbances caused by the Reformation or possibly as a canny use of what was available, a 14th or 15th century Church cross found its way to Greenaway and was employed

---

[1] The amount raised locally included contributions from the Parish funds, two bell trusts, the Dartmoor National Park Authority, Gidleigh Park Hotel, the Dartmoor Commoners Association, the proceeds of a concert in the Village Hall and private donations. The effort thus covered all sectors of the local community.

as a gatepost (evidently a Gidleigh tradition). In 1940 it was moved to the Churchyard where it marks the grave of William Sampson, long a bell ringer at the Church, who lived at Greenaway. Other graves record lives passed in more distant places and occupations: Alpheus Ross Wyllie, of Haldamulla, Ceylon, tea planter; Thomas Lane Stanley Fox-Pitt, Order of the Freedom of Zambia; Agnes Beddow, for many years "much loved matron" of a childrens' home.

The Churchyard is crossed by a leat and surrounded by a wall erected in the 19th century. This was possibly after the Rural Dean had noted with disapproval that villagers had the habit of spreading their washing on the tombstones. A Church or Poor House which stood on the other side of the leat was demolished and the stones used to help build the wall.

After Godwin in the 11th century there is a gap in the recorded priests. The first of which we have mention is of "Richard the chaplain of Giddelegh" who in 1238 was found dead on the highway. Since the death could not be accounted for but there was no evident foul play, only a fine was imposed on the jurors held responsible for law and order. [2] The registers from the time of Bishop Bronescombe (1257) trace the presentations and patrons from the mid 13th century. The living was always a poor one. The Taxation of Pope Nicholas IV (1288-91) gives the value as 20 shillings and therefore not taxed of its tenth.

The priests in the medieval period seem to have been local men: Michael de Leghe in 1259, Elyas de la Walle in 1276, Walter Prouz, appointed by his kinsman Sir William in 1284, Walter de Hertilande in 1384, Richard Chaggeforde in 1368, to name some of them. Under the system which was devised to balance the claims of church and state (or of the local landed proprietor at least). the Archdeacon was required to conduct an inquiry when a vacancy arose. The local vicars then reported whether the church was vacant by resignation or death of the previous incumbent, who the patron was and who the patron proposed. The Bishop then authorised the appointment. [3] Mostly this worked smoothly enough but from time to time difficulties arose. In 1452, for example, William Grose and Robert Prous were ordered

---

[2] H Summerson (ed), 'South Tawton Hundred Answers by Twelve Jurors', *Crown Pleas of the Devon Eyre of 1238*, p. 68. The finding in the terms of the day was "No Englishry, so Murder fine." Under a Statute of William the Conqueror if a man was found dead and could not be proved to be English he was presumed to be Norman and the hundred in which he was found was liable to pay a "murder" fine, as in this instance.

[3] Hingston-Randolph (ed), *Episcopal Register of Bishop Bronescomb (1257)*; G.Dunstan (ed), *The Register of Edward Lacy (1420-1455)*.

to sequestrate all the revenues of the church at Gyddeleghe "because the rector, Sir Nicholas Eggebury has left the church without services and for other reasons,"[4] The curate or priest of a nearby parish (most often Throwleigh) also served as the clergyman here on a number of occasions. Still, for most of the period up until modern times, Gidleigh was a separate parish with its own rector.

During what must have been the time of greatest upheaval in the mid 16th century Gidleigh had one rector, Richard Discomb (1549-1580). Whether his position was thought to be unsound or for some other reason, the next appointment to the living was made by the Queen. In the Parliamentary period the rector, Humphrey Gaye, was married by the Mayor of Okehampton since only civil ceremonies were allowed. He remained until 1683, however, and was able to perform the marriage service of his daughter at Gidleigh in 1658.

The life of the Parish seems to have been undisturbed, if not quiescent, in the 18th century. The rector reported to the Bishop of Exeter in 1821 that services at Gidleigh and Throwleigh were in the hands of a curate, that there were no papists or dissenters apart from an occasional Methodist preacher at Throwleigh, and that at Gidleigh communion was held four times a year and there were no children of a proper age to be taught the catechism. He added that he himself had permission to live in London.[5] The 19th century witnessed substantial changes as the Anglican Church sought to regain ground. At Gidleigh, where the accommodation available was described in 1821 as "unfit for a clergyman", a new rectory was built in the 1890s to provide suitable housing.

A list of the rectors of Gidleigh Parish since 1259, together with the patrons, is on a board in the Church.[6] The name of Godwin the priest was added through the bequest of Howis Croxford who lived at Throwleigh for many years.

The church had of course its own land in the past and was entitled to a share in produce or money in lieu (the famous tithe). Land owned by the church was known as glebe land, the origin of the name of Glebe Farm, and the assessment of the tithe was part of village life for centuries. The tithes and rent of the glebe in 1535 came to £15. The property at Forder was bequeathed to the Church in the late 17th century. In 1808 the living was valued at £44. A major re-assessment was made in 1843 and the papers and the map of the Parish in the Devon Record Office are an important source of information.

---

[4] Dunstan, op cit. III, p. 172.

[5] M Cook (ed) *The Diocese of Exeter in 1821,* vol II, p. 88, p. 174

[6] The names and patrons are listed in Appendix I.

By that time it was clear that the system could not be continued and the tithes were abolished as part of the Victorian tidying up operation. The Church lands were mostly sold and the proceeds put in trust; the Gidleigh Lands Trust still exists, a useful way for the Parish Church to arrange some of its business.

In the medieval period of the 12th to 14th centuries the church was the spiritual centre next to the manor house of the settlement (the "vill"). This pattern is well illustrated at Gidleigh where the Church and manor house (the Castle) stand close. The progressive separation of church and manor from the 16th century led to the parish becoming the main unit of local government, run by the leading members of the community. Under the Poor Law Act of 1601 parishes were made responsible for those in hardship and cases of vagrancy and the like. The Gidleigh Church accounts thus record payments to sailors using the Mariners Way which ran between Bideford and Dartmouth. In 1760 "Gave a sailor that had a pass, 1sh", 1774. "Giv'd Alms to sealor, 6d." The churchwardens also paid for the killing of foxes, seemingly part of parish responsibilities. In 1740 the Church accounts show

> "James Discombe - one shilling for killing six hedgehogs"
> "Thomas Newcombe for ale which they drank when they killed a fox 3/4d."

That seems quite a lot of ale for killing a fox!.

The principal task incumbent on the parish, however, related to the administration and distribution of the 'Poor Rate' levied each year. This was an unenviable job and in 1820, for example, Mrs Sampson and her son complained at the Parish meeting that the amount of £7-10-0 a year they received was not enough and unsuccessfully asked for more. Parish overseers, appointed in rotation for a year and commonly also serving as churchwardens, were responsible in addition for dealing with orphans and illegitimate children. A practice that is much documented, notably during the 18th century, is for the Gidleigh overseers to arrange for orphans and poor children from Exeter (mostly from St Sidwell Parish) to be apprenticed to farmers in Gidleigh (in effect adopted in our terms). This happened to children of the age of seven who became servants and virtual members of the family. There must have been cases of unhappiness, but many of the children seem to have settled down and married in Gidleigh. After 1834, individual parishes were no longer responsible for their poor and the task was handed over to Union workhouses.[7] Although the office of overseer continued into the next century, this change reduced the feeling of communal

---

[7] The matter is well summarised in R Sellman, *Aspects of Devon History,* chap 19, p. 56.

responsibility for the plight of one's neighbours.

The Church records date from the 17th century: Baptisms 1613-1812; Marriages 1599-1951; Burials 1599-1776; Churchwardens accounts 1736-1921; Church Lands Trust 1796-1904; Overseers 1754-1835; Apprentices Register 1803-1841; Rural Dean's Visitation Book 1823-1983. These are now deposited at the Devon Record Office in Exeter.

Turning to more modern times, the advowson passed from the patron to the Bishop in 1970 and all appointments since that time have been by him. In the 1970s the Parish was also brought together with Throwleigh and Chagford to form a united benefice. Services are held each Sunday at Gidleigh, thanks to the devoted efforts of the Rector, the Reverend Louis Baycock, aided by Lay readers and, for many years, the Reverend Joe Jury, who lived at Shilston in Drewsteignton. Besides those attending regular services, and the crowding of the Church at weddings and funerals, there are over 700 visitors a year. In future the three parishes will be put together with Hittisleigh, Spreyton and Drewsteignton under a single rector. He or she will have a heavy task. We have to hope that a country living still has its attractions as well as its demands, and the congregation will be prepared to take more responsibility for itself if the Church is to continue and flourish here. It has been at the centre of life in Gidleigh since the beginning.

Like the Church, **GIDLEIGH CASTLE** and **CASTLE HOUSE** are on the site of the original 11th century settlement.

The centre of the village was small, clustered around the Church and the main holding and it was from here that the rest spread in the following centuries. The Castle may have been the earliest stone building erected and is the first of which we have any real knowledge. It was built by Sir William Prouz, the fifth in line, around 1295. The date is known with relative accuracy because he used the same masons who were working at that time at Okehampton for the Courtenays. [1] Gidleigh Castle was not built as a major defensive stronghold and is more strictly described as the main part of a 'Hall house'. It was more extensive than the present remains; there were several stone built rooms on the north-west side where abutting stones may be seen, and the rest was probably of timber and wattle.

On the upper floor there is a solar or dining hall, with a recessed fireplace and three splayed windows. This has three entrances, one from the side where the rooms have disappeared (probably the

---

[1] S R Blaylock, *Gidleigh Castle: A Survey of the Standing Remains, 1991-2,* gives a detailed account.

sleeping chambers) and two from staircases, one at the front and the other leading down, inside the wall, to the undercroft. Aplite stone, a more easily worked stone that provides a better finish, was obtained from a quarry near Hatherleigh and used for the door jambs. The walls themselves are about seven feet thick. The undercroft, lit by a window at the end, is ribbed by three arches. The tower at the front, part of which fell down in the 1920s, extended to the top of the building. Photographs taken before that time (including some taken by Robert Burnard, one of the pioneers of Dartmoor studies) show what the tower looked like. It included a cruciform window the stones of which still exist. At the top of the building there was a sloping roof, some six or eight feet higher than at present, and a parapet.

The Prouzs had held the manor for the best part of a century before the Castle was built, which must have been part of a group of buildings. By the end of the 13th century a range of buildings would have collected around the manor: the Church, the dwellings of those working on the estate and barns and shelters for the animals. The manor pound is nearby (now threatened by Japanese knotweed, which Michael Hardy and Sam Holwill seek to keep at bay) and the Castle well, set in the wall by the road. There was a stone inscription giving the history of the well, which dated from before the leat was made, but some one went off with it in 1984. The well was in use up until about 1910 according to Margaret Osborne.

By the time the Castle was built around 1300 the amount of enclosed land had increased substantially. The Prouzs had by this juncture acquired other manors through judicious marriages. Sir William could thus call on the services of four or five hundred serfs in order to build his Castle, and since Gidleigh appears to have been the original home of this branch of the family, it was chosen as the site. He had no sons and the building may have been designed not only as a sign of strength and wealth but as an inducement for a successful marriage of his daughter. Marriages in those days were the equivalent of management buyouts today and as carefully plotted. At all events when in 1323 his daughter Alice married Sir Roger Moeles, himself the holder of a number of manors, she was a substantial heiress. From there Gidleigh passed by marriage to the Damarells in the 14th century and by the time of Henry VI (1422-1461) to the Coades, a Cornish family.

Since all these families had extensive estates and larger houses elsewhere it is likely that they did not live permanently at Gidleigh and the Castle was unoccupied. Between 1323, when Alice Prouz married, and 1628, when the estate, including Gidleigh Barton, was bought by Henry Battishill, an Exeter merchant, the land must have been farmed by bailiffs and tenants.

Battishill sold the estate to Bartholomew Gidley in 1638. Although he had land at Winkleigh, Gidleigh was his main residence, the first owner for nearly 300 years for whom this may have been the case. One of the indications that the Castle had been unoccupied for most of the previous centuries is that there are no signs of modifications made during this period. If Gidleigh had been the principal seat of a wealthy family or in the middle of a thriving town, it would have been altered and enlarged according to the demands of the time. When Bartholomew arrived therefore he would have found the medieval structure forlorn and crumbling, not at all the kind of place in which a thriving man and his family would have wanted to live. He could have pulled the Castle down or modified it, but fortunately he didn't. Out of respect for antiquity or shortage of cash, he chose to leave the Castle standing and built himself a new house nearby, using some of the stones of the Castle to do so, where Castle House now stands. [2] The cellars, now mostly filled in, date from his time. The medal he received shows a castle tower with a cruciform window so presumably he had a fond eye for the old building.

He was succeeded by his nephew and other descendants, but by the mid 18th century the Gidleys were in financial difficulties. After a long lawsuit the Reverend Thomas Whipham bought the estate, of which the Barton was the principal asset, in 1819. The Whiphams were to be in possession until 1916 when the last of them died. The first two, the Reverend Thomas and the Reverend Arthur Whipham, were clergymen in Kingsteignton, Hatherleigh and elsewhere. They never lived at the Barton or at most only briefly, but the first of them, the Rev Thomas, appears to have been responsible for converting the house that Bartholomew Gidley had built into the present one. The drawing showing the Castle as seen from the front door of the house, dated 1825, was made by Miss Hamilton Smith, the daughter of Colonel Hamilton Smith, one of the first to study Dartmoor antiquities on a serious basis.

In 1818 the tenant of Gidleigh Barton was a Mr Rogers, the agent of a Mr Crawford who sought to create an estate on the Moor. Both had come from Ireland where they had been engaged in the repression of an uprising. [3] A family named Southard (or Southward) who came from Ilsington, a village between Bovey Tracey and Newton Abbot, followed him between 1825 and 1831. Their family papers record that they lived in a house with ten rooms next to a look out tower. They had ten children and emigrated, oldest children first and then the rest, including the parents, to Upper New York State. From there they moved to the Middle West as the prairies were opened up. By the end of the 19th century there were several hundred Southards and the extended family now numbers several thousands. Their family newsletter, run from Houston, had an issue in 1985

---

[2] B Cresswell, *Notes on Devon Churches: The Fabric and Features of Interest in the Churches in the Deanery of Okehampton*

[3] See E Stanbrook, *Dartmoor Forest Farms* p 16 and Chapter Three below.

devoted to "The Southards at Gidleigh".

During the remainder of the 19th century the Barton was let to a series of tenants, the Southards being followed by Brocks (in the 1830s) and Endacotts (from 1865). The daughter of James Endacott, who was there in the 1880s, was the grandmother of Mr Dunning Morris who lives at Langstone in Throwleigh. Although the Barton remained one of the principal farms in Gidleigh, the decline in agriculture from 1870 on caused increasing difficulty and hardship to landowners and tenants alike.

The solution, apart from taking out bank loans, was to rent or sell off land and houses in a series of parcels. Gidleigh Barton ceased to be a working farm before 1914 and became, like most of the houses now, a private house. The lawn at the front of the house was earlier the farm yard, with buildings on either side .The remains of these can still be seen, the upright lintels and low walls, and the pillars of a horse mill. In 1910 it was rented by a Major John Gidley, one of Bartholomew's many descendants and whose plaque is in the Church. In the 1920s the McIlwraiths lived at Castle House while Gidleigh Park was being rebuilt after the fire there. They planted some of the trees that may be seen.

When the McIlwraiths sold the estate in 1933 and the remnants were broken up, Castle House, together with the Castle and surrounding land, was bought by a succession of owners. Few of them remained very long. Mrs Cleminson (John Milton's great aunt) was here with her husband between 1936 and 1940. Mr J Venn, the President of Queen's College, Cambridge, owned it between 1940 and 1945 and used it for reading parties.

Mr Geoffrey Hands, who lived at Castle House with his wife and family between 1962 and 1977, deserves special mention. He was relatively well off and bought (and sold) both the Old Rectory and Way Cottage during his time. A keen amateur archaeologist, he became convinced that Gytha's children, King Harold and Queen Edith, had been born here. There is no evidence for this so far as is known and it is extremely unlikely that Gytha would have come to such an out of the way place as Gidleigh in order to give birth to her children. It is a nice but improbable story. More seriously, he got engaged in several disputes with his neighbours, culminating in a case brought before Okehampton Magistrates Court when the Parish got bound over to keep the peace; which it has done ever since.

The Newtons followed the Hands, a resourceful couple who, besides bed and breakfasting, opened a restaurant at Castle House. It made the Good Food Guide but it proved difficult to sustain.

Michael and Swana Hardy bought the house in 1983. They have reshaped the hillside behind the house and planted a number of trees and shrubs. In the course of shifting the earth a tunnel was found in the compressed granite, almost six feet high if you got to its floor through the sediment,

"Gidleigh Castle from the House door"
1825

Keep of Gidleigh Castle in 1825

Drawing of Gidleigh Castle made by Miss Hamilton Smith in 1825, from the door of the house

and about 20 to 30 feet long before it had collapsed. It was not part of a tin working (the archaeologists were sure) and no one knows why it was built. Two old bottles were found (late 17th/early 18th century) a glass seal with the Gidley arms, and pieces of clay pipes. Perhaps Bartholomew went there for a quiet drink. The Castle has been re-mortared, to make sure it doesn't fall down and will still be here for a few more centuries.

GIDLEIGH PARK is the largest property in the village and it has been suggested that a two-storey thatched building with short wings projecting from the front, facing east towards the River Teign and known as Park House, existed on or near the site of Gidleigh Park in the late 1500s. No confirmation of this has yet been found in estate records, however.

There is thought to have been a house here in 1680, but it is not clear if the Gidley family lived there or whether it was simply a farm complex in the centre of the chase.

There is mention in later years of several properties in the park including a 'villa' and a collection of houses and farm buildings along the lines of the small hamlets of Chapple and Creaber. These houses were left abandoned for many years, but finally the Reverend Thomas Whipham carried out some work after he bought the estate from Chancery in 1818.

The first reference to residents of Gidleigh Park is in the list of persons entitled to vote in the parish in 1842, when there is mention of Arthur and Frances Whipham of 'Gidley Park'. Their son, Alfred Guy Whipham, was christened in Gidleigh Church on 6 January 1848.

This was a time when Chagford and its surroundings were being 'discovered' and the area appealed greatly to Victorian taste. In 1850, W. White wrote:

"A steep rocky descent from the park to the river Teign is studded by enormous rocky protuberances, whose level summits display many of the excavations called rock-basins. The roaring stream at the bottom of this descent, the wooded front of the bold bank that rises on the opposite side, and the vast masses of rock on either hand, grey with moss or dark with ivy, render this part of the park truly romantic." [1]

It is evident that the building of a suitable house took many years. An extract from a gentleman's travel journal in 1856 included the following trite report:

"Wednesday Aug 13th - By Holy Street to Gidleigh Park, a beautiful spot, well wooded with the North Teign running round the lawns; but neglected and overgrown. What should be the residence and ornamental cottage is only half built and falling into ruin, no part of it being habitable. It belongs to the Reverend Whipham, the Clergyman of Gidley who lives at Holy Street, where he is building and altering as usual with him having the character of never finishing what he has begun and spoiling everything he muddles with...". [2]

Park House was let to Wallis Nash in January 1869 for a period of 7 years but in 1881, the house and two other neighbouring buildings on the estate were uninhabited and the house and Park were

---

[1] W. White, *History, Gazetteer and Directory of Devonshire*, p. 194.

[2] Todd Gray (ed), *Devon Documents*, p. 94.

described as being "fruitful only in rabbits, but curious from its singular appearance".

Gidleigh is bisected here by the North Teign. The river runs through a gorge at this point crossed by a footbridge. The steep sides of the valley have never been cultivated and for much of the past centuries it was used as woodland and as a rabbit warren, where the river could act as a boundary.

Gidleigh Warren was an important asset of the estate, built in Lower Park on the other side of the North Teign River and well away from the farms. Rabbits were not indigenous to Britain and are thought to have been introduced as a source of food or for sporting purposes by the Normans in the early part of the 12th century.

Several warrens were set up on Dartmoor but the largest and best documented was Trowlesworthy Warren in Shaugh, which was granted to Sampson de Tralesworthy by Baldwin de Redvers, Earl of Devon, some time after 1135. There were various methods of warrening on the moor but the most common involved the construction of mounds of suitable earth to form a 'bury' or 'pillow mound' enclosed in gateless fields. Dogs were used to drive the rabbits into nets placed over the small number of entrances built into the warren; the meat was a source of cheap food to the community and provided welcome income for the estate.

The Whipham family grew steadily indebted with a plethora of mortgages. The house was put up for sale in 1862 along with the rest of the estate but was withdrawn after only a few weeks.

A visitor to Gidleigh wrote in 1907:

"Gidleigh Park, very wild and beautiful, really only a chase of the Prouz family. The trees, oak, birch and rowan, grow up among the rocks and ferns and whortle berry bushes." [3]

The last member of the family to live here was Alfred Guy Whipham, the Reverend Arthur's third son, who spent most of his life at Gidleigh Park. He was a JP, involved in local government as chairman of the Okehampton Board of Guardians and described as being "devoted to horses, and riding and driving have been his chief amusements". [4] He died without an heir in September 1916.

Charles McIlwraith, who bought the property in 1918, spent lavishly on the house and was responsible for building most of the newer properties on the estate including the lodges and the Village

---

[3] S. Baring Gould, *A Book of the West - Devon.*

[4] E. Gaskell, *Devonshire Worthies.*

Hall. The house itself burnt down in 1925 and Stanley Philpot, an architect from Tunbridge Wells, was commissioned to draw up plans for a replacement. The work took four years and in 1929 S.E. Winbolt wrote that Gidleigh "retains much of its wild character" and was "reached by a steep climb through woods [from Chagford] on rough roads, a car journey is not recommended". [5]

Florence Endacott worked there as a parlour maid in 1928. She said that, at that time, the house had six live-in servants: a cook housekeeper, two housemaids, a kitchen maid, a scullery maid and a parlour maid. The outside staff included a chauffeur, boot boy, two cowmen, an electricity man to operate the hydro plant and three gardeners.

McIlwraith proved to be a most popular owner but died young of tuberculosis in 1932, having lost most of his money in the Depression. The house and estate were sold to Major Rudolph (Rollo) Mayne for £15,000 in October 1933. Rollo Mayne and his wife, Caroline (Carrie), had no children but were constantly surrounded by family and friends including his sisters, the unmarried Cissie and the recently separated Claire Ogilvie and her two children. She was later to marry Lord Clifford of Chudleigh.

The Maynes were Catholics, distantly related to the Blessed Cuthbert Mayne, a 16th-century martyr from Barnstaple who was canonised in 1886. Another well-known Roman Catholic, Evelyn Waugh, visited the house on a regular basis when staying at Easton Court near Chagford writing *Brideshead Revisited*. He recorded in his diaries that he got stuck one day driving down Mill Street hill outside Chagford because he couldn't manage the gears of his car. [6] He was on his way to attend a service held by the resident Jesuit priest in the chapel built by the Maynes in the north wing of the house. (Waugh died in 1966, widely accepted as the finest comic novelist of the century.) The Maynes continued to improve the property and, amongst other things, were responsible for developing the water gardens and building the tennis courts.

Shortly after Rollo died, Carrie sold the house very cheaply to some nuns who never moved in but sold to a man called Barber for a quick profit. The house was converted to an hotel or guest house and passed through several hands, including Doug and Barbara Butler in 1966 and the Mathews family.

In 1977, the house and grounds were bought by ex-US Marine Paul Henderson and his wife, Kay, who had met as students at the University of Purdue, Indiana and moved from the United States to London in 1970. They reopened the small country house hotel to a chorus of silence. However,

[5] S.E. Winbolt, *Devon.*

[6] E. Waugh, *Diaries,* p. 449

after many years of hard work and considerable expense, they have turned it into arguably the finest hotel in the south-west of England.

Its reputation is now established internationally and guests come from all over the world to sample the excellent food and to enjoy the beautiful countryside that has attracted visitors to Dartmoor for centuries. The Hotel has been given many awards over the years, including Country House Hotel of the Year by the Good Food Guide in 1983, three red turrets and two stars by the Michelin Guide in 2000 and in the Condé Nast Traveller Readers' Poll in 1999, it was rated the best small hotel in Europe.

Among many regular visitors over the years was the late Poet Laureate, Ted Hughes, who lived not far away in North Tawton. Among many poems about his beloved Devon is one on the birth of Prince Harry called 'Rain-Charm for the Duchy' in which he mentions the rivers and places, including Gidleigh, that so fascinated him.

"And the Teign, startled in her den
By the rain-dance of bracken
Hearing Heaven reverberate under Gidleigh ..."

In a later poem he wrote:

"Older than mankind, the river swallows
The tale it has to tell.
Every bubble on it stares in envy
At Gidleigh Park Hotel".

On Gidleigh Tor, not far from the Hotel, lie the remains of Prinsep's Folly, a house and two towers built on the summit of the Tor in 1848 by Thomas Prinsep. It is believed he was related to the banker, William Prinsep, who left India to return to England in 1842. Together with the D'Oylys, the Prinseps were among the most gifted of the Anglo-Indian amateur artists and William was known mostly for his watercolours of Indian country scenes.

It is not clear why Thomas decided to build a house in so exposed and lonely a position because he never lived in it and his widow had the place pulled down and surrendered the lease soon after his death. All that can be seen of it today are the remains of a roofless octagonal tower with a pointed-arch doorway and a small window. The 250 acres of woodland surrounding Gidleigh Tor were recently bought by Mr and Mrs Peter Bayley from Oxfordshire.

CASTLE FARM, originally called Castle Cottage, was built in the 1920s by Charles McIlwraith for one of his employees.

It was bought for £950 from the McIlwraith estate in 1933 by George and Sarah Ann Osborne, together with about 30 acres on which they kept their herd of South Devon cattle. George died in 1944 aged 67 and Sarah in 1951; both are buried at Providence. Their daughter, Margaret, started a youth hostel, one of the first five to be set up in Devon and Cornwall.

It started life opposite Gidleigh Cottages as no more than a lean-to coal shed with sides open to the weather. By 1937 the present buildings at Castle Farm were completed comprising a common room, two dormitories and a kitchen.

Margaret ran the farm and hostel as well as the post office, almost single-handed, for over 50 years and her post office became an unofficial meeting place for villagers catching up with local gossip. She was invited to a garden party at Buckingham Palace to receive an MBE and celebrate her 50-year involvement with the Youth Hostel Association. Her death in 1988 saw the closure of the post office and youth hostel and a much-loved Gidleigh character was lost to the village. After her death and before the house was sold, a hoard of money, several thousands of pounds, was discovered hidden under the floorboards. It was passed to her beneficiary, a member of the family.

The house and land were sold to Mrs Parke in partnership with a man called Evans. He was responsible for building the Owls Foot Garage and offices on the road to Sticklepath. They applied for planning permission to build a 20 or 30 unit motel at the farm but local residents were strongly opposed to the plan. When it became apparent that permission for an extensive development would not be forthcoming, they sold the property to Nigel Hooper who also had plans to convert the farmhouse into a motel or country lodge but was unable to proceed with the venture. He had several projects in mind, including watching badgers in their setts at night through periscopes. He was also involved in taking out shipments to Romanian orphans and made several trips to Moldavia, where he hoped to open a bank and a furniture factory.

The property was divided up and sold in 1992. The house and some adjacent land was bought by Malcolm and Jennifer Bell on 10 September 1992, who set to work remodelling the building and transforming the garden which they open each year in support of a gardening trust. Malcolm, a graduate of the Royal College of Music, was Assistant Director of Music at the Royal Masonic School and now is greatly in demand locally as a piano tutor.

GIDLEIGH COTTAGE was built around 1650 and remained part of the Gidleigh estate for most of its history. It was originally two semi-detached thatched cottages which, together with the Castle and the Barton, formed the entire village of Gidleigh Town. 'Town' in the Moor vernacular does not necessarily mean a large collection of houses. A solitary farm with or without a couple of cottages is often dignified with this title; indeed, most villages were known as 'church towns' in the 17th and 18th centuries. In church records of baptisms, marriages and deaths, the address of the people living in 'The Cottages' in Gidleigh was simply shown as 'Gidley Town'.

In the 1870s J.L. Page, on visiting Gidleigh, wrote:

"There is the ruined castle adjoining the dilapidated manor-house, close hugged by the little church, with a tower unusually slim when compared with its brethren. And beyond the pool made by the bubbling brook beneath the churchyard wall are two thatched cottages, one the post-office, the other the residence of the worthy and not unintelligent parish clerk, where homely fare may be obtained, for inn there is none. The whole settlement - that is, the inhabited part of it - could be put into the waiting-room of a London railway station!" [1]

The cottages were occupied by a plethora of people in the 19th century. These included, in 1825, George and Keziah Bond in one and James and Mary Boarder in the other together with William and Elizabeth Turpin and their son James. In 1834, William Osborne occupied one of the cottages and the Brimblecombe family the other.

One of the cottages was occupied by William and Mary Mortimore (née Hill) in 1843 with their daughter, Mary Anne. Mary's sister, Eliza Hill, was living there in 1910 but by 1930 the cottage was occupied by Mary Aggett, her husband and their two children, Dennis and Marjorie. At that time the other cottage was occupied by Harry Cushman, a cowman at Gidleigh Park. A few years later this lower cottage was rented for a few years by a Miss Hadwin. In 1939, the lower cottage was occupied by Bert Osborne who worked at Castle Farm for his brother, George. In the 1950s, both cottages were purchased by the Aggett family for £800 with about seven acres of land and in 1992 Marjorie Aggett sold the property to Barry and Jackie Urmston who continue to live there with their son, Matthew.

The unpaved lane outside the cottage leads to Gidleigh Mill and shows clearly what most of the lanes in the region were like before cars and tractors arrived. George Endacott can remember delivery carts rattling their way down the lane to Gidleigh Mill in the early 1920s as he walked daily to school at Providence.

No account of Gidleigh Cottage would be complete without mention of the great beech tree beside the house. It was used as the village notice board for generations until it became diseased and had to be felled. Its loss was a sad day for the village.

According to Bonney Spiller, rumour has it that a Chagford sheep rustler was hanged from that tree many years ago.

---

[1] J.L. Page, *An Exploration of Dartmoor*, p. 94

WAY COTTAGE, originally known as 'Wayside', was erected in the late 1920s by the McIlwraiths for Percy Rice, a gardener at Gidleigh Park. It is thought to have been in an exhibition in London in the early 1920s and two similar, if not identical ones, were erected on the entrance road to Gidleigh Park.

George Endacott remembers that, when he was a schoolboy in the early 1920s, there was nothing but a cowshed where the cottage now stands. McIlwraith's widow, Madeline, sold it together with about a quarter-acre of land to Alfred Moore in 1933 for £300 and it changed hands regularly thereafter:

1938	Francis Wood	1968	Marjorie Sherriff
1945	Wilfred Soper	1970	Geoffrey Hands
1956	Francis Walton	1975	Reginald Birch
1963	Doris Callaway		

Reginald Birch was at one time the headmaster of Shebbear College and before he retired, he and his wife used the house as a holiday retreat. Bruce Dorey, who owned Holmanswood Tourist Park in Chudleigh, bought the cottage in 1993 and sold it to its present owner, Patricia Lee, in 1998. Pat, a retired pharmacologist, was Dean of the University of California Medical School in San Francisco.

This seems to be an appropriate place to make some mention of local schools and their teachers.

The first recorded school in the area was one for girls at Coldstone Farm (pronounced Catson) in Throwleigh, which started in the 1830s. The ground floor of the 'Vicarage House' in Throwleigh was used as a school in 1846 and within ten years it had 33 pupils. A school room was added to the chapel at Providence outside Throwleigh in 1869 and, finally, under the Education Act of 1870, a large and well-equipped school house was built down the lane from the chapel.

Amy Harvey who, for almost 40 years, was headmistress of Throwleigh and Gidleigh Junior School was born in Throwleigh in 1909, the daughter of Richard Hill, the local blacksmith. She left Throwleigh School in 1921 and after graduating from teacher training college in 1930, was offered the headship of her old school teaching a class of 32 between the ages of 7 and 14. In 1936 she married her second cousin, Alfred Harvey.

Talking of her years at the school, she said that she must at one time or another have taught most of the children of Gidleigh and Throwleigh. The school itself was a gem and it was a catastrophe that it closed in 1971 because of declining numbers and a demand to cut costs.

Amy Harvey related stories of the 25 'wild evacuees' from Battersea in London who were billeted in or near the village during the Second World War. They were kept at first in a separate class away from the local children. She tolerated no nonsense from any of them and in particular mentioned David Skeats, who years later told her that if it hadn't been for her he would probably have ended up in prison. Tom Wells, one of the last pupils, recalls how long the walk to Providence was from Creaber each day and remembers how absorbed they all were in the immediate life around them.

The demise of the traditional village school has been just one of several sad and probably irreversible changes suffered by small communities such as Gidleigh over the years. Children are now taken by bus and car to schools in Chagford, Okehampton and even farther afield.

(The Headmaster of Rugby School spotted an advertisement in a careers bulletin some time ago which made him question whether a drive for improved education was really necessary. The advertisement read:

"Wanted. Man to work on nuclear fissionable isotope molecular reactive counters and three-phase cyclotronic uranium photosynthesizers. No experience necessary.")

GIDLEIGH MILL lies at the bottom of the hill below the centre of the village and was served by a leat supplied from a spring on the Moor near Kennon Hill. It was acquired by Bartholomew Gidley together with the rest of the estate in 1638. In 1656, he built a new mill next to the Barton in the village, to be worked by water diverted from the tinners' leat which served the Bradford Pool tin mine.

In the belief that the mine, abandoned by the tinners at the outbreak of the Civil War, would never be re-opened, he diverted the leat at the 'the south highway' on Gidleigh Common and as a result sparked off the famous 'Bradford Pool Case' [1] which lasted for years and was won by Bartholomew's nephew in 1699.

The farmhouse, now a Grade II listed building, is of a three-room-and-through-passage plan, built across the hill slope facing south. It was never a longhouse in the strict sense of the word and there is no sign of the millrace or millpond that would have been needed to drive a mill. Allan Van der Steen believes that the mill was more likely to have been animal driven than anything else.

One of the buildings, which has since been converted by the current owners, was a threshing barn with a round house connected to it, indicating that animal power was used for a mill on the

[1] See L. Costello 'The Bradford Pool Case', *Trans Dev. Assoc.*, vol. 113, 1981, p. 59

property in the last two hundred years. Ernie Bowden, whose family owned the mill for some years, was told that the original water wheel and millrace were removed when the extension to the right of the front entrance was built at the time the mill was converted into a farmhouse.

Flour mills in small settlements such as Gidleigh catered for immediate local needs - three or four bushels of flour here and two or three hundredweight of barley there. The miller was also responsible for supplying cattle feed and malt for the local brew houses. These small local mills were replaced in the last century with the development of big steam-driven roller mills with their higher and faster rates of extraction.

The barn beside the lane running up to Gidleigh Church may have been built on the site of the original longhouse used by the miller and his family before the mill was converted to a residence. It is also likely that, in the early 1920s, the upper end of the barn was still in use as a farm cottage with the shippon at the lower end of the building. At some point in the late 1920s, the barn ceased to be occupied when the shippon roof and supporting wall collapsed.

In an Indenture dated 1733, William Northmore sold the freehold of Gidleigh Mill to Henry

Endacott and it remained in the Endacott family for almost 200 years.

William Northmore was the squire of Wonson Manor in Throwleigh, the same William Northmore, born in 1690, who became famous in the county as a rich gambling land-owning squire and politician.

The Northmores were an old Devon family, descended from ancient Saxon thanes. They owned several estates in the county, including the manors of Ash, Willey and Cleve and were, at the time, one of the richest families in the area. In 1690, John Northmore, William's father, built a large house on the site of what was known as 'The Mayor's House' in the centre of Okehampton. It was surrounded by gardens and farmland and became the most important residence in the town, clearly designed to impress. [2] King Charles I stayed in the Northmores' first house in July 1644 when passing through Okehampton.

William was addicted to gambling and threw lavish parties at Wonson Manor for his cronies, who travelled from all over Devon to enjoy nights of fun and games. One night in 1722, when he was 32 and plagued with money troubles, he risked a wager of £17,000, a fortune at the time, on the turn of one card, the Ace of Diamonds - and lost. As a permanent reminder of his folly he had a replica of the card painted on a panel in the parlour at Wonson Manor and it is said to be there to this day.

Before going to bed at night and every time he passed by, he would look at the image of the card and swear never to gamble again. In 1722 he began a process of mortgaging and remortgaging the Mill and other properties which lasted for 10 years. By 1733, his debt totalled £20,000 and the executors of Henry Portman's estate called in the mortgage on the Mill. Endacott, who already had a lease for 99 years, was able to buy the freehold for £50.

Clearly, William Northmore got over his youthful folly and prospered through the lesson he had learnt. He became Mayor of Okehampton in 1726 and in 1735 was elected a Member of Parliament. He died a rich, powerful politician, someone who so earnestly pursued pleasure that he had the misfortune to overtake it. Bill Hall, a retired lecturer in medieval history, has read the collection of ancient deeds relating to Gidleigh Mill and the Endacott family and believes they contain the names of the winners of the card game; Henry Portman of Portman Orchard in Somerset and Francis Seymour of Sherborne.

In 1832, the Mill and about 14 acres including fields called Long Close, Pan Close, Broad Field and Hebray Meadow [3] were in the possession of John Endacott, a farmer born in Gidleigh in 1805 who also owned the 29-acre North Creaber Farm. The Mill which, together with land at Haymans

---

[2] The Northmore town house is now the Town Hall, situated on the corner of Market Street and Fore Street.

[3] Hebray, as in Hebray Meadow in Old English, referred to a high meadow containing a burial place.

Park and a part of the Barton, totalled over 50 acres in 1878, was tenanted by Henry Scott, a farmer born in Chagford in 1843, his wife Maud and their four daughters and two sons, Alice, Jessie, Minnie, Mabel, John and Henry and two apprentices, Charity Foaden and Philip Stoneman. John Endacott retired to another house on the property in 1884 after his wife, Demaris, died and in the same year his son, William, took over the running of the farms.

In 1906, Frank Northcott took on the tenancy of the Mill before it was sold to Charlie Mortimore, John Holman's uncle, in 1921. John stayed at the Mill with his aunt and uncle for a couple of years while attending school at Providence. Charlie sold the farm to Percy and May Bere in 1926 and in 1943 they in turn sold to a man from London called Geldart who bought it as a refuge from the bombing around London.

In the same year, the Bowden family took over the tenancy of the farm and five years later, Ernie Bowden's father, Harry, bought the freehold from the Geldart family and farmed the 42-acre property with his wife Eleanor and their three children, Ernie, Tryphena and Kathleen. Tryphena married Joseph Thomas Neri in 1947 and Kathleen married Terry Beer in 1953. David Skeats, one of the 700 children evacuated to this part of Devon during the war, became almost an adopted member of the Bowden family at the Mill. Having arrived at Okehampton by train from London and been taken with 24 others to Throwleigh Tythe Barn, he had been sent initially to Wonson Manor (then owned by the Ashplant family), then moved to Forder to stay with the Bromells whose eldest daughter was Eleanor Bowden.

Her husband, Harry, continued farming Coldstone Farm on Ash Hill as tenant. The first piece of land that Ernie Bowden bought for himself was a field owned at the time by the Knapmans in Throwleigh parish, adjoining Coldstone Farm.

The family had a milk round for some years which supplied a large part of the village and sold clotted cream by mail order to customers all over the country, including the Houses of Parliament. Ernie remembers his mother carrying dressed turkeys on the bus to Exeter station, to be sent for sale in London in the early 1950s. In the late 1950s, TB testing of milk became compulsory and a number of farms gave up selling it. The Bowdens upgraded their milking parlour and were then able to sell and deliver cream and milk to neighbouring villages.

In 1960, when Ernie was 17, they bought a car and expanded the business a little. At this time the family was farming over 100 acres in Throwleigh and Gidleigh. Ernie took over Gidleigh Mill in partnership with his mother after his father died in 1962. Ernest Mortimore from South Zeal had a mobile shop and visited the farms in the area on Tuesdays and Saturdays. He also operated as a licensed slaughterman and dealt with any sick or elderly animals the farmers wanted put down.

In 1986, Ernie sold the Mill to Brian and Deidre Skilton, who spent the next three years completing lavish improvements and alterations to the property carried out with the help of Allan Van der Steen.

Brian Skilton spent 20 years at the BBC and is now an independent film director and producer. He has been responsible for several television and cinema films including a television production called 'Dartmoor – The Threatened Wilderness', filmed on Dartmoor in 1985. He also edited a book of the same name written by Brian Carter two years later. He and Deirdre have three children: Matthew, Jonathan and Emma Jane.

GIDLEIGH LODGE was built in the late 1920s by the McIlwraith family for their head gardener, Will Rice, and it remained a tied cottage until Dr Hans Hollander and his wife Leni bought it from the Mayne family in 1946. Hans, born in Moravia in 1899, was a graduate of Vienna University and a noted musicologist who became Director of Music at the Radio Station in Brno in the 1930s.

He and his wife arrived in England as almost penniless refugees and lodged initially in a farmhouse below Castle Drogo. They were befriended by the Maynes of Gidleigh Park who offered them the Lodge, rent free, for the duration of the war, an act of kindness they much appreciated.

Dr Hollander gave music lessons under the Exeter University Extramural Studies Programme and wrote books and articles, mostly about composers of the 1920s and 1930s. He is recognised particularly for his biography of the composer, Leos Janacek. He and his wife were well-known locally for their enthusiasm for collecting mushrooms and bilberries.

They were both enthusiastic ramblers on the Moor and lived on rabbits, pigeons and whatever else they could catch. Leni took a job as a waitress at the Mill End Hotel soon after they arrived, to make ends meet. Their daughter, Jenny, used to play with John Skeaping's children from Creaber Cottage. She recalls that, even as a child, Colin Skeaping's one ambition in life was to become a film stunt man, a career in which he has proved to be so successful.

Richard Leaman, whose father kept pigs nearby, was shocked when Hans Hollander asked if he could buy any still-born piglets that appeared. When asked why he wanted them, as they were normally thrown on the dung heap, Dr. Hollander explained that where he came from, roasted whole still-born piglets were considered a rare delicacy! Richard said he tried one and found it delicious. There is no doubt that, having got over the initial shock of the thought of eating an animal that had died rather than been slaughtered, the possibility of selling still-born piglets would appeal to any thrifty Devon pig farmer.

Hans Hollander, having rented the house for a while, bought it and some adjacent fields from Carrie Mayne in late 1946 and lived there until he died in 1986. Both he and Leni, who died in 1978, are buried in Gidleigh Churchyard. Their daughter, Jenny Wilson and their son, Tony, still come to visit the village from time to time. Tony's son, Tom, is a budding young actor and his daughter, Julia, an opera director.

Ernie Bowden bought the Lodge in 1986 after selling Gidleigh Mill and lives there with his two children, Ann and Julie. His wife Jean died suddenly in 1999 and will be remembered as a stalwart supporter of the Village Hall. The family farms about 100 acres of land, most of which once formed part of Gidleigh Mill. The barns and farm buildings are sited off the Chagford road, some way down the hill from the Lodge. Ernie's maternal grandparents, Ernest and Eleanor Tryphena Bromell, rented Forder Farm in Throwleigh from the Aggett family until Ernest died in 1952. Eleanor was a schoolmistress and rented out rooms during the war to supplement the family income. (The Aggetts also owned the 'New Inn', at Wonson, as it was then known, opening it after the 'Royal Oak' in Throwleigh was closed down.)

The Bowdens and the Kingslands (Jean Bowden's family) as well as the Endacotts, are members of the small Methodist community of Bible Christians, now part of the United Reformed Church, founded in 1815 by a Cornish farmer's son named William O'Bryan. At one time, in parts of north Devon and north Cornwall, the Bible Christians could match the mighty Wesleyan Connection in size. The local Providence Chapel at Throwleigh was built in 1839 and its burying ground lies a short distance away, containing the graves of several prominent ministers. By 1865 it had a membership of 33, compared with Chagford's 14 and South Zeal's 10. [1]

Chapel people found the Church of England intolerable and bitterly resented the tithe. [2] Many did all they could to cheat the system and some refused to pay altogether.

> *"We've cheated the parson, we'll cheat him again*
> *For why should a blockhead have one in ten?*
> *For prating so long like a book learned sot*
> *While pudding and dumpling burn to pot."*

[1] See 'Holy Enterprises: Victorian Folk Religion at Chagford', *Devon and Cornwall Notes and Queries,* Special Issue, 1996, p. 183

[2] The tithe was the payment of one tenth of their produce every year to the church enforced by law.

In 1836, Parliament passed the Tithe Commutation Act, which brought to an end this much re-viled and anachronistic method of supporting the established church.

Ernie's father was born at Tyneford and got a job at Higher Hurstone near Chagford where he met Ernie's mother, Eleanor Bromell, whose family were the tenants at that time. The Bromell family consisted of three daughters, all born at Hurstone: Eleanor, Elsie who married Donald Bentham and Marge who married Arthur Aggett.

Ernie Bowden's maternal great-grandmother was Tryphena Sparks, a 'cousin' of the famous Westcountry author and poet, Thomas Hardy (1840-1928) who was born in Bockhampton, near Dorchester, the son of a stonemason. Tryphena, the sixth and youngest child of James and Maria Sparks of Puddletown, fell in love with Hardy in the summer of 1867, when he was 27 and she 16. They lived close to one another, separated only by a couple of miles of Puddletown Heath and are thought to have been secretly engaged for five years.

While she was at college in London, however, a "ghastly and unexplained complication" entered their lives.[3] The engagement ended when Tryphena returned his engagement ring in 1872. Tryphena married Charles Gale in 1877 and bore him four children, Eleanor Tryphena (Ernie Bowden's grandmother), Charles, Frances and Herbert. Eleanor Tryphena married Ernest Bromell and one of her daughters, Eleanor Beatrice, married Harry Bowden, Ernie's father, in 1925.

Thomas Hardy married Emma Gifford in 1874 and soon after she died in 1912 he married Florence Dugdale (1879-1937). Tryphena, however, appears to have been the love of Hardy's life and the inspiration for his most famous work such as *Tess of the D'Urbervilles, Return of the Native, Jude the Obscure* and *The Well-Beloved*, as well as countless poems. Hardy died without ever revealing the name of his first passionate love or the details of the tragic, impossible affair.

> *"In years defaced and lost*
> *Two sat here, transport-tossed,*
> *Lit by a living love*
> *The wilted world knew nothing of:*
> *Scared momently*
> *By gaingivings,*
> *Then hoping things*
> *That could not be ….."*

Charles McIlwraith built **THE VILLAGE HALL** in 1927 for the benefit of his staff and the parishioners of Gidleigh. It was first used for a Gidleigh parish meeting in March 1928 and the annual parish meetings have been held there ever since. Prior to 1920, the meetings were held in 'John Hill's

---

[3] See Lois Deacon, *Hardy's Sweetest Image*, for more detail.

cottage' [4] and, between 1920 and 1927, in a tin shack in the Rectory grounds.

The Hall was very much the centre of Gidleigh social life and 'The Club' organised concerts, dances and lunches at various times of the year. On each August Bank Holiday, for example, a dinner-dance was held which attracted not only locals but people from as far afield as Chagford, South Zeal and Spreyton. John Holman recalls that when he was a young man, Gidleigh dances were a great favourite with local boys for miles around. They came by cart or simply walked, stopping for refreshment at one or other of the pubs on the way. In those days it was usual to arrive with your own supply of drink and John said that rum was a most popular restorative.

Membership of 'The Club' cost around 5 shillings [25p] a year and competitions in billiards, table tennis and darts were held annually. Though many of the original members were servants employed at Gidleigh Park, the Club soon attracted all the residents of the parish. Every Friday they held a whist drive

[4] John Hill's Cottage is thought to have been one of the cottages near the Church in the centre of the village.

in the committee room with sandwiches and tea, which gave the women a chance to exchange local news.

McIlwraith died in 1932 and his widow let the Hall to the village for 2 shillings [10p] a year. In 1961, after spending £200 on repairs, the McIlwraith family gave the Hall to the parishioners of Gidleigh to be administered by a group of six trustees, headed by the then president of 'The Club', Colonel Vicary. It was considered by far the best village hall in the area.

David Skeats says there was a rumour that during the war the valuable silver and plate from Exeter Cathedral was stored under the stage in the Hall in case the Cathedral was bombed. This story has not been repeated elsewhere and it would be surprising if it were true; nevertheless, it makes a good tale. Colonel Vicary, who took a very active part in everything that went on at the Hall, helped organise concerts and sketches that played to full and enthusiastic audiences from Gidleigh, Throwleigh and other neighbouring villages.

There has always been a certain amount of rivalry between Throwleigh and Gidleigh, each being proud of its hall and jealous of the events each other organises. Throwleigh is a considerably larger parish, having over 300 residents, but size has been no hindrance to Gidleigh's ability or willingness to put on rather spectacular shows.

In 1957, for example, one of the local newspapers wrote about a play entitled 'High Spirits' which was written by 12 members of Gidleigh Workers' Education Association Group and produced by them at the Village Hall. Evidently the idea of having so many authors proved most successful and an enthusiastic audience of more than 200 filled the Hall to overflowing.

Talk of competition between villages prompts mention of the story of two neighbouring Devon villages, that each year had a race from one church steeple to the neighbouring one and back again. A rider and horse were picked to represent each village and the winner held the joint fete the following year. On one occasion, Stanton village newsletter stated they had won the race convincingly. Culverton Parish Church Times, however, said they had come second and Stanton, second from last!

In an article in a local paper in 1961, the son of one of the original trustees of the Gidleigh Village Hall Club, Jim Hill, bemoaned the fact that so many of the youngsters of the parish, having by then acquired motor-cycles and cars, would "go out of the district for their amusement". He said that "television has spoilt all the fun we used to have making our own". Thirty-five years later, the same cry is heard from the current generation as they desperately find ways of interesting today's youth in support of the village hall and its activities.

When it was built, over 70 years ago, the Hall filled a gap in the needs and aspirations of the people living in the community at the time. Roads were bad and there was no transport to local towns other than an erratic local bus service as, apart from a few tractors, there were no motor vehicles in the village.

In rural areas at that time, English village halls provided the cohesive force that kept disparate farm communities bound together, offered the young a chance to meet one another and gave them the strong sense of belonging that survives to this day. It is not surprising, therefore, that people want to keep them going. This is not, as some suggest, in order to preserve them as monuments to the past or as 'exhibits' to attract or amuse urban visitors as they 'roam' the wilds of Dartmoor but, as in the past, to satisfy a need within the community itself.

Times have changed, as has the mix of people in the area. Exeter, Plymouth and even Bristol and London are now within easy reach with their theatres, cinemas and nightclubs. No longer is the farming community itself satisfied with tea and cakes and many of the incomers are retired or commute to work outside the area. They too need to feel they belong to the community and may have different ideas about how that can be achieved.

A great deal of effort has been expended in seeking ways of involving the whole community in support of the Hall and it makes sense that it should be used as much as possible by the people who live or work in the area. It is hoped that whatever is planned for the Hall will be long-lasting and well supported - and it is for that reason that the profit from the sale of this book will be donated to the Village Hall Fund for its future maintenance.

Currently work is being carried out under the watchful eye of Mike Date and with the help of several grants negotiated by Chris Smallwood and Brian Skilton, to replace the kitchen and undertake extensive internal renovation, as well as retiling the roof and providing a new water supply.

An extract about Gidleigh from 'The Western Times' dated 16 September 1870, demonstrates that the villagers didn't need much of an excuse for a party even before the Village Hall was built.

"DISTRICT NEWS - GIDLEY
THE COMMON RIGHT

On Thursday last week the 'Common Right' attached to this parish was renewed. The gentlemen farmers subscribed very liberally and supplied 'viands' of the real sort. The gentry of the neighbourhood were well represented by the Reverend Whipham, R. Cornish Esq, W.D. Brock Esq, Nash Esq, Budgett Esq, Burnell Jones Esq, Messrs J. Endacott and R. Underhill.

"They were also present Messrs. Northcott, Newcombe, Westcott, Scott and Sampson. Wrestling took

place after the return but the rain falling very fast, the party encamped in Mr Underhill's premises where a dance with the Dartmoor beauties concluded the eventful day. The church bells sent forth their welcome peals and the whole community seemed to be alive with delight.

The prizes for wrestling were awarded to Sam Hill, John Aggett and Silas Hill. Gideon Webber played a splendid contest.

Mr Holman, late of HMS Euryalus, supplied the refreshments, which were delightful to the hungry creatures assembled."

Some mention should be made of the telephone box outside the Village Hall. It is one of the standard BT 1960s type and, though most people in the village these days have a telephone and, indeed, many also have mobile phones, it is invaluable to visitors who get lost in the lanes on their way to visiting friends. British Telecom has been under pressure in recent years to get rid of these boxes as they are expensive to maintain, but the community would object strongly if it were removed.

THE OLD RECTORY was built between 1896 and 1897, when the Church of England decided that a larger and more up-to-date residence was needed for the rectors of Gidleigh. The house is faced with granite, some of which is said to have come from the disused farm buildings at the Barton, while the upper floor is built in mock Tudor style. The tin shed in the garden was used for annual parish meetings for some years, before the Village Hall was built.

The Reverend Burnett, the first incumbent of the new building, moved there in 1897 and was followed by a stream of rectors. A full list in the Appendix includes the likes of the Reverend J.K. de Havilland, Charles Capel-Cure and Joseph Rawson who wrote several articles on local history and is buried in Gidleigh churchyard next to his wife, Ellen.

In 1927, Charles Trounsell became the rector and he and his wife, Elizabeth, lived there for over 25 years. John Milton says that the Reverend Trounsell, a former coal miner, was a dreadful snob. He insisted that whoever read the lesson told him which school they had been to: the more famous the school, the more often he was asked to read the lesson. Trounsell was also as strong as an ox and on one occasion, when John's great-aunt's car got stuck in a ditch, the rector, single-handed, lifted it back on to the lane. After he died in 1952, his coffin was carried to the Church through the village by horse and cart.

The Reverend Scott, an ex-naval officer and larger-than-life character, was ordained the same year as his son and took over the parish in 1954. He wore a biretta hat, soutane and big leather belt. His daughter, Mary, married Peter Morton and lives in Chagford. His son, the Reverend Prebendary John Scott, is the Diocesan Bells Adviser and played a big part in getting the church bells restored in 1998.

The last rector to live at the Rectory was the Reverend Louis Coulson, who had a bit of a run-in with Geoffrey Hands regarding access to the Church along a path over Castle House land. Hands bought the house from the Church when Gidleigh, Throwleigh and Chagford were united into a single benefice in the 1970s and two years later sold it to Anthony and Valerie Moore, who lived there with their children, Suzy, Nick and Posy. Val's mother lived in the flat over the stables for several years and Jo Rowe-Leete

occupied a mobile home in the grounds and helped with the horses before moving to Creaber in 1988.

Anthony, who kept 10 of his own horses at the Rectory, rode Dunwoody, one of his mother's horses, in the 1983 Grand National. An accountant by training, he was Joint Master of the Mid-Devon Hunt with Chris Godfrey in the mid-1980s and, for a time, manager of Mole Avon Farmers Co-Operative outside Okehampton. He now lives in South Devon with his second wife, Annie. His first wife, Val, and her husband, Roger Baker, run a pub called the Atlantic Inn in Porthleven.

Rumour has it that a riderless horse haunts the house. Jo Rowe-Leete swears that she and Val Moore heard the sound of a horse galloping round the house one night. When they rushed outside to look, they saw nothing and none of the horses stabled at the house were loose. Other people have claimed to hear similar things there that no one has yet been able to explain.

In 1992, the house was bought by Peter and Caroline Bayley and is occupied by them and their children: Harriet, Hugh, Lily and Thomas. Gillian Mcfadyen lives in the flat above the stables.

Peter is a former merchant banker and Caroline, a keen horsewoman, rides out with the Mid-Devon and is involved with the social committee of the Village Hall.

SCORHILL derives its name from 'skurry hill', skurry fields being those on or near the Moor in which loose stones or clearance heaps have been piled. The name Scorhill is synonymous with the famous stone circle on the Common which the Reverend Samuel Rowe described as "by far the finest example of the rude but venerable shrines of Druidical worship in Devonshire". [1]

The stone circle has suffered over the years but remains unrestored. There are about 25 stones still in situ, with signs that some stones have been attacked; at least two have been holed for splitting. Fortunately the culprit was caught and encouraged to seek gateposts elsewhere. An American woman visiting the site was overheard telling her companion that "the manager at the hotel said the stones have been here since time immemorial, but I reckon they're much older than that."

In the Assize Roll of 1332, John de Scoriawall is listed as the owner of the property but by the last half of the 16th century, it was in the hands of the Tincombe family. In 1600, John Tincombe died leaving the farm to his son, Alexander. It passed to Henry Tincombe in 1633 who farmed there until he died in 1644. A Mr Hole was either the owner or tenant of Scorhill, according to references to him in the 'Bradford Pool Case' in the Stannary Court at Chagford in 1653.

---

[1] Rowe, *A Perambulation of the Ancient and Royal Forest of Dartmoor*, 1848.

The Rowe family acquired Scorhill around 1730; in the Land Tax Assessment for 1742, it is listed as being owned and occupied by Andrew Rowe and his stepmother, Susanna, who also owned Berrydown and Batworthy. In 1788, his son James inherited the farms and in 1824 James and Mary Dodd took on the tenancy. The farm fields at that time included names such as Reave Close, Backsey, Berry Park, Cutland, Water Park, Bottom and Smiley Park. [2] During the 18th and 19th centuries, the Rowes had many tenants at Scorhill but none stayed for long. It was a time of short tenancies and the life of the small hill farmer was hard and unrewarding.

The 1850s saw the start of the agricultural depression in England, which reached its peak in the 1870s with the rise of imported lamb from Australia, grain from North America and beef from South America. Farm rents stayed relatively constant, however. With the price of lamb and beef collapsing in local markets, the small farms became increasingly dependent on the sale of milk, cream, cheese and eggs, for which there was only local demand at the time. Farm incomes dropped rapidly and rent arrears were common, which led to bankruptcies and evictions.

Among the list of tenants at Scorhill during this period are the following:

1828	William and Frances Counter	1844	William and Lydia Brock
1832	John and Margaret Stone	1856	James and Ann Osborne
1841	Edward and Mary Busel		

In 1866, George Glanfield bought the farm from the Rowe family and sold it five years later to the Reverend Richard Cornish, who brought in John Gay as tenant. In 1873, James Endacott bought the farm and sold it in 1879 to Robert Stark of Chagford, who started to rebuild the house. At that time, the tenant of the 76-acre property was Thomas Rowe, an unmarried farmer born in 1849, who lived there with his servant, Mary Tarrant. In the same year, Gidleigh Common is shown to be in the hands of George Gidley who lived nearby with his two young sons and a daughter.

Robert Stark was the father of the famous writer and explorer, Dame Freya Stark. She was born in Paris in 1893, and by the age of three could speak three languages. She attended Bedford College,

---

[2] 'Berry', 'Bury' or 'Barrow' as in Berry Park refers to a ploughed-out Bronze Age barrow or hut circle or prehistoric bank or earthwork. 'Brake' refers to rough land where bracken [fern to a farmer in Devon] and brake weed grow. It also suggests land fit to be 'brake' or broken up.

London University, and later studied Arabic at the School of Oriental and African Studies. She became a fearlessly independent and courageous geographer and historian who always travelled alone.

Unconventional in her style of life, she was befriended by many of the famous characters she met on her travels including Field Marshall Wavell, Sir Sydney Cockerell and Bernard Berenson. She produced more than 30 travel books, including *Travellers Prelude* and *West is East*, and married a diplomat, Stewart Perowne.

Though she lived most of her later life in Italy when not travelling, she visited Scorhill in the early 1950s. Her artist mother, Flora, and her father loved the wilds of Dartmoor. They were regular visitors to Gidleigh, staying at Berrydown while work was being carried out at Scorhill.

Robert rebuilt part of the old farmhouse at Scorhill but is better known for the enormous number of trees he planted round the property, many of which blew down in the great storm of 1989. He sold the property to the Reverend Ernest Brownlow Layard of Worthing in Sussex on 12 April 1898 and moved the family to Asolo in the Dolomites.

The Reverend Layard was a bachelor who leased the farm to Thomas and Mary Rowe [née Cullen], who kept house for him on his occasional visits. Percy Lowe Norrington and his wife Clara bought Scorhill from the Reverend Layard for £3,375 on 30 November 1907. They were responsible for a great deal of the rebuilding work and the present layout of the house.

Percy Norrington died on 20 September 1922, aged 53, and Clara sold the property, including the farmhouse and lodge, to Lt. Colonel Alexander Vicary two years later. The contents of the house were sold separately at auction. Clara built 'After' or 'Park' as it is now known, where she lived until her death in 1936. Arthur and Katie Williams occupied the lodge on the entrance drive to Scorhill in 1925.

Colonel Alexander Craven Vicary and his wife, Kathleen, moved in 1929 with their family to live at Scorhill after he retired and four years later bought 800 acres of Gidleigh Common. He had joined the 2nd Battalion Gloucestershire Regiment in 1908 and served in China, France, Salonika, southern Russia and India during the First World War. He was mentioned in dispatches on six occasions and awarded an MC and DSO and bar.

Though he retired from the Army in 1930, he re-enlisted when war broke out in 1939 and from 1944 to 1945 served in Italy and Burma and was made a Commander of the Bath. He was Lord of the Manor of Gidleigh, chairman of the Parochial Church Council, a governor of the Royal Devon and Exeter Hospital and of Chagford and Throwleigh schools, an Okehampton rural councillor and a member of the Dartmoor Commoners Association from its inception. He was also instrumental in helping to revive the Mid-Devon Hunt in the 1930s and was a Steward at Newton Abbott racecourse.

In 1931, Colonel Vicary originated what became known as 'Gidleigh Sports', a series of pony and horse races over an arduous 1.5-mile circuit on Gidleigh Common.

In August 1935, Gidleigh Parish carried out the traditional 'Beating the Bounds', a custom that has been honoured almost without break every seven years since 1639 and is a way of confirming the boundaries of the Parish. As in previous years, there was a foot race for the children to the food waggon at Wild Tor which was won by Will Webber of Buttern Farm, followed by 14-year-old Charlie Hill and, thirdly, by Dorothy Lentern. The youngest entrants on the day were Monica Hill and John Vicary, Colonel Vicary's son, both 12 at the time.

There have always been disputes between neighbouring parishes over their exact boundary lines and it is for that reason, as well as others, that 'Beating the Bounds' is so important an event in the area. Over the years, there have been many cases of boundary stones being moved, defaced or taken away all together. The Duchy of Cornwall is no exception and in the past has been accused of tampering with them. [3]

All Hallows, a small Catholic preparatory school with only 13 pupils started by Mr and Mrs Dix in Bognor Regis in 1938, took over the house after the outbreak of war in 1940 when concern about the school's safety in Bognor forced them to search for a safer place. Scorhill proved to be an ideal spot far from the coast and tucked away, as it is, on the edge of the Moor. Soon after the school arrived at Scorhill two boys, Michael Hartley from Torquay and an Austrian Count called Maurice Coreth, together with their riding instructor, 19-year-old Monica Hill from Ensworthy, retrieved an American airman who bailed out of his aeroplane and landed near them on the moor - but more of this later.

In the early years boys walked (on empty stomachs) to Mass each Sunday at Gidleigh Park provided by a priest called Father Pederick from Okehampton. In later years they had their own chapel at Scorhill served by monks from Buckfast Abbey. By the time the school left Scorhill to move to Cranmore Hall near Shepton Mallet at the end of 1945, it had grown to over 70 boys with some 'billeted' in annexes at Berrydown Farm and the house next door known as 'After'. The boys walked everywhere, Petrol was strictly rationed and the only times transport was provided was for away

---

[3] In 1808 when a wall was built as part of a newtake across Gidleigh Common the villagers protested and tore down the wall. The incident is described further in Chapter Three, pp. 168-9, below.

matches and at the start and end of each term when Mr Thomas, who ran a taxi and bus service in Chagford, took the boys to and from the station in Okehampton in his ancient coach. They walked to Chagford and back to watch the Dartmoor Pony Sale in the Autumn Term and to Kestor and Fernworthy reservoir as a regular Sunday afternoon activity. An old boy called, John Ford, said that one of the penalties fathers suffered when visiting their sons during term time was to be bullied into giving a talk to the boys on their wartime experiences. As a result they heard General de Guigand, Montgomery's Chief of Staff when on a 48 hour leave from Normandy and also the future Admiral Gladstone while he was on survivors' leave just after his ship, HMS Fiji of which he was the Commander, had been sunk in the Mediterranean. There were two girls at the school at this time, Moyra Bateman from Batworthy and Mima Luisa Pellew (now Lady Iddesleigh).

Major Arden brought the Mid-Devon hounds to meet at Scorhill once a season and this was always an excuse for the boys to have the morning of work. Lessons also stopped whenever hounds were hunting nearby or on the Moor.

The School Chronicle in 1942 contained an article by Robin Couchman, which he wrote when he was 13, and about to leave the school to begin his first year at Beaumont College. It captures the mood of the times and describes the house, its surroundings and the people he knew.

"Of all the places I have seen in England, I am convinced that there is not one can rival Scorhill in beauty. It is perched on a hill commanding a view over the moors, and behind it is a pine wood which is a protection against the keen winds. Below is the river Teign, which rushes down in pools and waterfalls, and in winter the rain often swells it into an awe-inspiring torrent of brown water, so strong that it moves even the huge boulders, which stand in its path. The house is nearly surrounded by the moors, their beauty lying in their bleakness and utter solitude. Near at hand are memorials of ancient days - the Sacred Circle of Scorhill with the stone avenue leading to it, the Round Pond and many other hut circles from the stone age.

What adds to the beauty of Scorhill is the colouring, supplied by the rhododendrons, red, white, pink and mauve, the grey granite, the yellow gorse and the purple heather. For all nature lovers Scorhill is an absolute paradise as it abounds in birds and animals, such as foxes, badgers, otters and rabbits; and there are many fish - trout and peel - in the river.

The house itself is a fine granite one and is most adaptable for a school, having many large rooms and dormitories. In the adjoining fields we have, with quite an amount of hard work, made a very respectable cricket ground, on which we have already played several matches.

We know a good many of the local people and they are all characteristic of the kindness and hospitality of Devon folk - Mrs Endacott and Mrs Rowe who have given us treats on special occasions, Mrs Hill who provided the 'pack' tea, Mr Vallance who so liberally rewarded our potato picking, and Nash always so kind and ready to join in any enterprise to the making of a cricket pitch to the setting up of a stage for our end-of-term plays.

I shall never forget my pleasant days in Devonshire; the early morning bathes in the Teign; the cricket in the meadow below the house; the picnics on school holidays; the scouting games on the brake; the walks across the heather-clad moors and much beside.

I have spent two years at Scorhill and know they will stand as two of the happiest years of my life."

  C.R.Couchman

Robin Couchman sadly was killed a very few years later in a parachute accident shortly after joining the Army.

Ernest Nash, referred to in Couchman's article, was the gardener and handyman at Scorhill. John Ford remembers him as "- a very kind and patient giant of a man who was regarded with great awe and admiration being credited with feats of incredible strength". He and his wife Annie lived in the Lodge with their son, Victor, who worked in the school as a House Boy for a time before joining the RAF. Nash had been a Colour Sergeant in Colonel Vicary's regiment and when the Colonel retired, he asked Nash to join him to help around the property. He was clearly very popular with the boys, who knew him simply as 'Nash', and was always willing to do what he could to help them with their projects, including the laying of a cricket pitch.

The Mrs Endacott mentioned by Couchman was Florence Endacott from Berrydown, who opened her house to some of the boys and spoiled them rotten. For years after the War, many old boys returned to visit her and to enjoy one of her renowned cream teas. Mrs Hill, Monica Hill's mother from Ensworthy, helped with the boys' riding lessons and provided packed lunches and cream teas.

John Ford said of his time as a schoolboy at Scorhill,

"Although we did not appreciate it at the time, we were really extraordinarily privileged to spend our formative years, during a World War, in such wonderful surroundings and in such a safe and healthy environment."

The Colonel's wife, Kathleen (née Hilton-Green), died in 1942 and their 20-year-old son, John, was killed while serving with the 17th/21st Lancers in North Africa in 1943.

The Colonel was de-mobbed in January 1945 and moved into Kestorway with his daughter, Peggy, until the school moved from Scorhill later that year. In 1947 he married Bridget Hale (née Hunter), who had lost her husband during the War. She had three young sons who were subsequently brought up at Scorhill. Meanwhile, the Colonel's daughter Peggy married Edward Madgwick, an officer in the Canadian Navy, in 1943 and three years later sailed for Canada on a 'Bride Ship' (The Mauritania) with her one-year-old son, to join her husband who had by then returned to Ottawa.

Edward Madgwick was born in Gloucestershire and served in European waters with the Canadian Navy on Atlantic and Russian convoy duty during the war. He served again in Korean waters in 1951 and was awarded the DSC. They have three children, a son in the Royal Navy and two married daughters. Peggy Madgwick inherited the property after her father died in 1975.

Percy Norrington built **SCORHILL FARMHOUSE** in 1909, to house his tenant farmer, Tom Rowe and his family. Mrs Madgwick now owns it.

Tom Rowe ran the 40-acre farm with the help of his wife, Mary, until he died in 1939, when his nephew Willy Cullen, who lived with them, took over the tenancy. Mary died in 1950 but Willy continued to run the place for almost 40 years, helped by his two spinster sisters Elsie and Emily. Elsie died in 1962, Emily in 1982 and Willy in 1984.

Rod Webber rented the house briefly for a few months before it was taken over by Michael and Carol Gaillard-Bundy in 1985. They lived there for 10 years until his tragic death in 1995, at which time Carol moved to Moorlands in Chagford. Michael was a well-known wood carver who carved, among other things, what is known as 'The Bishops Chair' in Exeter Cathedral and several pews in Chagford Church. In 1987 he presented the Church in Gidleigh with a beautifully carved wooden altar cross and ran courses for further education in wood carving. They both adored springer spaniels which they bred at their previous house, Brimstone, and later at Scorhill.

Jo Rowe-Leete rented the three-bedroom house in November 1995 and moved there with her children, Daniel and Rebecca (Becky).

Clara Norrington built **LOWER PARK** or Park House in 1923. She moved into the four-acre property in 1924 and initially called it 'After' because she moved there after selling Scorhill to the Vicarys. However, it has also been known as 'Greystones' and 'Park' over the years. Clara died on 16 June 1936 and left the house to her niece, Molly Clare Adye, who sold it in the same year to Horace Mann and his wife, Annie.

It has had many owners since, amongst whom have been Albert Lunn from Culford Lodge Farm in Bury St Edmunds (1940) and Lt Colonel Reginald Benwell from Frinton-on-Sea in Essex (1948). During the War the house became an overflow for boys and staff from All Hallows School which had taken over Scorhill in 1940.

John and Winnie Kingsland, who worked for Colonel Benwell, occupied a flat in the house where their daughters Jean and Di were both born. Winnie Kingsland (née Mortimore), is a first cousin of the late Norman Mortimore, one of the great and much-loved characters of the area who held court for years in the Northmore Arms at Wonson.

In 1955, Colonel Benwell sold the house to a schoolteacher called Walter Santer who renamed it 'Greystones' and it changed hands almost every two years thereafter until 1977:

1958	Lt Colonel Leonard Watkins	1966	Harold Gore
1960	Mrs Starling	1975	George and Thelma Carr
1962	Frederick and Elvena Rist	1976	Derek Reed

Ronnie and Mary Rankin who bought the house in 1977 sold it to Air Chief Marshall Sir Peter Squire and his wife, Carolyn, in 1996 and moved to a smaller property in Chagford, though they keep in touch with people here and are regular visitors to the village.

CHERRYFORD, originally a bungalow, was built for Amy Pardon Rowe in 1938 on a two-and-a-half acre plot forming part of the Rowe family farm at Berrydown.

In 1946, George Lentern and his wife, Annie (Amy's sister) bought the bungalow from Amy, who continued to live there until she died in 1954. Before he retired, George owned Norden Thatch Farm, now known by its old name of Northdown, near Murchington.

Their daughter, Dorothy, married Jack Lewis of Haycroft Farm in Murchington and they moved into the bungalow in 1952. Their son, who runs the garage in Chagford, was born there soon after. The cottage was sold after George Lentern died in 1959 and was occupied as a holiday home by Dr Edward Gratton and his wife Fay for a few years.

A property developer called Charles McKelvie bought the bungalow at auction in 1990. A year later, he commissioned plans from an architect called Roderick James to demolish it and construct a large green-oak framed house on the site. The project gained approval from the Dartmoor National Park Authority, but plans were shelved when the bottom fell out of the property market.

Bill and Pam Bourne, who bought the property in 1992, demolished the bungalow and built the present house. In 1998 they sold it to Graham and Pauline Leedom who provide bed and breakfast accommodation. The food is outstanding, as Graham was a chef at the Dorchester Hotel in London for some years, completing his catering career by teaching at Westminster College.

NORTH CREABER is a Grade II listed farmhouse and is one of two in the hamlet built in the 17th century on the site of earlier dwellings. Like others in the parish, it was owned by 'venville-right' holders.

The word 'venville' is a corruption of the Latin words 'fines villarum', meaning the rents of the vills.

Various farms in the parishes surrounding Dartmoor Forest were said to be 'in venville' if they enjoyed certain rights for which they paid a very small fixed rent to the Duchy. These rights allowed them to graze their animals on the Common. However, the number they could turn out was supposed to be limited to the number their farms could support in winter, a restriction known as 'levancy and couchancy'. This was in contrast to the rights of the ancient tenement holders who had free rights to the Forest only, but who owed certain services such as forming manor court juries and assisting in cattle drifts on behalf of the Duchy. None of the Gidleigh farms, however, are included in a list of manors and hamlets paying venville rents in Henry V11's accounts in 1505 perhaps because at that time Gidleigh formed a part of the

neighbouring manor of Throwleigh. [1]

Today it is impossible to be sure how many animals are grazed on the moor but in 1939 there were 29,000 cattle and 108,000 sheep in all the parishes bordering Dartmoor. Today the Ministry of Agriculture records might show a figure greater than the actuality.

Exactly when Dartmoor became classified as a 'forest' is not known for certain but in 1615 Manwood wrote;

"A Forest is a certain territorie of woody grounds and fruitful pastures, privileged for wild beasts and fowles of the Forest, chase and warren, to rest and abide in the safe protection of the King, for his princley pleasure." [2]

According to Allan Van der Steen, who was the architect responsible for the thorough refurbishment and enlargement of the house in 1986, the farm probably started as a single-roomed dwelling in the 1500s where the kitchen now stands. In the 17th century it was extended to include a shippon beyond a cross passage which had the effect of turning it into a form of long house.

Little remains of the original interior as the house was nearly derelict when work began on it in 1986. However, the fireplace in the parlour is probably late 17th century. The only carpentry not replaced in 1986 is a soffit-chamfered half beam across the front of the kitchen chimneybreast above the granite ashlar fireplace.

The recently refurbished threshing barn faces north-west and is built down the hillslope. It is probably earlier in construction than the house, being of 16th-century origin but with few if any signs of former domestic use.

Oliver Aggett paid rates for the farm in 1747 but by 1780 it was in the hands of the Knapman family. James Endacott bought it from the Knapmans in 1781 and took on eight-year old William Turpin as an apprentice. James's son, John, inherited the farm in 1827 and leased it to William Sampson in 1846. By 1876, William's son Edmund (b 1845) and his wife Charlotte, the daughter of William Westcott of Batworthy, took over the tenancy of the 30-acre property. Edwin Hill and his wife, Maria, lived there briefly in 1881 with their three children.

John Endacott died in 1885 and left the farm to his nephew, William Endacott

---

[1] *Worths Dartmoor* pp. 343-345 No mention of Gidleigh or any farms.

[2] Manhood, *Treatise of the Laws of the Forest,* 1615.

"during his life without impeachment of waste and from and after his death to the use of the first and every son of the said William Endacott successively according to their respective seniorities in tail......".

The entailing of estates and even small farms up to 1925 was a device used by successive owners to ensure the retention of property within a family and also to avoid the payment of any fee or duty on the transfer of ownership when one individual in the family died. All measure of devices were used by lawyers to transfer property.

One was known as a Lease and Release Conveyance, common between 1650 and 1840. This was a procedure for conveying a freehold without the need for registration and hence the payment of duty. A freeholder who wished to sell a property without publicity would first lease it, say for a year, to the intended buyer, for maybe five shillings - in other words he sold a lease, leaving himself with a future interest or reversion. The following day, the freeholder would release the reversion which, being incorporeal, or in other words an intangible right, could be conveyed by deed alone to the buyer or tenant and the conveyance, allowed by the Statute of Uses, was complete. The Release would have contained the full details of the conveyance.

In the past, the subject of land ownership and transfer seems to have been most complicated and evolved over the ages through a morass of legal hyperbole and contrivance. In feudal theory, all land belonged to the sovereign who did not occupy it himself but granted or conveyed parts to some of his subjects, who held such land as tenants-in-chief.

They in turn could grant some of this land to others who held it as tenants. Those tenants could grant a lease to others and so on indefinitely. However, the tenant at the bottom of the pile was the owner of the land as we understand it today. Each feudal superior was entitled to his cut in the way of service and payment from his tenants. [3]

It gets more complex because there were two kinds of lease. In a Lease for Lives, an owner

---

[3] The transfer of property as a result of the feudal theory of land ownership often caused frightful problems, so in 1535 the Statutes of Uses and Enrolments were introduced. The first made the original freeholder the actual owner of property and liable to pay Relief to the Crown when the property was sold. The second made the enrolment of conveyances compulsory and prohibited secret conveyancing. The result was that owners began to arrange complicated lease arrangements entering into one year deeds of grant, retaining for themselves a reversion that could be conveyed without livery of seisin. This system of Lease and Release remained in general use until 1841.

parted with a property based on the lives of certain named individuals. The lessee paid a fairly large fine, or capital sum, and a small rent and the lease was granted for the lives of three persons, usually by an institution such as a college, university or cathedral.

Then there was a Lease for Years, the more usual kind of lease, where an owner parts with the property for a stated period of time but retains the freehold.

In the case of North Creaber, however, the deeds show that in 1885 it was sold freehold without hindrance and had fields with names like Pit Meadow, Cleave, Witthay, Higher and Lower Water Park, Brake and Long Close. [4]

To return to the Endacotts, John and Maud Endacott took over the tenancy of the farm from Frank Cook in 1917. They left Glebe Farm and moved into Castle House for a few months with their three young children, John junior and the twins, Harold James and George, who now lives at North Forder.

Three other children were born at Creaber - Tom, Muriel and Dorel - and when they were young all six walked each day from Creaber to school at Providence.

After John Endacott died his eldest son, John, took over the tenancy in partnership with his mother. The owner, William Endacott (no relation), who spent most of his life at Gidleigh Mill, died in 1924 and left North Creaber to his eldest son, John George.

He arranged, with the agreement of his two surviving brothers Rolf and Ernest, to disentail the property and in 1951 sold it to the tenants, John Endacott and his mother Maud. John died intestate in 1965 at which point his brother, Tom, bought the remaining four-fifths of the property owned by his surviving brothers and sisters and farmed the property for the next twenty years.

Tom bought an Allis Chalmers in 1941, one of the first tractors to be seen around the village and the cause of some excitement in the neighbourhood. In the end, he chose to live in a caravan in the grounds rather than in the dilapidated farmhouse and died there on 4 November 1984.

John and Jennifer Milton bought the old farmhouse and 5.5 acres from Tom Endacott's estate on 20 April 1985. Their children Adam, Simon and Candia and their families, are regular visitors to Gidleigh. The Miltons have done a massive amount to the property over the years with the help of Allen van der Steen, converting the barn into an open-plan studio and guest wing.

Jen Milton died sadly in April 1999 after a long battle against illness and at a Memorial Service in Gidleigh Church one of the largest congregations seen there, paid there respects. John has since

---

[4] Cleave means a steep cliff-like field. Brake Close refers to an enclosed field of rough unbroken land, probably full of 'fern'.

married Judy Appleton, a long-time friend of the family.

John tells stories of his Great Aunt Hilda and her husband, Robert Cleminson, who lived at Castle House. Robert, having left the army, went to Canada "to shoot bears and grow peaches". The couple then moved to Jersey were they appear to have made a living playing bridge. John says that, as far as he can remember, Robert did little work other than collect stamps, a hobby he shared with King George V1.

He remembers packages arriving marked "Top Secret - OHMS". At the time, the rumour went round that he worked for MI5 but John feels certain that it was more likely they were simply swapping stamps! After Robert died, Great Aunt Hilda moved first to South Creaber and then to St Johns in Murchington.

As a schoolboy sent to relations in the country to get away from the blitz, John recalls life on Dartmoor at the time; long walks across the moor for riding lessons with the Hill family, trotting down deserted lanes with the smell of peat hanging over the village and then home to oil lamps and a tin bath in front of the fire. As a 10-year-old he was fascinated by the invasion gliders practising over the moor and the tense activity generated by the approaching invasion of France.

Great Aunt Hilda used to drive her car down the narrow lanes around Gidleigh by following the grass strip in the centre. When she drove to Okehampton on the main road, she drove down the white line in the centre of the road because, after all, that's what she always did! One can only guess at the reaction of her fellow road users.

On one occasion, she parked her car on the way to Okehampton and when she came to drive away she reversed into a car parked behind her. She caused quite some damage and was taken to court by the car's owner. Her defence was that the car behind wasn't there when she parked - and they let her off. She must have been quite a character. (Incidentally, her car ended life as a chicken house when it was left behind at Creaber after the move to St Johns).

According to *Worth's Dartmoor*, there is an ancient stone slot-and-L gate on the property, complete in all respects and preserving its original dimensions.

The name Creaber, sometimes spelt Creber or Creubergh, is old English for 'Crow Hill' and the name first appeared in documents held in Devon Record Office files dated 1238.

SOUTH CREABER is a Grade II listed farmhouse built in the early 16th century of granite stone rubble including a section of large coursed blocks of granite ashlar. There is evidence of 17th-century improvements and the house was modernised and partly rebuilt in the 1920s, with further modernisation in the 1980s. The rebuilt portion is plastered and the whole house has a slate roof which before 1920 was probably thatched. It was originally a 3-room-and-through-passage plan house and is reputed to have been a Dartmoor longhouse. The kitchen is a mid-17th century extension and a corridor connects it to the hall passing through the dining room, the former dairy.

It is evidently a house with a long and complex structural history and much of the early fabric may survive behind the later plaster. The court is surrounded by a collection of traditional Devon farm buildings that date, in part, from the early 1650s. Like North Creaber, it is thought to have been held in venville.

Creaber Pound, just below the farm, was the drift pound for the east quarter of Dartmoor. Unlike the other quarters, however, the drifts to Creaber were not the responsibility of the holders of the ancient tenements but rather local 'moormen' or venville farm owners.

In 1680 James and Agnes Vogwell owned the farm, cousins of the Vogwells of Moortown. They died within a month of one another in 1687. John Jarvis paid tithes for the farm in 1742, followed by James Tiddy in 1780. Eight years later it was acquired by Bartholomew Gidley with Christopher Head as tenant. In 1843 Bartholomew's son Gustavus inherited it and passed the tenancy to John Dunning. John bought the farm from the Gidleys in about 1860 and it remained in the Dunning family for many years thereafter.

Richard Dunning of Thule Farm took over the freehold of Creaber in 1873 and, together with George Frost of Greenaway, was appointed an overseer of the parish in 1898. This seemed to be of some importance in those days. Apart from any sense of public spiritedness, parishioners were obliged to pay 'rates' that, prior to 1834, included a 'Poor Rate' which had to be assessed in advance each year. It was collected with some difficulty and distributed by the overseers in a variety of ways.

People in need of help would apply to the overseers who would assess their case. All the villagers and their circumstances would be well known and local men were often in a good position to judge their needs accurately and fairly. It was an unenviable job, however, carrying with it a good chance of being accused of favouritism or neglect.

The parish had no obligation to support anyone who did not have a settlement (a right to live in the parish) and this depended on a variety of circumstances: place of birth, place of last work and so on. Illegitimate children were always likely to be a charge on the parish so the overseers' job would be to trace the fathers of these children and get them to pay maintenance. After 1834 the

parish was no longer responsible for its poor and part of the overseers' job disappeared. [1]

Richard Dunning died in 1899, aged 68. His sons, Alfred and Bob, took over the running of the farm which at the time had fields with names such as Rush Close, Journey, Post Close, Higher and Lower Parson's Hay, Hurdle Plot and Yonder Brake. [2] The freehold was transferred to Bob in 1910 and he and his sister, Anne, lived in the house with Percy Tucker, the farmer and Elsie Canning the cook. In 1920 Agnes Packard also moved into a part of the house.

After Robert Cleminson died his wife, Hilda, (John Milton's great aunt) moved from Castle House to join them and at the end of the war they all moved to St Johns in Murchington. Anne Dunning died on 4 January 1956 aged 90 and is buried in Throwleigh churchyard.

There is no doubt that Bob Dunning was a great local character. He is quoted by just about everyone who visited Gidleigh as being an expert on all subjects from ancient cure-alls to stories about the folklore of the moor. Peggy Madgwick said that he lived almost entirely on cider that he called 'pure apple juice' and was never far from a glass of it.

John Holman and George Endacott remember him doing little work around the farm. He spent a good deal of his time sitting outside the house with his binoculars, keeping an eye out for visitors. George remembers him driving his horse and cart and empty hogshead through the village on his way to Spreyton on regular cider buying expeditions.

In the introduction to a book that contains drawings of Creaber, he is said to "know the moor well and is himself widely known". [3]

Brian Sillem bought the farm from the Dunning family on 31 May 1947 and sold it in 1954 to

---

[1] By the end of the 17th century, the parish poor relief system was well established and the payment of rates to fund it was considered a reasonable price to pay to care for the impotent poor and as a result prevent social disorder. Overseers continued to be appointed in some parishes in Devon up to the outbreak of the First World War, when district councils were established. They were basically unpaid officials who fulfilled various roles, including being churchwardens and overseers of the highways or waywardens. Together with the parson and the squire, they made up the government of the village, the Vestry as it was called, administering national law on a parish scale.

[2] Yonder Brake refers to a piece of rough unbroken ground a fair distance from the farmhouse. Higher and Lower Parson's Hay probably refers to some long forgotten arrangement whereby the priest got the hay from those fields in lieu of tythe.

[3] Allen W. Seaby, *Dinah - the Dartmoor Pony.*

a Frank Mitchell, who appears to have spent much of his time making and trying to sell clay model animals. Having sold Creaber, Sillem bought the Warren Inn near Postbridge, on the road between Moretonhampstead and Princetown.

In 1962, the Wells family acquired the farm for £2,950. It was offered at £3,000 but John Wells said they managed to get £50 knocked off the price "because there were no drains". John and Alice Wells farmed the 42-acre property until 1999 and were regularly visited by their children Ben, his wife Vicky and their six children Sophie, Georgia, Juliet, James, Charles and Thomas; Katherine, (Tabbin) married to John Almond, and their children Lucy and Edward and finally Tom, his wife Katie and their children William and Henry.

John Wells was chairman of the Gidleigh Parish Meeting for over 30 years and he and Alice are joint secretaries of the Mid-Devon Hunt, which has the north-eastern quarter of the moor as its country.

The history of the Mid-Devon dates back to 1604, though the book containing these early records was destroyed in a fire at Furlong, near Chagford, the Bragg family home. According to surviving records, the Braggs provided the Master from 1793-1822 and then for most of the 19th century. Masters such as Colvill Hayter Hames, John Byers-Leeke, Gilbert Spiller and Gerald Crawshay-Ralston followed them.

The country was hunted continuously from 1793 up to 1915 when the then Master, Captain Huntriss, was called up to join his regiment. The Mid-Devon was restarted on May 1 1937 and with little upset has thrived ever since.

The reports in the press of those early days are a joy to read, full of quotes and details of each day's sport. The author of the articles written between 1892 and 1907 doesn't hide his enthusiasm for the sport and often breaks into verse to illustrate his enjoyment of the day's hunting.

> *"No longer like a flash of fire*
> *He flies o'er mountain heath and mire*
> *No longer level with his back*
> *But dark bedraggled, soiled and slack*
> *He bears his brush".*

In those days the Mid-Devon met at, among other places, Fernworthy, Bennetts Cleave, South Zeal, Postbridge, Throwleigh, Okehampton and of course Chagford where the traditional Boxing Day meet is held. After another day's sport the enthusiastic hunting poet wrote:

"Nothing daunted -on they pull
Their breeches spurs and boots
Some in red and some in black
And some in other suits
A few appear on wheels that day
And two have come by rail
But if I counted all who came
twoud make too long a tale".

The South Devon Hunt week in April 1896 consisted of ten days' hunting on the wild moorland country on East and North Dartmoor. In all, five packs contributed towards the week's sport and people came from all over Devon and Cornwall to enjoy it.

On April 8, Mr Sperling's hounds met at Okehampton and on the 9th Mr St Maur's hounds met at Grendon. On the 10th it was the turn of the Mid-Devon that met at Fernworthy and then on the 11th, Mr St Maur's again at Heatree. Believe it or not, Mr St Maur's hounds met yet again on the 13th at the Rock Hotel and on the 14th Mr Sperling's hounds met at Postbridge.

On the 15th there was a large gathering for Colonel Garratt and the East Devon Hounds at Widecombe, followed on the 17th with the Dartmoor at Brimpts. Finally the ubiquitous Mr St Maur and his pack of tireless wonders provided what turned out to be the best day of the week at Manaton.

In those days, people kept several hunters so finding fresh horses was not a problem. However, they had to ride miles to the meet and then, after an exhausting day's hunting, ride back to their stables at night. There must have been a few sore bodies by the end of that week.

A short verse in memory of the landlord of the Warren Inn written by George Bragg, Master of the Mid-Devon, sets the scene:

"Don't pass this house, but call on Joe Warne
An honest old fellow as ever was born;
Two good things he keeps, they are brandy and peat,
The one warms the stomach,the other the feet."

In 1898, an article in a local paper described what sort of horse was needed to hunt with the Mid-Devon:

"He must have all good qualities save one - he need not be a water jumper. He must, however, be strong, fast, a good bank jumper and should possess the cleverness of a cat. He will at times be called upon to get up and down banks as steep as the side of a house; nothing but a galloper can live with hounds over open country."

For the hunting man, Dartmoor is described as rough country, with wild tough foxes. The rich land-owning squires may have faded away but they have been replaced by a much more democratic mix of local enthusiasts, from farmers to building workers, from shop girls to lawyers.

Keen followers of the Mid-Devon Hunt today include characters such as Will Hutchins, one of the 'terrier men', Heather Parr and her father Herbie, George Lyon-Smith, Robert Curtis and Diane and Crispin Alford.

The Bentinck brothers from Yelfords, near Chagford Common, became keen followers of the Mid-Devon hunt in the 1950s and Guy Bentinck said that, had it been possible, he would have hunted five days a week and gone cubbing on Sunday. Everything would stop on the farms when the hunt passed by and the nearest vantage point was sought to watch the tricks of the fox and the skills of the hounds.

There are tales of past masters and characters of the day, such as Major Arden, for example, who had only one leg. He rode with the stump in a holster and his wooden leg in a bag over his shoulder. Charles Hooley, a wild man who loved to play the trumpet, switched from being Master of the Mid-Devon to become Master of the North Dartmoor Beagles. Another character was Harry Davis, a local poacher and keen hunt follower.

In spite of the anti-blood sports lobby of recent times, hunting has as large a following as ever in the area. In a recent survey conducted by an independent group, over 90% of the farmers who farm in the Dartmoor National Park said they support hunting on their land. The Mid-Devon remains a most popular hunt with joint Masters Michael Hickmott from Whitestone, Graham Pope from Throwleigh and Hugo de Ferranti from Parford House near Chagford.

There was a paragraph in the newsletter of a Devonshire Equestrian Club a year or two ago which read:

"Colonel ..... said he could not abide sloppiness; girls who rode to hounds should ride dressed properly or not at all."

Finally, here is an extract of a newspaper report of the first day meet of the Mid-Devon Hunt 100 years ago:

"THE MID-DEVON HOUNDS - Oct 31st 1898

The opening meet was on Monday at Fernworthy, a moorland farm situated in the heart of Dartmoor. A large field, perhaps the largest on record, welcomed the Masters, Messrs, Ralston and Spiller. Those present included Mr and Mrs Hayter Hames, Mr Byres-Leake, Mr Charles Cumming, Major General Holley, Mr Richard Dunning, Mr A. G. Whipham, Mr Ferrier Kerr and many others - but alas! For the first time for years - no sporting parson!
On the Assycombe Hill a fox is viewed stealing away to Hempson Rocks. Hounds settle on his line but he's headed back and makes his point up the valley to the New Take Gate and on to New House, past Warren Tor, on to Birchy Tor where just opposite Grimspound he was marked to earth. The run was throughout slow. Then followed a long draw, on to Gidleigh Park, where hounds quietly got on the line, but scent was bad and a slow run ended in earthing him on the south side of the Park.
The day was very enjoyable, the air keen and bracing and though not a classical sporting one, was very satisfactory as showing great possibilities for the future.

"Ye Gods what a fox, what a punishing pace
it is less like a hunt than a steeplechase!"

John and Alice Wells have been keen Dartmoor Greyface sheep breeders over the years and entered their ewes in all the local shows.

On Dartmoor, Scotch Blackface sheep have largely taken over from the Dartmoor Whiteface but in Devon as a whole there are several other breeds such as Devon Closewool, Exmoor Horn, the Devon Longwool, South Devon as well as the Dartmoor Greyface. In recent years, many new breeds have been created by crossing foreign sheep such as Romanov, Friesland, Spanish Merino and others with the native breeds but the pure-bred Dartmoors continue to hold their own against an invasion of multi bred stock.

John and Alice sold the farmhouse to their daughter, Tabbin and her husband John Almond in 1999 and retired to a bungalow near their favourite pub, the Northmore Arms at Wonson. The flat at South Creaber was occupied by Jo Rowe-Leete and her children between 1988 and 1995 and then, until recently, by Steve and Lorna Gallimore who also now live at Wonson.

Agnes Packard built **CREABER COTTAGE** as a family holiday home in the 1920s. Her daughter, Iris, married the Reverend Charles James Selwyn Ward, the Vicar of Langham, on the Suffolk and Essex border. Coincidentally, the artist, John Constable's wife was the daughter of another earlier vicar of Langham.

The Reverend Ward's daughter, Morwenna, married the artist and sculptor, John Skeaping in 1934 and they lived at Creaber Cottage, on and off, until 1940 when John left to join the Army in the early stages of the war.

Skeaping was one of the most brilliant of the young British sculptors who came to the fore in the 1920s. He won all the important scholarships available for sculpture - the British Institution, The Royal Academy Gold Medal and in 1923 he won the Prix de Rome and proceeded to marry the runner-up, Barbara Hepworth, shortly after.

He worked in close association with her and Henry Moore until differences of temperament and style made the relationships impossible. Barbara left to live with Ben Nicholson while John Skeaping had a brief affair with a buxom seductress called Eileen, whom he met at riding school. He was befriended by a number of celebrities of the day such as the distinguished biologist, Sir Ray Lancaster, Bernard Shaw, Arnold Bennett and H.G. Wells.

He once told a story illustrating how Wells' caustic wit got him into trouble at a dinner party. A young lady had spent most of the evening flirting and swapping banter with him when clearly he showed little interest in her. She said to him – "There, Mr Wells, I can give tit for tat". "All right," said Wells, "tat!" The conversation ended.

David Jacobs, the television and radio presenter, knew Skeaping well and said that he enjoyed having him on the panel of his shows together with people like Francis Day, Bill Owen and Katie Boyle.

While living at Creaber Cottage, John started work on a pair of gigantic granite tortoises in a yard owned by Bertie Gratton, a stone carver in Sticklepath. To give some idea of the hardness of granite, John said that were this to be measured in figures, "ordinary Portland building stone would be 250 whereas the reading for granite would be 1,350". When he finished the tortoises he was justly proud of the fact that, though they would never be on public display, he could carve granite, something no other living sculptor could do.

He spent hours chatting to the characters who hung around Bert's yard watching him work, droning away in that lovely Dartmoor dialect with all the words joined together, "sounding like a swarm of bees hovering over a flower-bed". He also built up a kennel of greyhounds and trained ten of them himself. He raced them at tracks in Marsh Barton and the County Ground in Exeter with some success. Guy Bentinck remembers being taken dog racing by John who, at the time, had something of a reputation as a 'smart boy' when it came to the dogs.

Skeaping enjoyed life on Dartmoor and when he wasn't racing greyhounds or working on his granite sculptures he was riding over the moor to fish for mountain trout or to visit one of his favourite pubs, the Warren Inn. In his autobiography, he mentions these trips across the moor and how the only person he ever met was 'old stony Adders'. [1] Adders was a stone carter who slept and lived on the moor. He wore an old bowler hat, green with lichen, with a red poppy in the band that looked as if it had been there since the end of the First World War.

In another of his favourite pubs, the Cawsand Beacon in South Zeal, he, Morwenna and his friends, Bert Gratton, the Endicotts and Billy Rowe the butcher, heard on the wireless that war with Germany had been declared. During the war he served in the Intelligence Corps and the SAS. On one occasion a ship called Strathallan, taking him and 6,000 troops to North Africa, was torpedoed in the Mediterranean. He was one of the few survivors rescued by a British destroyer moments before the troopship sank.

In 1945 he returned to his "beloved Devon" and bought Puggiestone, "a large ugly house" with thick granite walls and about 15 rooms near Chagford. David Astor, a friend and patron whom he met during the War, lent him the money to buy the house and Morwenna and the twins, Colin and Chris born in 1945, moved in. Nicholas arrived in 1947.

In 1949, John moved to Mexico for three years and soon after his return was appointed Professor of Sculpture at the Royal College of Art and elected an Associate of the Royal Academy. At about this time, Jean Drewe was taken on as a kennel maid to look after the family's 15 standard poodles. She says that in time she also helped to look after the children, did some cooking and acted as a general help around the house.

She remembers Skeaping's love of tickling salmon in the rivers round the moor and his friendship with the racing crowd, particularly John Hislop and Peter O'Sullivan who were godfathers to the twins, Colin and Chris. In 1959, however, he decided to leave England for good and moved to the Camargue in the south of France. Morwenna continued to live at Puggiestone until it was sold in 1968. Skeaping died on 5 March 1980.

His work includes the statue of Mill Reef at Paul Mellon's Rokeby Stud and the statue of Brigadier Gerard at Newmarket. He also made the famous bronze statue of the 1933 Derby and St. Leger winner,

---

[1] John Skeaping, *Drawn from Life*

Hyperion, that stands at Lord Derby's Stanley House Stud and was modelled in clay at a studio in Chagford. His work can be found in museums all over the world, including the British Museum, the Adelaide Art Gallery, the National Museum, Tokyo, the Tate Gallery and the Yale Centre for British Art in the United States. He is remembered as one of the most creative of modern British sculptors.

Another proud owner of Creaber Cottage was a Mr Perrott, a chemist from Martock in Somerset. He became famous in the community for owning the first television set to be seen in the village. His wife, a practising midwife, adopted the surviving twins of a woman who died in childbirth.

(This mention of childbirth prompts the story of a local lawyer who received a form filled in by a client which included the question: "Are you a natural born British subject?" against which the client had written: "No, by Caesarean operation".)

BERRYDOWN is a large Grade II listed farmhouse built mostly of blocks of granite ashlar with a slate roof. The old farmhouse was of a 3-room-and-through passage plan, built down the hill slope and facing south. The newer block, facing east and built at right angles to the original section, contains the principal rooms.

It has been greatly altered and gentrified over the years but it is still possible to see where the cross passage was in the south-facing farmhouse. It contains all the usual massive granite fireplaces, some dating back to the late 1500s, while others were built later than 1800 when the newfangled 'feather and tare' system used for splitting stone was first introduced.

This confirms the belief that the house underwent considerable rebuilding in the early 19th century, including raising the ceilings by almost three feet. It was certainly one of the most important farms in the parish at that time and had fields with names such as Shuta Park, Middle and Lower Grattner, Bowey, Great Neat Down and Sheellands. [1]

According to the Assize Roll of 1322, Berrydown was the home of Ralph de Beridon. It got its name from the word 'Berrow', Celtic for 'hilltop'. In 1332 the Assize Roll shows the property in the possession of his son, Simon. On a list of Jurates in the Stannary Court of Chagford dated 1532, the first of a plethora of John Rowes of Berrydown appear and again in 1572, the Tawton Rolls have a 'John Rowe of Berydon' in residence.

The Stannary Courts were created by a Charter of Richard I, over 600 years ago, to police the tin-mining industry of Cornwall and Devon. They were not abolished until 1896. In the 16th

---

[1] Shuta, as in Shuta Park, is Celtic for orchard. Grattner or Gratton, as in Middle and Lower Grattner, means cultivated field.

century there were more than 12,000 tin miners in the West Country, known as 'Spalliards' and described as the roughest men in England.

The power of the Stannary Courts was legendary. Richard Strode, a Member of Parliament, experienced this power when he was arrested by the tinners and thrown into jail in Lydford Castle after trying to stop them polluting the rivers of the South West. He was left there to rot for three weeks on a diet of bread and water; on his release he persuaded the Commons to pass an Act allowing Members of Parliament freedom of speech in the House without threat of prosecution.

William Browne wrote:

> *"I oft have heard of Lydford Law*
> *How in the morn they hang and draw*
> *and sit in judgement after.*
> *At first I wondered at it much*
> *but soon I found the matter such*
> *as it deserves no laughter."* [2]

There is an entry in the Gidleigh Parish Register dated 1603 recording the marriage in Gidleigh Church of Stephen Berrye to Joan Downe. How appropriate the marriage would have been had they lived at Berrydown. They didn't, of course, as it was already in the hands of the Rowe family.

The initials 'JR' (John Rowe) were carved above the entrance door in 1655 and it was at that time that the main part of the house was built and the earlier house underwent a series of major alterations. The Rowe family owned the property from 1532 to 1938, apart from a brief interlude in the 18th century.

John seems to have been the most popular name for boys in all branches of the Rowe family over the years and it is all but impossible to determine which John owned which farm, when.

In the Subsidy Roll for 1624, a John Rowe is in possession and again in 1654, mention is made of a John Rowe marrying Joan Messenger in Gidleigh church and moving to Berrydown. Samuel Rowe, however was the owner in 1780 and his son, John, took over in 1815. He owned Berrydown, Scorhill and Batworthy, a total of 200 acres, which he farmed with his son, William, who took over the farm when his father died in 1832. In 1843 they paid tithes of £14 and Berrydown itself was listed as being 58 acres in size.

The Rowe family has had its ups and downs over the years; in a way it is remarkable that it held

---

[2] William Brown, *Lydford Journey*

on to the property for as long as it did. A more detailed account of the innumerable members of the Rowe family who owned the farm over the years can be seen in the 'Tale of Berrydown' written by P.R. Whiteaway for the May family in 1986.

An extract from 'Trewmans Exeter Flying Post', dated 26 January 1837, announced:

"On January 12th at Chagford aged 90 years and 8 months, Mrs Margaret Rowe, widow of the late Mr James Rowe of Gidleigh, yeoman, leaving 9 children, 59 grandchildren and 65 great grandchildren; she was one of the good old Dames and was much respected by a large crowd of relatives and friends."

With so many relations, it is surprising that ownership of the property passed out of the control of the Rowe family, as it did with Amy Rowe in 1938.

There is a story told of a horse and cart falling into a tunnel in one of the fields on the farm, and the belief that the tunnel is connected to the Castle adds a little glamour and romance to the area. Exactly why a tunnel should exist between the Castle and Berrydown Farm has never been explained but the 'tunnel' might just be part of the leat that was built by Bartholomew Gidley in the 1650s and is said to run past Creaber and Berrydown to Gidleigh Castle.

There are stories of tunnels all over Devon of impossible length, such as the one from Denbury to Tavistock being 30 miles through solid granite and another from Gidleigh Park to Prinsep's Folly. How these rumours of tunnels start is not clear but it is supposed that dimly remembered connections between buildings owned by the same or related owners assume underground links that never existed. It must be said, however, that 'secret passages' or tunnels in general cannot be very long due to the difficulty of construction and ventilation.

In the Census Return of 1881 James Rowe, a 39-year-old farmer, his 30-year-old wife Jane and two daughters, Bessie and Annie, are recorded living on the farm, together with a 23-year-old landscape artist called Frank Beswick from Cheshire. It is likely that the farmhouse opened as a guest house at around this time. In 1930, Lawrence Worskett and several other people were living at Berrydown including John and Hannah Tattershall, Alice Akers, Beatrice Brimblecombe and Charles Earland.

John Caroll Johnson from Brighton bought the farm on 30 November 1938 from Amy Rowe for £2,600 and in 1939 let it to William and Irene Bowsher. They ran it as a guest house for several years, charging 2 1/2 guineas a week most of the year and 3 guineas in high summer. An overnight stay cost 10/6d or around 52 pence (equivalent to about £50 today). In the 1939 Electoral Register, the people eligible to vote and listed as resident at Berrydown, apart from the Bowshers, included Florence Darby, Mary Kensington and Robert Ponsford.

In 1943, Arthur Charles (Charlie) and Florence Endacott moved to Berrydown from Higher Murchington Farm. They rented it from John Johnson, who died a couple of months later on 14 July 1943, after which it was inherited by his daughter, Erica, who sold it to the Endacotts on 29 April 1946.

Florence Endacott had moved from Wales when she was 17 to work for the Sutton family at St Olaves in Murchington. She left to work at Gidleigh Park as a parlour maid for the McIlwraith family for four years before returning to St Olaves where she met her husband, Charlie. They married in 1940 and moved in with Charlie's parents at Higher Murchington Farm for a while before taking over the tenancy of Berrydown.

Florence tells a story about Charlie, an avid hunting man who, when out ploughing one day with his two horses, heard the hounds calling beyond Gidleigh. He stopped, unhitched both horses, tied one to the hedge and leapt on the other to follow the hunt leaving his furious father to finish the ploughing.

Charlie farmed the 56-acre property for 30 years, turning it back into a working farm while Florence used the house to take in lodgers. In those days, it had 12 bedrooms and a loo and bathroom upstairs, and five sitting rooms, two kitchens, a dairy and pump house downstairs with an outside loo. It had running water supplied from the leat which ran through the grounds. During the war, the Endacotts took in boys from All Hallows School at Scorhill as boarders and opened the house to the parents when they came to visit them.

Like so many of the farmers in the village, Florence made and sold clotted cream, butter, eggs and milk to the visitors that came to stay. Their two children, Evan born in 1941 and Val born in 1948, helped on the farm. Val can remember the family driving their stock to market in Chagford on foot, collecting the odd beast from neighbours on the way.

Val married Graham Loram, a carpenter from Chagford, at Gidleigh Church in May 1970 and they moved into a flat at Berrydown. On her wedding morning she found her father standing in the kitchen in a bit of a lather. While changing at the last moment he had mistakenly rubbed shaving cream into his hair instead of Brylcream and so, dressed in all her wedding finery, she put his head in the sink and washed his hair for him. They got to the church on time but it was a close shave!

Val and Graham's daughter, Kay Marie, was born in Okehampton Hospital on 11 February 1972, the first child born to a Gidleigh resident in 10 years. When he heard the news of Kay's arrival, their neighbour, John Wells from Creaber - who had three children and was known to boast that he had fathered three-quarters of the children in the village - told a local newspaper reporter: "Now I'm only the father of three fifths!" Gidleigh, with a population of only 80 at the time and most of those quite elderly, saw a newborn baby as quite a novelty.

Evan Endacott, who married Julia Rice, works at Moortown Farm and lives in Chagford. His daughter, Catherine, is the General Manager of Gidleigh Park Hotel. Charlie Endacott died in 1981 and is buried at Providence. Florence, hail and hearty as ever, lives at Little Paddock in Throwleigh.

In 1971, the Endacotts sold about 20 acres of land to Colonel Terry of Ensworthy and in 1973 they sold the rest of the farm to Henry Oakley, a dentist from Chagford and his wife Barbara. The Oakleys altered the place quite a bit, including removing the attractive bay windows from the south and west fronts.

In 1977 they in turn sold to Denis Wilkinson, a property developer from Humberside, who started a plant nursery next door called Berrydown Products (Gidleigh) Ltd specialising in heathers and conifers.

Gary Mortimore worked at the **NURSERY** for three years as a teenager. Denis Wilkinson would collect him and a couple of school friends off the bus in Chagford for work at the nursery, potting up plants in the summer months. Wilkinson, who built the Brettville Close development in Chagford, evidently had hoped to convert the property into holiday flats but that plan was discarded. He sold a couple of fields and the house known as Moorhurst (Little Berrydown) to Roy and Bridget Barnett in 1977.

The Nursery business was sold to two partners who ran it for a few years before they too sold in 1994. A house had already been built on the site and outline planning permission had been given subject to an agricultural tie. The house has recently been sold with the agricultural tie lifted on condition that plant tunnels and other equipment is removed.

The rest of the property was sold in 1984 to Syd Moore, who lived there for a couple of years with his wife, Gabrielle and her parents. He described himself as an Australian-Armenian and his nickname among the locals who knew him was 'Hissing Syd'. He was a larger-than-life character, large in every sense of the word, who involved himself in the local hunt and seems to have spent most of his time dealing in local property when prices were going through the roof. John Milton tells of being invited to the house to see Syd's latest acquisition, what he described as an 11th century bed! "Trouble is," said Syd, "I had to cut the legs off to get it in!"

Neville and Jill May bought the property from Syd Moore in July 1986 and commissioned the history of the house prepared by Mr Whiteaway. The booklet contains far more detail about the farm and the Rowe family than would fit in this book.

John and Brenda (Bee) Barford bought the property from the Mays, having sold Puggiestone in Chagford. They, in turn, sold it in 1999 to Alan and Yvonne Roberton who moved in with their children Charles and Victoria (their eldest offspring, Zoe lives in Berkshire), three of their five horses and several peafowl. They came to Gidleigh from Oxfordshire; for Yvonne, whose family farmed near Haytor, this was a return home.

LITTLE BERRYDOWN, originally known as Moorhurst, was built for a member of the Rowe family and like Berrydown Cottage it remained part of Berrydown Farm for many years. In 1908 it was let to a Mrs C J Hobson, who wrote to the Church Commissioners asking if they would sell her a small piece of land nearby so that she could build a cottage. They appear to have rejected her request and she moved a few years later. At some stage prior to 1920 it was tenanted by a Miss Akers for a few years.

It burned down in 1939 when occupied by the Pilcher family, who were away at the time, and the cause of the fire was something of a mystery. The burnt-out shell, with its tin roof, was used as a barn by the Endacott family for many years. In 1977, however, it was bought by Roy and Bridget Barnett with about five acres of land. They lived in a caravan nearby with their two children while working on rebuilding the house.

At about this time, the name was changed to Little Berrydown Farm which caused some confusion. When it was sold to John and Carol West in 1981 they dropped the word 'farm' and call it simply Little Berrydown. They have since acquired more land and created a garden in the field opposite.

BERRYDOWN COTTAGE, built in about 1700 as a farm worker's thatched cottage with two acres of land, originally formed part of Berrydown Farm, owned by the Rowe family for 400 years. It was known simply as The Cottage, Berrydown. According to the Electoral Roll in 1902, it was tenanted by Anna Alexandrina Grant and by 1910 it was in the possession of a Miss Hanfield.

In 1910, William and Alexina Ferrier-Kerr were shown as living there in what was at the time described as 1 Berrydown Cottage. William was a keen hunting man and he is listed as one of the field out with the Mid-Devon at Folly Gate in 1896.

It was sold by Amy Pardon Rowe on 29 September 1937 to Millicent Lely from Eastbourne in Sussex and occupied by two maiden sisters called Tattershall soon after. At some point in the late 1930s or early 1940s, the thatched roof burnt off and was replaced with tiles.

On 8 October 1946, the cottage was sold to Agnes, the widow of James Black from Tiverton, who moved there with her son Gerard. Agnes died in 1962 and the cottage was eventually sold to Robert Woollcombe from Petworth in Sussex on 29 September 1967. He used it as a retreat, a place to write and escape the pressures of life in the Home Counties.

Robert Woollcombe applied for and got confirmation from the Devon County Council of grazing rights for the cottage on Gidleigh Common. He died in 1996 and left the property to his children.

GREENAWAY, in the 12th century, was the home of Ralph de Greneweyesfote or 'green way's foot'. The house was probably built as a longhouse in the 1650s on the site of an earlier wood-frame building. Like so many farms in the area, however, it has been altered considerably over the years. Much of the original character of the longhouse, however, can still be seen. The through passage is now the entrance hall with the living area, now the kitchen, to the left. It contains the original fireplace and a gap where the bread oven has been removed.

The kitchen has always been the centre of life in Dartmoor farmhouses and was ruled over by the farmer's wife. In medieval times, farmhouses contained one large room, open to the roof with a central fire, in which all food preparation, cooking, eating and sleeping took place. Wall fireplaces were known in England since the 11th century at least but were uncommon in Devon farmhouses until much later.

Residents ate off wooden platters, (sometimes square sometimes round), with a scoop on the rim for salt. Their jugs and bowls where often made of leather or tin. Later in the 17th century, pewter plates and mugs were introduced and were much prized by the families in this part of Devon, often being passed from generation to generation together with heavy brass cooking utensils. Finally, imported china or porcelain was introduced by the squirarchy in the 17th century and silver, by the gentry, in the 18th.

In later years, many of the larger farms had several specialist rooms such as dairies, still rooms, smoke chambers, butteries and so on. Butter was kept until needed in a butter-cooler or butter well. This might have been a simple arrangement of slates over a stream or something more elaborate.

Cheese was dried by the larder window and it is interesting that these windows were exempt from the Window Tax introduced in 1795, as long as they had the words 'Cheese Window' clearly painted in large black letters on the lintel above.

Until recently, it was quite normal for a farmer to give his wife no housekeeping money at all. She was expected to keep the household going, feed the family and all the farm servants, make clothes and buy china all from her own earnings. From the 18th century, butter, cream, bacon, cheese, honey and eggs were all very saleable in the local markets or were shipped to Exeter, Bristol or London and beyond.

Every week or so, a farmer's wife would set off to market in a pony and trap, or riding side-saddle on a pony with a packhorse on a rein behind her. How much she had to sell would depend largely on her own industry and that of any farm servants her husband employed.

Somebody once said they had seen a sign in a farm window in Devon which read: "Eggs are good value - still 12 to the dozen".

In the 16th century, chimneys became common to all Devon houses and were often built into the thickness of the walls. Above the hearth would be a massive granite beam which supported the weight of the chimney. A mantelpiece, or in Devon parlance a 'clavy-tack', was attached to it on which a jar for salt, a pestle and mortar perhaps and other small household items such as candlesticks and a rack for clay pipes could be kept.

The head of the family had a chair or settle close to the fire. These Devon 'bacon settles' had doors in the back for storing food. In the centre of the room there would have been a large kitchen table surrounded with benches, at which the whole extended family would eat including the farm servants.

After 1750, the potato ('tetties') became the principal food of farmworkers in and around Chagford and Moretonhampstead. They replaced rye bread that, together with 'risty' bacon and 'vinid' cheese, formed the basic diet on the poorer moorland farms. In the 17th century, salt fish and 'tetties' was a common meal in all parts of Devon when salted Newfoundland cod called haberden was shipped over from the waters off the east coast of North America. Served with beans, 'hastings and runcivall' or marrow fat peas, sometimes carrots and cabbage, it made a wholesome and filling meal. [1] [2] The dried,

---

[1] Thomas Tusser, *Five Hundred Points of Good Husbandry*, 1580, describes the diet of the people living in the Westcountry at that time in great detail.

[2] Broad beans are the only indigenous bean in this country. All other types of bean were introduced to England from North and South America during the 17th century.

salted fish stank to high heaven and was often referred to as 'toerag' by the farmers in Devon.

Christmas was a great feasting time, however, and the 12 days of Christmas really meant 12 days' holiday. Most of the year's harvest was still in store and at Christmas they ate extremely well.

"At Christmas be merry and thankful withal
and feast thy poor neighbours, the great and the small!" [3]

By the early 18th century, most vegetables familiar today such as carrots, onions, parsnips, spinach, lettuce, leeks, parsley and radishes were grown in country house gardens; but it is not certain how common they were outside the big towns.

Here at Greenaway, the extension to the north on the far side of the through passage and opposite the old kitchen is a Victorian addition which gives the front the impression of being two houses joined together. The extension to the west was built in the mid-1950s. Outside are three splendid old barns. A room in one appears to have been a residence and shows signs of having been lived in until quite recently. It contains a fireplace and what might have been space for a stairwell.

In the last part of the 16th century, the farm was held by the Rysdon family and in 1607 Henry Rysdon died, leaving the farm to his son, John. In 1677 William and Mary Preston and their son, John, were in possession of Greenaway. In 1742, William Bennett was shown as owner of the farm and in the Land Tax assessment of 1788, Mrs Ann Whiteburn is listed as owner with Digory Lee as tenant.

Greenaway was bought by the Aysh family in the early 1820s. John and Ann Aysh farmed the 42-acre property with their eldest son, Richard and five other children. Richard took over in 1841 when his father retired. He found it hard to survive on so small a property and decided to sell to John Endacott in 1860. The new owner gave the tenancy to William Sampson. At this time the farm had very unusual field names such as North and South Wales, North and South Ireland, Cherry Park, Great Meadow, Middle Close, Mousey Field and Rixey Meadow. [4]

John Endacott, born in Belstone in 1830, moved to Greenaway with his 33-year-old wife, Caroline and four children - John junior, Margaret, Harriet and William. John senior died in 1889 and between 1890 and 1893 his sons, William (nicknamed 'One-eyed-Will') and John junior

---

[3] Robin Stanes, The Old Farm - *a History of Farming Life in the West Country,* gives much detailed information about food and drink consumed on Dartmoor farms over the centuries.

('Grenway Jan'), worked the farm helped by a labourer called William Symonds.

John Holman tells an amusing story about 'Grenway Jan' and his brother, 'One-eyed-Will'. For some reason in the early 1920s John Endacott would visit Greenaway Farm once a year to collect £12 which was thought to be an annuity or mortgage agreed on the sale of the farm some time earlier. He and his brother 'One-eyed-Will' would then go off on a bender and take three or four days to get home via the Wonson (as the Northmore Arms is often known) and all the pubs in South Zeal. John says he remembers 'Grenway Jan' drinking in his father's pub solidly all day. At closing time the brothers would sleep in the barn behind the pub or anywhere else they could find, waking the next day to start all over again until the money was spent.

In 1897, Greenaway was tenanted by George Frost and in 1903, Edmund Sampson and his wife Charlotte bought it from the Endacotts. In the same year, Edmund and his cousin, Edward Sampson from Thule, became overseers of the parish. Edmund died in 1921 and Charlotte a year later. Their son, William and his wife Eva, took over and farmed the land for over 20 years.

Will and Florence Aggett moved from Chagford to work on the farm with William Sampson and after he died in 1940, the Aggetts bought the farm from his estate, selling it to Eric Sillem eight years later. Eric's brother, Brian, who owned South Creaber for a while, was landlord of the Warren Inn for some years in the 1950s.

Ronald Kingsland and his wife, Dorothy, moved to Greenaway in 1949 and worked on the farm for two years. A day or two after his 15th birthday, Ronald lied about his age and tried to join the Territorial Army. When war broke out they discovered how young he was and threw him out. He worked for Mr Dunning in Throwleigh for some years before starting his own farm contract business.

After the war, Ronald remembers meeting Dorothy for the first time when her donkey cart got stuck carting 'vags' off the moor near Shilstone. [5] Ronald claims that Dorothy, who had just left the WAAFs, tried hard to get him to take her to the cinema but he told her he was far too busy and

---

[4] Farmers liked to give their fields easily remembered names to make sure their workers knew which ones to work on. Often the use of names of other countries, such as North and South Ireland and North and South Wales, meant they were some distance from the farmhouse. They also liked to call fields 40 acres, for example, when in fact the field would be no bigger than four or five acres. They would joke that they had finished ploughing their '40 acres' and were off home in half a day. Meadow, as in Great Meadow, implies a hilly field with water running through or around it.

[5] Vags were the top end of peat slices which were burnt in place of wood or coal by many families on the moor.

had no time for that sort of thing! Playing hard to get must have worked, however, because they ended up getting married in 1949.

After they left, Eric Sillem went into partnership with Tom Endacott from Creaber and they farmed the properties jointly until, in a fit of depression, Eric committed suicide in 1953.

The house, by this time in a very rundown condition, was sold to a quantity surveyor called Trinnick and ceased to be a working farm. He spent a considerable amount of money on it and was responsible for adding the extension to the west, which included a new staircase and what became the drawing room. He also did a lot to the barns and outbuildings, as well as the structure of the house itself. A good deal of the land surrounding the farmhouse had been sold off over the years and Mr Trinnick tried to buy it back.

On his death in 1978, the farm was bought by John Jordan of Moortown who kept the land but sold the farmhouse and garden to John and Pam Weeks. In 1987, they sold the property to Commander Alastair MacIver RN and his wife Pam. Alastair became known as something of a 'saint' in the area and was very popular, especially with those who relied on his hospital car service. He had joined the Royal Navy in 1943 and served in various ships, including submarines, until 1967 when he decided he wanted to spend more time with his family. Pam was known to have the power of third sight and was renowned as an aromatherapist and reflexologist.

They had regular visits from their children; Kirsty, married to Julian White, a chiropractor in New Zealand together with their children, Alastair, Angus, Hamish and Elsbeth. Amanda, married to Steve Scheuermann, a Colonel in the United States Airforce and their children Andrew, Neil, Susannah and Alastair; and finally David MacIver and his wife, Sarah and young daughter Marnie.

The MacIvers sold the farmhouse to Hanneke Richters from Jurston in 1996 and moved to Ulverston in the Lake District. Hanneke did a lot of internal restructuring, including the building of a new staircase and the creation of a self-contained guest wing. She sold the farm to Dennis and Angela Bexson in March 1997 and moved to St Just in Cornwall.

Dennis and Angela have three children, Rosalind 33, Christina 31 and Andrew 30, all regular visitors to Gidleigh. Angela, a state registered nurse from one of the London teaching hospitals, has been married to Dennis for 35 years. Dennis, a petroleum chemist, spent over 22 years in the motor industry. He is now semi-retired and after ten years with one of London's top strategy consulting firms, started his own management consultancy. He is involved in a number of local causes and is a member of the Moretonhampstead Hospital committee, chairman of the Chagford Young People Development Fund and a member of the Grant Application Committee of the Gidleigh Village Hall.

© Chris Chapman (Helicopter pilot - Stephen Bond)

Will Webber's field at Buttern Newtake

Holy Trinity Church, Castle House and Gidleigh Castle, from a photograph around 1890

Holy Trinity Church, Castle House and Gidleigh Castle, from a postcard around 1908

Coronation celebrations at Gidleigh Castle, 1937

Gidge Webber

Will Webber of Buttern

Tommy Fox-Pitt of Chapple

Marjorie Fox-Pitt plucking a turkey

George Endacott outside
North Creaber

© Chris Chapman

Will Webber and Norman Mortimore cutting 'vags' on Gidleigh Common.

Margaret Osborne of Castle Farm (right)
and earlier Osbornes (above)

© Chris Chapman

Batworthy in the snow

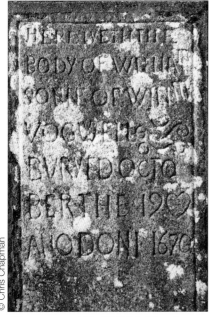

Gravestone outside Gidleigh Church

The 14th century Wallen Chapel near Chapple Farm

Geese and a rainbow at
Little Ensworthy

© William Hannaford

Scorhill Circle

© Chris Chapman

The Rev and Mrs Everett Dasher and Monica Alford revisit the scene, 1979

Tom Endacott showing visitors the Moor at Batworthy Fields in September 1947

Sheep shearing

Charles McIlwraith, who owned the estate from 1918 until he died in 1932, was responsible for building the Village Hall

Mrs Bromell presenting prizes to members of the Gidleigh Village Hall Club, April 1955. From left - David Nailor, Den Bishop, Leonard Kingsland, Jim Hill, John Vallance, Will Hill and Will Aggett.

Beating the Bounds, 1997

Inspecting the Boundary stones

The clapper bridge over the Wallabrook

Along Mariners Way

Outside Way Cottage and Gidleigh Cottage in the 1920s

In documents dating back to the 17th century, the house has been called, variously, the Old Rectory or the Parsonage until finally it became known as **The Glebe** or **Glebe Farm**. The word 'glebe' refers to land owned by the church and used for the support of the parson apart from the tithe which applied to all other land in the parish.

The fact is that, up to the end of the 18th century, the majority of Westcountry parsons were parson-farmers with a strong bond of common interest linking them to their rural congregations: a bond only put at hazard by the contentious issue of tithes.

The house was built in several stages, the first part around 1590 and more in the 1800s. The modern extension to the east was built by Howard Skewes in the 1920s. It was probably never a longhouse in the strict definition of the term, but was built to accommodate a parson and probably a farmer and his family. The barn at the side of the house abuts the oldest part of the building and is thought to have contained an early shippon at one end and a room for a farm labourer at the end closest to the house.

The chamber above the kitchen has a separate internal stone staircase which at one time would have lead directly outside and enabled the farmer or farm workers to have separate access to their living area.

In many Devon farmhouses, these rooms with separate access were often referred to as the 'boys' chamber or 'mens' room'. They were also used for storing dry goods such as farm tools, cheese vats, dried fish and barley. They would accommodate three or four men who slept on 'douse' beds. [1]

The parson, William Downe, took over the property in 1625. He died three years later and was buried in Gidleigh churchyard. His successor, Humphrey Gaye, moved here in the same year with his young wife. Their three children were all born in the house and baptised in Gidleigh Church between May 1632 and December 1648. Their eldest daughter, Sarah, died in childbirth in 1654 and was buried in Gidleigh churchyard.

The terrier written by Humphrey Gaye in 1679 lists all the property belonging to the parish of Gidleigh. This is the only contemporary description of a house and its contents in the village in the 17th century:

> *"A true coppie off the houses and glebe lands belonging to the Rictorie off gidleigh, onn hale, onn hale chamber, onn kitchine chambre, onn little chambre over the butterie, on little chambre over the entrie. The wales of the kitchine and hale of hewen stone. onn shipon, onn brewhouse & entrie onn barn and*

---

[1] Douse beds were mattress covers filled with chaff.

these are waled with ruft moore stone. The inner houses are floored with earth & stone, Onn little med-
dow lying the west side of the house ajoyndeing to the free hold of Ralin Bennet widdow.
The gardin Lying one the north west of the house contaning twenty pole or 20 land yards ajyning to
the Land of George Oxenham a gent man. All the rest of the ground belonging to the said passonage
lieth alltogether a joyneing to the high way of one said Bartholomew Gidley Esquire. His land and
George Oxenham his land the other said the gret bower 3 acres the little bower halfe an eaker the
broad Parke 2 eakers & halfe the waye Parke 2 eakers the middle Parke 2 eakers the Cassell parke 3
eakers the little parke onn eaker & halfe the lower meddow 2 eakers the letle meddow halfe The whole
sum of fourteen eakers and halfe."

Mention of the brewhouse on the property prompted some research into beer and cider making in the Dartmoor area. Hops arrived in this country only around 1534 according to the rhyme:

Hops, Reformation, Bays and Beer
Came into England all in one year.

Previously the farmers on the edge of the moor tended to drink a lethal concoction made from 'oaten malt' as described by John Hooker:

"The husbandmen of the edge of Dartmoor be very skilful in their husbandry and do dress their grounds very well yet in the north part thereof about Okehampton and Hatherleigh and other places thereabouts, the oats they sow be all spoiled oats and the drink they do make thereof is spoiled drink … yet what ever creature do taste thereof it do make them to vomit … be it man horse or hogge." [2]

Little cider was produced in this part of Dartmoor, though a considerable amount was consumed and any farmer who offered his workers only water at harvest time was hard pressed to find men willing to work his land the following year. Cider is an ancient drink and records show that it was known as 'sicera' in the middle of the 12th century. Cider, meaning 'strong drink', is mentioned in the Lollard English Bible of the early 14th century that is still preserved in the chained Library at Hereford.

Cider was certainly made in Devon as early as the 13th century and became the most popular drink on the farms. A gentleman visiting Devon in 1856 observed in his travel journal:

"Of apple trees there are scarcely any. The crop has been a failure for several years and the cyder which forms the usual drink of the labouring classes has been made from French apples. It is melancholy to see the numerous orchards with scarcely a bushel of apples in each." [3]

There was a 'pound house' years ago next to the Barton in neighbouring Throwleigh, which was

---

[2] Robert Stanes, *The Old Farm*, p. 62. John Hooker was a contemporary of Richard Carew, who wrote *The Survey of Cornwall* in 1602.

[3] A 'Gentleman's Travel Journal on Dartmoor in 1856', *Devon & Cornwall Notes & Queries* (Special Issue), Todd Gray (ed), p. 93.

used for crushing apples to make cider and each cottage in the village grew some apples for it. Here, however, each farm made a small amount of cider for their own consumption if they produced enough apples. But it would not keep and as a result was treated as more of a seasonal drink in Gidleigh.

The apple pulp was crushed in a circular stone trough in which a heavy stone wheel was dragged by horses walking continuously in a circle. There are a couple of these troughs in the garden of Glebe Farm which are now used as bird baths. The apple-mill, invented in 1664, enabled the manufacture of commercial quantities of cider, though farmers continued to make it with hand presses for many years.

Cider was cheap: in 1750 it sold for 2d or 3d a gallon (1p) when a man's wages were perhaps 7 shillings (35 pence) a week. One way of getting the hoeing done quickly was to put a firkin of cider at the end of each row and many farmers paid their workers partly in cider until the late 19th century, when legislation ended the practice.

Devon farmers made a cider spirit not unlike French Calvados. It was called 'still liquor' and was made from what was known as 'snarleygoggs', the sticky yellow mass found at the bottom of empty cider barrels. It must have been very powerful stuff indeed and the way it was made would send modern-day 'health police' into total decline.

The pulp was mixed with fresh bull's blood and contained the carcasses of rats, lambs and even pigs who often collapsed, drunk, in the piles of rotting apples at harvest time and ended up in the presses. The liquor was extremely empyreumatic and at one time was known as 'necessity' since without a dose of this brew the colic couldn't be cured.

The operation of these stills was illegal of course and the smell produced by them could be detected miles away. The trick was to delay the visiting policeman as long as possible when he came to check the farm while the brew was poured away, the still dismantled and the parts hidden around the farm or disguised as bits of farm equipment. It is not suggested that the vicars of Gidleigh were in the habit of producing illegal spirit - on the other hand, they certainly brewed their own beer.

After the middle of the 16th century, the quality of the ale made on farms hereabouts steadily improved. Many of the gentry had their own brew-houses and even illegal stills. Ale in those days was not a strong beer and would often be drunk by all members of the family, including the older children. An average-size parson's family of ten would probably have consumed around three hogsheads of beer a month; that is about 1,600 pints, or an average of five pints per person per day!

In 1683, Bartholomew Gidley gave the living to Edward Seddon who was also the rector of Throwleigh. The Reverend Richard Skinner occupied the Glebe in 1769 and took on seven-year-old Elizabeth Osborne as an apprentice to work in the house and on the farm. When her apprenticeship ended, he took in another young girl from the poor house called Mary Moore in 1789. Between 1832 and 1838 George Peardon tenanted the farm and lived here with his wife Ann and their three children John, William and Joseph.

In 1842, John Newcombe, who lived at Thule at the time, took over the tenancy and the size of the farm increased to just over 29 acres with fields with names such as Higherway Park, Bowey, Great Castle Park, Lower Broad Park and Parsonage Meadow.

In 1851, William and Susanna Brimblecombe and their son Thomas took on the tenancy, followed in 1859 by James and Ann Hill and their two children. In 1864 John Belworthy, a farmer born in Crediton in 1817, took over the farm with his wife Eliza and in the same year his daughter, Ellen Mary, was born. In 1872 the Rector of Gidleigh, 81-year-old Owen Owen and a 13-year-old student called Frederick Young moved into what was then known as the Parsonage, with the Belworthy family.

Richard Leaman's great-grandparents stayed at the Glebe for a few months in 1884 before moving to Waye Farm, Throwleigh which they purchased later that year. In 1889, Eliza Belworthy died and William and Ellen Endacott and their son James took over the tenancy.

Attendance at church was somewhat erratic over the years but it is amusing to recall the experience of a vicar in a small Devon village who one Sunday was faced with only one farmer's wife for a congregation. He wondered whether or not to hold the service and ended up asking the woman what she thought.

"If I take a bucket of corn to feed my chickens and only one turns up, I don't send it away hungry", she replied. The vicar, impressed by this simple response, continued the service and gave the longest and most heartfelt sermon of his life. When he had finished, he asked the farmer's wife what she thought of it.

"When only one chicken turns up, I don't give it the whole darned bucket", she replied testily.

One of the oddest and, in a way, saddest things about church life is the unwritten rule that when a parson retires from a parish, usually having lived in a particular village for many years, he is expected not only to move from the house that has been his home for that time but to move out of the district as well. He is often left without a house to move to or the capital or income to support a mortgage to buy one.

The present rector of Gidleigh, Louis Baycock, is the parish priest and minister incumbent of Chagford, Gidleigh and Throwleigh and when he chooses to retire, his replacement will be expected to look after an additional three parishes, Hittisleigh, Spreyton and Drewsteignton - with no increase in the stipend.

The days of the parson's freehold (the mediaeval right of the parish priest to his property and income) are seemingly over, silently removed in most cases by administrative order with minimum debate in the Synod.

Parish priests were once placed in a parish for life and feared nothing from their bishop. Only a third of parsons have this protection today; the remainder have become employees of the bishop, without employment rights and can be removed from their living given three months' notice to quit. Parish mergers have provided the church with not only a cache of attractive country properties to sell but also with fewer salaries to pay.

The result is a break in the threads of village life that helped bind the farm communities together. Lone farms and families in distress may now be lucky to see their priest on rare occasions as they tear round the villages like an army of beleaguered bedlamite banshees.

After the rectors moved to the new Rectory in 1891, the house became known simply as Glebe Farm. In 1894 it was in the possession of John and Mary Ann Hill whose son, John Silas, was born here on 16 September 1894. In 1902 the Reverend Douglas McLaren had Thomas Cullen as tenant.

John and Maud Endacott lived at the Glebe between 1914 and 1917 before moving to take over the tenancy of North Creaber and their son, George, was born here in 1915.

The Webber family took over the lease in 1917 and Gideon (Gidge) Webber, who served in the Army during the First World War, walked from Okehampton station with his friend, Thomas Holman, to return to their families in Gidleigh after being demobbed in 1918. The Webbers had a son and eight daughters and must have found the Glebe very small as the family grew because they moved two years later to Manaton, to work on the Kitson estate. Amy Harvey remembers her friends, the Webber girls, walking each day from here to school at Providence.

In 1920 Howard and Lilian Skewes bought the Glebe from the Church and set about building the extension to the east. Howard, a retired tailor, together with John Endacott from North Creaber, took their turn as overseers of the village until the practice ended in 1926.

Miss Hilda Pestell moved to live at the Glebe in 1930 and, according to a Deed of Grant dated 1933, Skewes acquired the right to run water pipes from a holding tank in a field owned by William Sampson of Greenaway. Prior to this, water was drawn from a well beside the small enclosed garden to the southwest of the property. It was at about this time that the house became known as the Old Rectory.

The farm was owned for a few years during the war by a Mrs Vining and her sister who sold it to Lt Colonel George Gorringe. He in turn sold in 1947 – for the sum of £3,250, to Mrs Joan Ensor, who lived here with her mother, Ethel Iredell and daughter, Sally Bragg. Ethel died in 1972 and Joan in 1991.

Guy and Mark Bentinck, whose family lived at Yelfords, near Chagford Common, used to ride over to visit Joan and Sally. They recall that in those days you had to boil the drinking water and the house had a tin roof that made a dreadful noise when it rained. They used to race their horses across country with their friends from Cawsand Beacon to Kestor, a 3.5-mile chase, and from there to the Warren Inn, a race most often won by Johnny Rowe.

Joan Ensor sold the fields on the far side of the lane to Ernie Bowden's sister Kathleen and her husband Terence Beer in 1974. These fields formed part of the Glebe lands which formerly belonged to the parish church and lie between the farm and what is now called the Old Rectory. In the same year, Joan Ensor sold the farmhouse, outbuildings and a field known as Croft, in total five acres, to Primrose Brett Young who lived here until she died in 1991.

Primrose was a much-loved character who encouraged the local pony club to use her field for an annual camp. She was married to Noel Brett Young, brother of the well-known author. Her brother, Colonel Peter Varwell, lives at South Zeal and one of her daughters, Elizabeth, married Bill Pybus and lives at Shilstone in Throwleigh.

The Grumley-Grennan family bought the property on December 18 1991 and their children, Jason and Alix, are regular visitors to the house.

THULE, Thowle or Thuell, which in old English means 'tuft' or 'clump', was originally the home of Henry and Richard de la Thivele (or atte Thyvele). Most of the present house was built in or around 1560 and an oak beam in the drawing room photographed in the 1940s has the date 1566 scratched into it. This suggests that either the house was built in that year or a major reconstruction occurred at that time.

Richard Aysh paid tithes for the property in 1745 and, in the 1788 Land Tax Assessment, James Endacott of Gidleigh Mill and North Creaber was listed as owner with William Northcott as tenant. According to the parish register, Joseph Edgecombe was in possession of the farm in 1826 and he installed John Newcombe as tenant a year later. John's son bought the property from the Edgecombe family on 8 January 1872 and, the following day, appointed William Sparke as tenant. At this time, fields on the property had names such as Lay Close, Grist Park, Croft, Great Broom

Close and Shuta Park. [1]

Thule was once one of the largest farms in the area, with over 120 acres of land. Apart from sheep and a herd of milking cows, it would have had a few pigs scavenging in the farmyard and around the lanes. Healthy and omnivorous, they were left to wander loose, living in hovels or under ricks until they were ready to be fattened. Pigs are intelligent and are not frightened of humans. They could certainly be dangerous and are known to have attacked and killed small children.

The old-fashioned South-West pigs were descendants of the numerous swine that rootled for must, acorns and roots in the extensive Devon woodland. During the 15th and 16th centuries the domestic pig had a distinctly boar-like appearance, its snout long and aggressive looking and its legs long. In the 18th century Devon had more recorded swine than any other county in England.

When pigs were brought in to be fattened, they were shut up in small close hutches, where they ate and dunged and were fed to a great size. They were never let out or given straw to lie on. They lay on a bed of mud and became covered "with a thick coat of mail". This was not idleness on the farmer's part. "Fat pigs should lie wet, it keeps them cool; if they lie on dry warm litter it melts their fat." They were not expected to waste energy moving about and were fed boiled barley meal, potatoes, apple pulp and scraps. 'The People's Health Police' and the RSPCA would no doubt find this practice unacceptable today but this kind of fattening was common until recently and produced the fat bacon, with little lean, so beloved of Devonians.

Just about every bit of a pig was eaten in some form or other. The head was stripped of its meat which was made into brawn, the hams and gammons were salted and hung for smoking. Lard was produced from the fat of the stomach, the intestines were cleaned and fried with onions to make 'chitterlings' or 'pigs fry' and the fat bacon gave the labourers the energy to work ten-hour days in the fields.

Returning to Thule, in 1881 the tenancy was taken over by George Leaman, a 55-year-old farmer from Throwleigh and his wife, Harriet. Their son Henry and daughter Emily, together with a 16-year-old apprentice called Eli Brock, helped on the farm. George died in 1908 aged 77 and Harriet in 1918. Edmund Sampson, who had bought the freehold of the farm in the 1890s, sold it

---

[1] Grist as in Grist Park was an enclosed field where young pigs were reared. Lay Close described a small field with a barn or shelter; Croft in Old English was the name for a small enclosed field; Broom as in Great Broom Close described a field where broom grows; Shuta as in Shuta Park is Celtic for orchard but in Old English 'Shute' or sometimes 'Shuta' was used to describe a corner or angle of a field.

after George Leaman died to James and Annie Colridge. They farmed here for about ten years before selling to Tom Vallance in 1919. Tom, who bought Thule as an investment for one of his sons, farmed at Aller in Bovey Tracey and also owned neighbouring Chapple Farm.

Thule, which at this time consisted of a farmhouse, barns and over 78 acres of land with extensive Rights of Common, was tenanted by George and Annie Lentern until September 1922. Jim Hill rented the house, but not the land, for a few years before moving to Ensworthy and Monica Alford (née Hill) was born here in 1925.

Tom Vallance sold the farmhouse and 38 acres of land to William and Beatrice Walker on 14 Dec 1934. William Walker died four years later but Beatrice continued to live at Thule until she died in 1985. She let out rooms and operated the farm as a 'bed and breakfast' guesthouse for several years. There is a record of her offering accommodation to airmen who had suffered burns during the war requiring plastic surgery. They used to convalesce there and appear to have benefited from her homely care and the excellent food and clotted cream she produced.

Like so many farms in the area, Thule generated its own electricity until the late 1950s, using a generator next to the battery room in one of the outbuildings. Before the war, any farm with a DC power facility was considered very up-to-date and at Thule all the old light fittings are still in place in the barn.

The sleeping arrangements on these larger farms was complicated in the early days, as all the upper rooms led one into another with no corridor. As an example, in 1890 on a large farm near Winkleigh, there is a record of 20 people sleeping in four rooms. Because the bedchambers were inter-connected, the girl servants were sent to bed first followed by the daughters of the household in the next room and then the menservants in a room at the other end of the house and so on, with the 'maister' and his wife in the main room at the head of the stairs.

What exactly happened in the mornings is not explained but it is doubtful anyone was able to lie in and there was little privacy. The apprentices and farm servants slept three to a bed and as many as five or six to a room. They slept on 'douse' beds (douse being the waste that came out of the end of a threshing machine once the corn and straw had been separated).

People went to bed and rose with the sun but if light were needed, they used home-made tallow candles in candlesticks which were lit using a tinder box. Whale-oil lamps were introduced early in the 19th century and paraffin lamps arrived towards the end. At night, the countryside must have been almost totally dark with just the flicker of the occasional candle in a window to show any sign of life.

Farms in the area were well-served by tradesmen from Chagford in the early 1920s. Bread, for example, was delivered six days a week; Holman from South Zeal called on Thursday, Endacott on Wednesday, Rowe from Chagford on Saturday, Monday and Tuesday, and old Charlie Hill on Friday. The butchers from Chagford had a regular delivery as well; Holmes & Son delivered meat on Tuesday and Saturday and Alfred Haydon delivered to order but usually on a Friday.

Mrs Walker let the farmhouse to a widow, Mrs Jackson, in the 1930s who lived there with her son, Tony, before buying the Old Rectory in Belstone. There is a story about this Mrs Jackson flying back from New Zealand when she was over 80. She had been told that one of her old retainers at the rectory in Belstone had run into some problems and she came back to help him out. Her son Tony and his wife Jan from New Zealand came and visited the house recently. At some point in the 1950s, the thatch caught fire and was replaced with tiles.

Thule farmhouse and a little over five acres of land was bought by Jill and Edward Mellersh

Jackson from Beatrice Walker's estate on 23 October 1985. In her will, Beatrice Walker had left Thule Cottage and a small amount of land to a Roma Callis. In September 1988 the Jacksons bought the cottage and their daughter, Amanda, lives there now.

The name **MOORTOWN** derives from the original owner, John atte More, who lived here with his wife Matilda and daughter, Cecilia, in 1327. It is mentioned in Devon Record Office files in 1537 as 'Moretun' (tun or dun meaning hill or mound). It is a 16th century, Grade II listed farmhouse built of granite rubble with large dressed quoins and later 17th-century improvements. The front is roughcast and the stacks are of the original granite ashlar with moulded copings.

Inside, it has three rooms and a through passage facing south-east. There is evidence that it was originally an open hall house with the upper floor being part of the 17th-century improvements. Some 50 yards from the farmhouse is an 18th-century butter well made of large slabs of roughly-shaped granite. It is a box-like structure with sides and a flat roof made from single pieces.

In 1585, a Sybil Comyns was summoned to the Court at Lydford because the gate at Moretown was in ruins and in 1606, records show that William Tincombe had possession of the farm.

From 1640 Moortown was in the hands of Alexander Vogwell, a large landowner in the area, who appears to have owned most of Gidleigh parish. He married his second wife, Constante Pomsford, in 1658 who died in childbirth a year later. The Vogwell family were great benefactors of Gidleigh Church and in 1674 when churchwarden, Alexander gave the parish the fourth bell that bears his name and still hangs in the tower. William, Alexander's eldest son by his first wife, Rebecca, took over the farm in 1683. He died in 1697 and John, a second son, died the following year and is buried in Gidleigh churchyard.

The Vogwell estate at that time, apart from Moortown itself, included Broadway, East and West Chapple, South Coombe in Murchington, Lamb Park, Tadely Park, Metherell, Gidleigh Common, North and South Forder, Meldon and a large part of Chagford Town.

In 1742 Thomas Dodd was a tenant on part of Moortown whilst William Hoale farmed the rest. Robert Martyn is shown as 'moorman' at Moortown in 1780, for which he paid land tax of £2. On his death his wife, Anna, received an annuity of £12 for life, to be paid from the income from the farm. Robert was the only son and heir of Robert Martyn the elder of Throwleigh whose wife, Joan Vogwell, born in 1707, was the only daughter and heiress of William and Mary Vogwell.

The farm was placed under the supervision of Anna's two half brothers, William and Oliver

Langmead, who arranged to let it to Lyle Bloxham for a few years with the provision that rooms be made available to Anna 'undisturbed and for the term of 90 years if she should live so long or during the term of her natural life'. Edmund Knapman is shown in possession of the farm on the Land Tax Return in 1788 and in 1792 he took on an eight-year-old girl from the poor house as an apprentice housemaid.

He was succeeded as owner by a Richard Underhill in 1827 and in 1843 Richard's son, James, took over the farm. In White's Directory of 1850, William Brunning is shown to be the tenant on the

67-acre property which at the time had fields with names such as Long Ley, Square Close, Burrows, Bake's Park, Croft, Higher Wallands and Twenty Acres (which in fact was only one acre in size). [1]

Ownership of land has always been important in England but never more so than prior to 1832. Before that date, you could vote in elections only if you owned property valued for land tax at more than 40 shillings a year. (Incidentally, you also had to be male, a combination that some might argue was nothing but sense.)

In 1869, George Underhill's son Richard, born in Throwleigh 1837, married Jane Newcombe, the daughter of John Newcombe of Thule, and took over the running of the farm. By 1880 they had three daughters, Annie, Emily Grace and Alice. Richard died in 1900 and his brother, George, who lived with them died in 1913. Their 68-year-old uncle John, a retired farmer, also helped on the farm together with an apprentice called George Ash. They also had a servant called Elizabeth Brimblecombe, who helped around the house.

Alice Underhill inherited the farm after her uncle George died and on Lady Day 1913 Edwin Jordan, a 'horseman' at Throwleigh Barton and his wife Mary took over the tenancy of Moortown from W.G. Edwards. Edwin Jordan and his family stayed at Forder for a while before moving to Moortown with a herd of 20 South Devons, a flock of 45 grey-faced Dartmoor ewes and some ponies. In 1933, Edwin's son William married Emma Jane Hill and took over the tenancy after his father died.

Alice Underhill died in 1947 leaving the freehold of the farm to William in her will. She stipulated that he was to pay set sums of money to her relations when they came of age. William's only son, John, took over the farm from his father in 1974 and runs what is now a 300-acre property with the help of his wife Diane and their two boys, Robert and David. Diane's father, Douglas Kellow, is a retired farmer and renowned horseman from Lostwithiel in Cornwall.

William Jordan died on Christmas Eve 1985 and his wife Mary, as fit as ever at 87, continues to live in the cottage at Moortown Gate. She is the daughter of John Endacott of Belstone and married William Jordan at Belstone Church in 1945. She was William's second wife, his first, Emma, sadly having died during a minor operation.

Over the years, the Jordans have greatly increased the acreage they farm at Moortown. They run

---

[1] Ley as in Long Ley implied an open field of untilled land; Square Close a small field close to the farmhouse; Croft is old English for a small enclosed field; Wallands as in Higher Wallands, as the name implies, referred to one or a series of walled enclosures but in old English it also meant 'land of the Britons'.

200 suckler cows, a mixture of Galloways and South Devons and a flock of 850 ewes, Scotch Blackface and North County Cheviot, mixed. They also keep more than 40 Dartmoor ponies on the moor and half-a-dozen pure-bred Dartmoors at the farm for showing. They are well-known in the county for their Dartmoor ponies and the walls of their farmhouse are covered with rosettes and cups.

Until the early 1950s there was no electricity, or mains water on the farm and the Jordan family only bought their first tractor in 1952. Until then, the work on the farm was done by William Jordan's shires, Prince and Flower.

Ponies on Dartmoor lead the most natural life of all the moorland stock. Though they wander the moor apparently wild, they are in fact all owned by someone. The stallions run out on the moor with the mares throughout the year and most foals are born between April and June. The Dartmoor is the descendant of the original feral Celtic ponies that have bred and fended for themselves in the forests and moorlands of Britain since prehistoric times. It is a fact that the true-bred Dartmoor pony is the only domestic animal that can breed and fatten simultaneously on the open moor.

The two existing breeds of Devon cattle are red, the Red Ruby of North Devon and the more orange South Devons or South Hams. There is some evidence to suggest, however, that in the Middle Ages and up to the first half of the 18th century, local cattle were often small and black rather like Kerrys, Dexters or the Welsh Black; Celtic cattle in fact. In the middle of the 18th century, black cattle were being driven down from Dartmoor to St Budeaux to fatten for the Plymouth market and were described as being

"very small, black, short nosed, coarse-boned. I saw black cows and bulls weighing only three to four hundredweight". [2]

The pedigree of modern-day Devon cattle can be traced to the Quartly family of Great Champson, who are reputed to be the founders of the red North Devon breed. By 1750 there was a nucleus of red-brown cattle in the South Hams which no doubt were the first South Devons or old Marlborough Reds. Their origin, however, is obscure, though they are almost identical to the French double-muscled Limousin breed and similar to the Sussex.

The province of Limousin in central France was an English possession from 1152 to 1369, so

---

[2] See George Worgan's *Agriculture of Cornwall,* 1809; Worgan was a schoolmaster and leaseholder from Liskeard.

there is no reason why the two breeds should not at that time have been one. Certainly the South Devon ports have always done a brisk trade with France and an exchange of cattle would be more than a possibility. [3] The double-muscling found in the Limousin breed sometimes turns up in South Devons but it has never been bred for, because it is inclined to lead to calving difficulties.

William Marshall wrote of Devon cattle in 1796 that they were "in many respects the most perfect breed of cattle in the island and the best workers I have anywhere seen". [4]

Marshall did not make much distinction between the two Devon breeds but to Charles Vancouver, an early 19th-century writer, the difference was clear. The North Devon was a red beast, redder and much meatier than the South Devon and produced much less milk. [5] Tests have shown that the two breeds are related, however, and there may well be an addition of Channel Island blood into the South Devon which might account for the high butter fat and the yellow colour of the milk.

Breeding was the hobby of the richer farmer or landowner; the ordinary farmer bought what was available at market. Under the old three-life lease it was common practice for the landlord, right up to the 19th century, to demand and receive the 'heriot' at the death of a tenant. This was the best beast in his herd, handed over without payment to the landlord. [6]

There was always a great demand for South Devon store beasts to be fattened on the Somerset levels and elsewhere and then sold in Bristol, London or Banbury. Today, Devon cattle are immensely admired and continue to win prizes at national shows all over the country. The Dartmoor-bred South Devons are popular with graziers from as far away as Northumberland who find that these strong moorland beasts will "go away and do" anywhere.

To return to Gidleigh and Moortown, Mary Jordan is full of stories of life in Gidleigh over the years. She remembers when in the 1950s clotted cream sold for 1/3d a quarter (around 6 pence) and turnips for a penny. She also misses the days when everything was delivered to the farm: the grocer came once a week on a Monday; Ashby the fishmonger made a regular visit on Wednesdays and so did the butcher. The family would give its order one week and receive it the next. There was no need to shop elsewhere and in fact a shopping trip to Chagford or Okehampton would have been quite an expedition.

---

[3] M. Havinden's chapter in Gill (ed) *Dartmoor - A New Study*, p. 167.

[4] W. Marshall, *The Rural Economy of the West of England*, 1796.

[5] C. Vancouver, *General View of the Agriculture of Devon*, 1809.

[6] R. Stanes, *The Old Farm - a History of Farming Life in the West Country*.

At the turn of the 19th century, travelling tailors and dressmakers would call and stay on one or other of the farms for days at a time, in order to make suits and dresses for the family. The men wore suits of strong serge, woven on local looms from the fleece of their own sheep. The cloth, often finished at the factory in Chagford, was designed for years of wear rather than style.

The first cars arrived in about 1925. Until then, the only way of getting around would have been by horse or pony and trap. Mary's father used to be given a shilling a week pocket money by his father and would ride his horse from Fernworthy to Moretonhampstead on Saturday nights for a drink with his friends in one of the pubs. In those days a pint of beer sold for 1d.

Part of a route used by sailors travelling between the ports of Bideford and Dartmouth known locally as the 'Mariners Way' crosses Moortown land on its way south to Glassy Steps below Gidleigh Tor and then to Frenchbeer, Yardworthy and Jurston. This was not a track existing in its own right but simply a route which used roads and lanes where possible and elsewhere crossed fields.

ENSWORTHY (OR MOORTOWN) COTTAGE, a farm worker's cottage attached to Moortown Farm, appears to have been built in the late 18th century. Although little is known of the occupants before 1860 they would all, more than likely, have been employed at Moortown Farm.

George Willcocks, a local thatcher and his wife, Mary (née Hill) moved into what was then called Moortown Cottage. They lived here for a number of years but by 1874 it was occupied by James and Susan Webber. From 1881, the house and the surrounding 10 acres of land were rented by George and Jane Endacott. George was a retired farmer born in Throwleigh in 1816. They were followed in 1902 by John Stevens and in 1925, by George Comter.

As the Jordan family had no workers on the farm at the time they leased the cottage to Gertrude Harding for a few years from 1939 and then to George and Lilly Webber who lived there briefly before taking on the tenancy of Buttern Farm. They in turn were followed by someone called White.

It reverted to being a tied cottage occupied by Dorah and William Hannaford who moved there with their son in the 1950's. William Hannaford worked for Fred Scott on a farm in Drewsteignton before moving to Gidleigh to work for William Jordan. His son, Billy, a keen photographer, rents the cottage from the Jordans now and works for a local builder, Keith Redstone in South Zeal. He cycles there to work every day along the edge of the Moor as he has done since 1960.

DONKEYS CORNER (Previously **BROOK COTTAGE**) appears to have been built for employees on the Gidleigh estate in the early part of the 19th century. In 1881 it was occupied by John Brimblecombe, a gardener born in Throwleigh in 1828, and his wife Thirza. His brother-in-law, William Endacott and his two daughters, Mary Jane and Elizabeth, lived with them.

On 24 June 1918, the cottage and 2.25 acres surrounding it were bought by Arthur Collins from Reginald Arthur Whipham of Queensland, Australia. Reginald Whipham had inherited the Gidleigh Estate from his brother, Alfred Guy Whipham, who died in 1916 having mortgaged most of the property in 1908. George and Ada Webber occupied the house in 1920 followed in 1939 by Caroline and Christopher Hughes.

Joy Whateley and her sister Betty lived here for 50 years and it was during their ownership that it became known as Donkeys Corner because the young ponies and donkeys on the moor used to congregate in that sheltered corner near Moortown Gate.

Joy and Betty were the daughters of a solicitor from Godalming in Surrey and bought the cottage after their father died in 1948. Betty, the elder of the two, was very much in charge and tended to be the organiser. Joy was an accomplished motor cyclist and in the early days was regularly seen tearing round the lanes on her motorbike. After her sister became ill and housebound Joy, a nurse during the war, took care of her until one day she fell, breaking a leg in several places. She managed to crawl to a telephone and was rescued by Alastair MacIver and David Lyon Smith. She spent many weeks in hospital and Betty, unable to take care of herself, was moved to a nursing home where she died six weeks later.

Both sisters were extremely popular in the area and Joy was secretary of the Parochial Church Council for a number of years. She earned a healthy respect among the locals when each spring in May she moved into a tiny unheated summer house in the garden and stayed there, regardless of the weather, until October. She died in 1996 and is buried in Gidleigh churchyard.

HINGSTON was built in about 1919 on land acquired by the Collins family when they bought Brook Cottage in 1918. The Reverend Joseph Rawson lived there for some years after retiring as Rector of Gidleigh but sold the house to Donald and Elsie Bentham in 1941.

Elsie was a retired school teacher and a member of the large Bromell farming family. Her mother, Eleanor Tryphena Bromell, who lived at Forder, was also a school teacher for many years. After Donald died, Elsie moved to Chagford and sold the house in 1994 to Val and Mike Date's daughter Penny and her husband Adrian Rowe, a Colonel in the Royal Logistic Corp. Adrian and Penny have two children, Charlotte and Rebecca, both keen riders who are out on their ponies in the lanes and on the moor at every spare moment of the day.

The Rowes have enlarged the house considerably and it bears the nickname 'Tardis' because, although from the outside it gives the impression of being a small bungalow, it now has six bedrooms, a bathroom, two main reception rooms and a very large kitchen. Adrian and his father-in-law have done most of the work on the extension, to the point of rewiring the whole house.

Hingston was built on granite pillars with granite walls covered on the inside with 'beaver board', a Canadian type of plaster board. The granite pillars meant the wind whistled under the floorboards, making it extremely cold and damp in winter but this has now been remedied.

Most of the old farmhouses in the parish were built of granite without foundations and had little in the way of floor insulation. In some cases the floors were paved with granite slabs and in others, the rooms had nothing to cover the beaten earth but rush matting. The traditional farm kitchen may have had blue slate slabs for a floor but the most common flooring was lime ash or grip. [1]

Gidleigh and the area surrounding it had a plentiful supply of granite for building and the smallest structures where built of it. The mushroom-like straddle stones were used for supporting ricks and granaries, while some pastures still have posts of stone around 5ft high for cattle to scratch and rub against. There is a story that these scratching stones were known as 'Argyles' because a Duke of Argyle made them fashionable. There were few chimneys in farmhouses in Devon prior to the middle of the 16th century and a visiting parson wrote in 1580:

"There are old men yet dwelling in the village where I remain which have noted three things to be marvellously altered in England within their sound remembrance; one is the multitude of chimnies lately erected ...". [2]

The oldest farmhouses were single-storey buildings consisting of one open room or hall with a central fire on which all food was cooked. There was little concession to privacy. Children were conceived and born more or less in public perhaps concealed behind the odd wooden partition or screen, six or seven feet high.

Many of these early mediaeval hall houses were 'ceiled' in the late 16th century or remodelled. Chimney breasts were built into the thickness of the walls and upper stories placed over the whole length of the house, including the shippon, with bedrooms tucked into the roof space. These were often reached by a newel stair housed in a semi-circular projection called a caracole, or a straight flight of stairs set along a back wall. Although hall houses continued to be built well into the 17th century in this part of Dartmoor, there is evidence that the 'modern' two-storey house was being introduced and hall houses converted at about the same time.

The change from hall house to upper-storey house reflected not only the increasing wealth of the farming community but also the size of families, including farm workers and apprentices, who required more living space. Ironically, the gentry in Devon preferred to preserve their halls as a symbol

---

[1] Grip was the name of a floor covering consisting of a mixture of lime, coal ash and clay.

[2] William Harrison, *Description of England,* 1580

of status and could afford to build servants' quarters on the side or rear of the original houses. During the late 18th and early 19th centuries, however, there was a move away from hiring 'bed and board' farm servants and the system of 'day-labourers' became the norm in the Westcountry, thus reducing demand for larger accomodation.

Apart from granite stone rubble and, in later years, granite ashlar blocks, cob was used as a building material in some houses and farm buildings in the parish. Cob is a carefully blended mixture of sub-soil, straw and animal dung with some sand or gravel to add ballast. As long as the cob was kept dry - "All cob needs is a good hat and a good pair of shoes" - it will last for hundreds of years and is no less secure than brick or stone.

There is no doubt that most early dwellings that we now call farmhouses or cottages were occupied by people of a somewhat greater prosperity than the ordinary labourer. None of the tiny wattle-and-daub hovels that were built on corners of common land, or surrounding the Castle and the Barton, have survived. They have sunk back into the ground from which their materials were so laboriously taken, leaving no trace.

Remains do exist, however, of 18th and 19th century granite rooms in barns that would have been occupied by apprentices or farm labourers. These tiny dismal spaces had fireplaces and earth floors with little more than a loft above reached by a ladder. The doors were made of vertical boards with slabs nailed across to hold everything together. Nails were hammered right through the wood and bent over to prevent them pulling out.

The inside of external walls were given a thick application of plaster made from clay reinforced with horse or cow hair and lime to bind the mixture together, then finished with lime wash. Windows were seldom glazed until at least the end of the 17th century and were little better than holes in the wall with some vertical wooden bars or stone mullions. [3]

Rural villages in England, however, were much more prosperous and better kept than in Europe in the 18th century. A Frenchman on a tour of Britain in 1765 was amazed to see that labourers had shoes on their feet and instead of grey rags wore good cloth on their backs. In contrast to the mud cottages of the peasantry of France, all the dwellings he saw were "built of (stone or) brick and covered with tiles (or thatch), and have glass windows!" [4]

---

[3] The small room in the barn attached to the Glebe contains a small window with a rare granite stone mullion.

[4] Andre Parreaux, *Daily Life in England in the reign of George III*, p. 45.

LITTLE ENSWORTHY (MOOR COTTAGE) was originally a very small one- or two-room cottage, probably built in the early 19th century on about an acre of land. It lies off the narrow lane that crosses the edge of the moor between the farms of Moortown and Ensworthy and is well known for the ducks and geese that occupy the stream beside the lane.

Charles Mortimore, who owned the cottage in 1843, sold it to John Underhill in 1851. After only a couple of years the Underhills leased the property to George Endacott. William Webber's son, James, married Susan Hill in 1874 and they occupied the house until 1910 when the tenancy was taken over by William Wonacott. William moved out in 1915 and James and Elizabeth Endacott took over the tenancy briefly. James (b.1841) was the son of Theophilous Endacott of Waye Farm, Throwleigh, and he married his cousin, Elizabeth, in Gidleigh Church in 1876.

James Dunning, Lord of the Manor of Throwleigh, moved into the house in 1922 when he retired from Wonson Manor. He made extensive alterations to it, increasing the size and numbers of rooms and laying out the garden. A retired solicitor from London called Monroe bought the cottage in 1945 from the Dunning estate after James died, and sold it in 1951 to Monica and David Alford, who have lived there ever since.

The most exciting event that affected the residents of Ensworthy in recent years occurred during the Second World War. The story of what happened that day is contained in an article written by 19-year-old Monica Hill for a local newspaper at the time:

"January 23rd, 1943, dawned a bright clear day. It was indeed a marvellous and a red letter day for me and two young school boys from Scorhill house who accompanied me on horseback to the rescue of an American airman.

About a quarter to four in the afternoon we were enjoying a canter across Dartmoor when a large aircraft was sighted. Almost immediately six parachutes were seen descending gradually nearing the earth. Could they be German or were they English? Someone should be informed. All these thoughts flashed through our heads. The plane flew low over us and three more parachutes appeared making a total of nine - the plane was soon lost to sight but our eyes were fixed on one of the last three parachutes. This particular parachute came lower and lower and landed on a hillside nearby.

While the parachute still fluttered in the high breeze, the man lay motionless for a few seconds. With our eyes fixed on him we galloped at the fastest possible speed to the side of the hill, having no thought of the paths our horses took, leaping over granite boulders and splashing through thick black mud where peat had been cut during the past summer. We slowed up as we neared the spot feeling now rather timid and wondering what nationality the parachutist might be.

The younger of the two boys, Michael Hartley aged 12, was very brave. He drew out a cowboy knife from his pocket and waved it above his head with the blade flashing in the sunlight. Such a brave Commando! Coming close, one behind the other, we saw the back of the airman who was trying to gather in his parachute but he was obviously still feeling a little dazed. He looked strange to us in his flying suit and helmet. Then speaking with a funny accent he asked for the nearest military camp. My reply came swiftly and sternly: "I don't know who you are and what you are doing here?"

He replied: 'We are over here to help win this war' and he gave us his name. Still not feeling too certain I asked to see his identity discs which he showed us.

"We then knew that this mysterious but fine looking fellow was one of our Allies - an American. Michael all this time was holding his knife ready but Maurice Coreth, the older boy, kept muttering that he knew it was an American plane all along.

The three of us dismounted and helped to gather up the parachute. The horses seemed unconcerned as they nibbled the gorse and heather. Our new friend's one regret seemed to be that he had left most of his chewing-gum behind in the plane. We walked over the hillside and persuaded our American friend to ride. We learned that his home was in Georgia, USA and many other interesting things.

We arrived at our farm feeling quite ready for a cup of tea. The police, who had quickly been informed of the whereabouts of the parachutists, arrived to collect our guest and they brought with them the news that the other eight men were safe and also the pilot who managed to land the plane some miles away. We were very sorry our guest had to leave us so soon but we were pleased that he would rejoin his companions.

With a handshake and words of goodwill we bade him adieu. My mother, remembering the words to the American song, 'Oh Ma, I miss your apple pie', produced an apple tart for him and together with his parachute he left to join the other brave members of the crew.

A day which will never be forgotten !"

The young Monica Hill lost her job as a riding instructor at the school for supposedly putting the boys at risk and allowing the story to reach the press.

But Top Sergeant Everett A. Dasher, the young radio operator on Werewolf, a B17 flying fortress, made a point of keeping in touch with the family at Ensworthy Farm, and in particular the young Monica Hill. He visited them several times during the rest of the war and was eventually wounded and invalided back to the States, having been awarded the 'Purple Heart'.

He returned in April 1979 as the Reverend Everett Dasher, a minister of the Lutheran Church from Camden, South Carolina, with his wife, Helen. He wanted to visit the place where the plane crash-landed 36 years before. Monica was with him during the visit and later said that, though they had kept in touch all those years, it was the first time they had met since the war ended.

The following year, Monica and her husband David, together with her sister Gwen and her husband, Dennis Bowles, visited America and spent three weeks touring the east coast. They ended their visit with a week as guests of the Dasher family at their home in South Carolina. Monica said of the visit to New York: "It was awe inspiring - so many people going so fast in such a small space!"

In January 1993, exactly 50 years after the dramatic incident on the Moor, the 72-year old Reverend Dasher returned to Dartmoor with his wife and family. They were guests of the Alfords and came to see the spot on Kennon Hill where he bailed out and the site at Starcross, near Dawlish,

where the huge plane landed. The Mayor of Dawlish, Fred Cann, gave a civic reception for the Reverend Dasher and his family.

The Flying Fortress landed on some playing fields and, because of the shortage of B17s, a repair crew was set to work to repair the damaged plane. Six months later, it took off along a runway specially cleared and bulldozed across hedges and fields in the direction of Botchill, to continue the fight. Sadly the pilot, Lt. Oxrider, was killed later in the war.

Talk of this incident prompts mention of a comment seen in a prospectus produced by a firm of stockbrokers in the City of London wishing to raise money for a company owning hot-air powered airships. They helpfully explained that "casualties in aviation are generally caused by involuntary vertical movement towards the ground".

Monica married David Alford from Okehampton at Gidleigh Church on 11 April 1949. She is now one of the pillars of Gidleigh village life and watches over the church where she plays the organ each week. David is renowned for his manipulation of little sticks or 'bones' which produce a rhythm similar to castanets. Some are made of ivory, some of dried pony or calf ribs. He has appeared on television a number of times and in 1953 played the 'bones' at a concert given by the English Folk Dance Society at the Albert Hall in London.

Monica remembers her mother sending clotted cream in special tins through the post to people all over the country. One of their most loyal customers was the film star, James Mason, who wrote and asked for cream to be sent to him and his daughter, Portland, at the Dorchester Hotel whenever he returned to London. The MP for Falmouth at the time, George Pilcher, stayed at Ensworthy Farm regularly and made a point of recommending their cream to Mr Hoare-Belisha and other members of his London Club.

In 1954, Monica's parents retired and moved into the cottage with Monica and David, while their son took over responsibility for farming Ensworthy. Monica reminds us that in her grandmother's day, the village of Gidleigh consisted of no more than the Church, Gidleigh Barton (Castle House) and the cottages next to the big beech tree. The rest of the buildings that form the village proper, including the Village Hall, Way Cottage, Castle Farm and the Lodge were all built after 1920.

Crispin, the Alfords' son, is married to John and Anne Holman's daughter, Diana, and farms nearby. Crispin recalls that when he was young and working on the farm at Ensworthy, he was up and out by 6am most days, having had 'tea-sups' (tea with lumps of bread soaked in it). He was back for 'lunch' at 10am, which was always a big fry-up, dinner at 1pm followed by tea at 5pm which often consisted of 'Thunder and Lightning' bread, treacle and clotted cream. Supper was had when work on the farm was finished for the day, usually around 8pm. Caroline, Monica's daughter, married Bill Murray whose songs and recitals keep everyone amused at village gatherings.

The name Ensworthy derives from the old English for 'Afan' (a persons name) and 'Worthy' or 'Worthig' meaning enclosure. The stream now known as Forder which runs by the farm was originally called Afan Brook. The first recorded owner of the property is John de Afenysworthe, who is shown as occupying the land in 1326. He was followed by his son Richard in 1337. Documents in the Devon Record Office dated 1340 refer to the house as Avenesworth.

GREAT ENSWORTHY is a Grade II listed Devon longhouse, of which the earliest surviving portion probably dates from the late 15th century. One of the most beautiful homes in the village, it was built in two phases, the first being the low end to the east which is three bays long and forms the shippon end of the longhouse. The second phase, the two-bay hall added to the west, probably dates from the early 16th century.

The longhouse plan, therefore, is the product of a second phase in which the new hall was added and the existing building converted into a shippon, with the provision of a second entrance for livestock in place of the shared cross-passage entry.

When recent restoration work started on the house it was discovered that the lower end of the building was originally one room split between a small hall and a shippon separated by a timber screen. The original smoke-blackened roof timbers show that the longhouse was open to the roof from end to end, possibly divided by low partitions and heated by an open hearth fire. In the late 17th or early 18th century, a stone outshut was built to the rear of the house, though its original plan and form is no longer clear.

The barn to the left of the house was built in the 17th century of granite stone rubble and roughly squared blocks on large boulder footings. It has been suggested that it was converted from a bakehouse into a cottage, with the shippon end transformed into a barn. Detached bakehouses of this type are very rare and of great interest to students of vernacular architecture and it is even more unusual for one to be associated with a threshing barn.

---

[1] Further detail about the history of the construction of buildings on the property is contained in a report by the Royal Commission on the Historical Monuments of England, December 1996.

However, because the remaining ceiling carpentry is considerably superior to that found within the house, it does suggest that this building was designed to be more than a kitchen or bakehouse. In any event there is no evidence of there ever having been an entrance on the north wall facing the house and without such access the relative positions of the buildings would have made the transfer of food inconvenient. The fireplace is built of granite with a soffit-chamfered and step-stopped oak lintel and a massive granite oven under the stone stops of the newel stair. [2] The building was occupied by Will Webber's grandmother about 100 years ago. Like the cottage at Chapple it has been used as a barn for the last 80 or 90 years.

Ensworthy is the only farm in Gidleigh Parish listed separately as being in venville in 1502 (albeit listed under Throwleigh parish) so at that time it was possibly one of the larger of the outlying farms in the area.

In a Conveyance by Bargain and Sale with Feoffment dated 1647, the farm was sold by Alexander Aysh to John Ford of Sampford Courtney for £100. The tenant at the time was Alexander Risdon who held a lease for the rest of his life and for the lives of two others. His tenancy was not interrupted by the sale and after he died the tenancy passed to his son, John.

John Ford died in 1655 and left his interest in the farm and all his other properties to his son-in-law, Robert Burgoyne, who conveyed the farm to John Risdon in 1693 in a complicated Final Concord of Fine. [3] By a Lease and Release conveyance in 1730, John Risdon transferred the property to Thomas Hawkes, an innkeeper from Okehampton, for an advance of £100 but remained in possession.

He must have been quite heavily in debt at this time and appears to have arranged a similar transaction with Thomas Northcott in 1747. Thomas Hawkes's son, Henry, leased the farm to Joseph Walton for 11 years from 1758 for an annual rent of £13 and then to Thomas Hatherly in 1781. William Brock bought the property from the Hawkes family in 1817 and, together with East and West Chapple, farmed a total of 100 acres in the parish.

There must be something in the air at Ensworthy that warrants further research - between the

---

[2] Department of National Heritage, 'List of Buildings of Special Architectural or Historic Interest', District of West Devon (1987) describes this building as a detached bakehouse but the Royal Commission Report raises some doubts and suggests the building was intended as a separate dwelling similar to those at Chapple and Creaber.

[3] Because medieval land law, still in use in the late 17th century, prohibited the sale of entailed land, the courts developed fictitious legal systems to bypass the prohibition - the Final Agreement or Fine is one is one of these.

years 1825 and 1849, over 20 children were born to families living and working on the farm.

Fields on the property in the mid–1800s had names like Honeypool, Thorne Park, North Down, Lower Gratton, Higher and Lower Cleave, Garden Park and North Meadow and it had substantial grazing rights on Gidleigh Common. [4]

George Leaman was the tenant in 1863 when the farm was acquired by the Kennard family of Okehampton. The following year James Hill, a farmer born in Throwleigh in 1825, took over the

[4] Gratton as in Lower Gratton means ploughed or cultivated land; Higher and Lower Cleave imply that both fields, the one closer to the farmhouse than the other, are very steep.

tenancy and moved there with his wife Anne and their children, William and Ellen and a grandson, Charles Parker.

The Northcott family, which included 76-year-old William Northcott, his son Thomas, daughter Mary and grand-daughters, Bessie, Emma, Mary Anne and grand-sons Frederick and John Leaman, held the tenancy briefly in the early 1880s. William (Ginger) Hill, married Emma Jane Mayne in 1888 and returned to Ensworthy as tenant in 1892. In the years 1898, 1905 and 1917 Ginger was an overseer of the parish and heavily involved in local affairs for over 20 years.

His son Jim (b.1892) and his wife Mabel, rented Thule farmhouse from the Vallance family after they married and their daughter, Monica, was born there in 1926. Jim's father died three years later and the family, including Monica's three-week-old sister Gwen, moved to Ensworthy and took over the tenancy. Monica's brother, who bought the farm from the Kennard family after his father retired in 1954, sold it four years later to Colonel Terry and his wife and took on the tenancy of a farm called Langley on the Fulford estate at Dunsford.

The Terrys renovated the house and among other things removed an original stone staircase from the interior. The property was sold to Allen and Rachel Van der Steen on 6 September 1997, who live there with their children, Eve, Joseph and James. A number of improvements have been made to the farmhouse and most of the land is let. Allen is a well-respected local architect and much of his work involves the rebuilding or converting of property in the Dartmoor area.

The name 'Buttern' derives from 'outer' and an acceptable nomenclature would be Outer Farm on Outer Hill. **BUTTERN FARMHOUSE** was built later than most of the others in the parish and was one of the last of the 'newtakes' on this side of the Moor. The earliest part of the building dates to the latter half of the 18th century and the farmhouse, known for a time as Higher Ensworthy, has been extended twice by the current owners.

When still a part of the Gidleigh estate, the farm was tenanted by George Endacott in 1892 and in 1901 he was elected an overseer of the Parish. In 1910 Jim Lentern and his wife, Lucy, took over the tenancy. Jim was succeeded by George Webber and his wife, Ada. George had two brothers and a sister. Gidge Webber, a farm bailiff at Lindscotte near Moretonhampstead, who retired to live at Hazelwood, Frank who lives at East Weeke and their sister, Suzy.

Two of George's children, Gwen and Will, who remained unmarried, ran the farm as partners after their father died and Colonel Vicary sold the farm to Will on 3 October 1951. George and Ada had a total of 11 children; Dorah, Jim, Louise, George, Fred, Anthony, Emily, John, Frank and Gwen and Will who moved to Wyndhurst at Wonson when they retired.

The Webbers are a famous moor family and there is an excellent photograph of Will Webber hanging in the Northmore Arms at Wonson. Will reverted to the practice of his ancestors - the cutting of vags on Headon for use as fuel after many years of paying heavily to have coal delivered to the house.

A charter of Henry III granting the right to take peat from the Moor referred to it as coal and, in the 18th century, the people who cut and sold it were known as colliers. Peat used for the domestic hearth came from the top layers of turf known as 'vags' while the darker, richer bog peat was sold for industrial use and was taken from deeper levels. Peat slabs were generally 20 inches long, 7 inches wide and 2 inches thick and a good peat-cutter could cut 3,000 slabs a day. Petrol, tar oil and acetic acid can all be distilled from peat but no-one so far has been able to do so commercially on Dartmoor.

Exploitation of the peat beds round here has fortunately been limited over the years and does not match the aggressive cutting near Glastonbury which saw over 50,000 tons a year removed for horticultural use. Such an amount would have proved disastrous for Dartmoor.

Devonians depended on peat to fuel their fires and these were not suited to roasting meat. As a result they tended to cook joints in what was described as 'baking ovens'. These were large cast iron pots with lids which, when filled with meat and whatever else was to be cooked, were buried in the hot ashes of the peat fire for several hours.

"Peat fires! What fires can surpass them? They do not flame, but they glow, and diffuse an aroma that fills the lungs with balm ... Every farm has its peat-bog and in the proper season a sufficiency of fuel is cut then carried and stacked for winter use. I may be mistaken, but it seems to me that cooking done over a peat fire surpasses cooking at the best club in London." [1]

By the turn of the century, farmers in Devon were eating very well indeed. For the main meal at mid-day, they had a joint or a stew most days of the week. John Holman recalls that when he was a boy, around 1925, his favourite meal was rabbit stew with 'doughboys' (dumplings) and he can remember being sent out with two great slices of homemade bread and a quarter-inch-thick slice of fatty bacon between them.

[1] S. Baring-Gould, *A Book of Dartmoor*

One local farmer said that when he was young, in the 1920s, his family would be up and out by six and back for a full cooked breakfast at nine, 'dinner' at one and tea at five followed by supper at eight. They had clotted cream and fresh bread with each meal and didn't appear to put on a pound in weight.

In 1542, a dietician called Andrew Boorde said:

"Clowted Crayme and nawe crayme put together, is eaten more for a sensuall apptyte than fer any good nouryshment."

Commercial cream production in the South West dates back to the 13th century. Clotted cream has been sent by post to all parts of the country and was once packed in stoneware jars labelled 'To be kept dry and cool not on ice or it turns fusty'. [2]

Other dishes common to farm kitchens in Devon durng the 17th and 18th centuries were chicken dumplings and beef stew in cider with parsley dumplings, revel buns, Exeter pudding and Devonshire junket. In 1816, Richard Polwhele wrote of Devon pies:

"The squab pye, the herb pye, the leek and pork pye, on which clouted cream was profusely poured - the goose and the parsnip and the fish and apple pye were frequent...".

Best of all was the 17th-century recipe found in Allison Ainsworth's book for lark pie:

"Take as many larks as you please, season them with pepper and salt, put some forcemeat in the bellies and balls of the same in the pie with them. Lay some very thin slices of bacon upon the larks if you like, if not put some butter, put in a little thin gravy when it comes out of the oven give it a shake; to have a good lark pie add a few Palates - lamb stones or sweet breads, hard yolks of eggs, asparagus tops, dried mushrooms; make a ragoo of all these things and when the larks are baked open the pie and throw it over the larks, give it a shake, let it stand quarter of an hour by the fire."

The idea that the local farmer in the 17th and 18th centuries ate only "poor ale, vinied cheese and rye bred" is somewhat misleading.

---

[2] Allison Ainsworth, *West Country Larder*

Returning to Buttern, at the foot of the hill, on the other side from the farmhouse, is an ancient stone circle with only five of the original 30 stones still standing. It has a diameter of about 80 feet and in the early 1930s the turf in the centre of the circle was removed for fuel. No-one knows what purpose was served by these circles though the use of hut and retaining circles is clearly understood. Close by are traces of the ancient Buttern Lane, an early bronze age track to the moor.

Stuart and Jill Abrahall bought the farm and its 32 acres from Will and Gwen Webber on 24 March 1981 and then, in January the following year, sold it to the current owners, Robert and Christine Hurdle who farm there with their son, Richard. Christine's father, Archdeacon Fisher, was among those who helped out at Gidleigh Church after he retired in the early 1980s. Richard and his wife, Juliet, live in the new extension with their young daughters, Katherine and Rachel.

Bob Hurdle described the warm welcome they received the morning they moved to the farm from Betchworth in Surrey on a freezing cold, blustery January day. Their new neighbour, Monica Alford, arrived at the door with a basket of bread and hot soup to welcome them in. With no hot water or heating in the house, nothing could have been more welcome.

Bob is an enthusiastic apiarist and cares for several hives in Gidleigh Park. His honey, sometimes sold locally, is excellent and not tainted with the overpowering flavour of rape so common these days. Honey was the principal source of sweetness up to the end of the Middle Ages. As cane sugar was not readily available until imports arrived from the Caribbean plantations in the 17th century, there is little evidence of tooth decay on Anglo-Saxon skeletal remains found in the area. Honey was a precious commodity and medieval farmers considered themselves fortunate indeed if they were able to tempt a swarm to settle in their thatch.

Bob Hurdle also makes his own excellent mead which unfortunately he does not sell. During the Middle Ages mead, a super-sweet alcoholic drink with quite a kick, was brewed from the remains of honeycombs and became the drinking man's choice beverage in some parts of the Westcountry. [3]

It is assumed that the tiny hamlet of **CHAPPLE** is named after the Wallen Chapel, which stands nearby on Moortown land. **CHAPPLE FARM** or **EAST CHAPPLE** as it was called, is the most substantial building in the hamlet and was probably built as a longhouse of plastered granite stone rubble in

[3] Hagen, *Second Handbook*, pp. 230, 231.

the 16th or 17th century. It has been altered dramatically over the years, with many additions and renovations in the 19th century. Most of the interior of the farmhouse is the result of 19th- and 20th-century refurbishment but the fireplace in the inner room is contemporary. It is built of granite ashlar with a hollow-chamfered surround and a 17th-century crossbeam. The old kitchen

fireplace is next-door, behind the oven housing and alongside a cream oven. It has a plain chamfered oak lintel with similarly treated crossbeams.

The original house has been added to extensively over the years and was split into two for most of the 19th and 20th centuries. There is a small disused cottage across the road from the farmhouse, built in the late 16th century of coursed blocks of granite ashlar with some granite stone rubble patching. It is small but of good workmanship and, though it was never a longhouse, it is a good example of a further type of 16th-century house. This small dwelling is thought to have housed the smith and his family before they moved to Throwleigh in 1920.

A flight of external steps leads to the first-floor doorway and there is a timber casement with glazing bars on each floor. The interior is mostly 16th-century, with an oak lintel over the granite fireplace and remains of stone newel stairs alongside it. The ground-floor partition has been re-moved and the first-floor structure is supported by a 20th-century beam. Gidge Webber can remember someone living here in about 1920, but the building has been used as a granary for the last 50 years or so.

WEST CHAPPLE, next to the farmhouse, was used as a cow house for many years. However, it re-tains even now much that confirms its origin as a genuine early 16th-century Devon longhouse of sophisticated workmanship with some remarkable features.

There are many farms in Devon described as longhouses but few can easily be identified as such today. In a true long house, animals and people share the same entrance. [1] That was certainly the case at West Chapple, although modernisation has inevitably erased much of the character of the original dwelling.

The house has a main range on a slight slope with an added rear wing, all built of granite. The original part is the main block, which would have been a 3-room-and-through-passage plan open to the roof from end to end, divided by low partitions and heated by an open hearth fire. Through the late 16th century and early 17th century, the rooms where progressively floored over and the hall stack was inserted. The main doorway had a porch that was, until recent years, roofed by a single slab.

The shippon, to the left of the door, is largely unaltered with three slit windows on the east wall.

---

[1] N. Alcock 'Devonshire Farmhouses, part III', *Trans Dev. Assoc*, vol 101 (1969), p. 83, contains a detailed account and sketch of Chapple

The north and south walls have signs of larger square windows which were probably dung holes. The wing of ashlar blockwork at the rear was added in the 17th century to provide a heated parlour and chamber. It has a circular stair with a slit window and a large fireplace with hollow moulded stone jambs. On the east wall is a probable original door with a large boulder as a step outside.

In the sale particulars of Chapple Farm dated 1924, West Chapple is described as two labourers' cottages. The room at the rear of the house was one cottage with two rooms above, while the right half of the front of the house was the other with the shippon to the left.

South of Chapple Farm is a very attractive and unusually complete Dartmoor threshing barn, built in the 16th century of large blocks of granite ashlar. There is a window high in the uphill gable which contains a 16th-century oak round-headed doorframe which fits well into the opening.

In the 19th century, a horse engine house was added to the rear of the building. These engines

were developed in the north of England at the very end of the 18th century and presumably arrived in Devon soon after. The engine house was attached to the barn's outer wall so that a drive shaft could be connected through it to the threshing machine housed within. Threshing was dry indoor work on the farms and a source of employment in the short days of winter. For this reason, threshing machines became unpopular with farm labourers as all the work could be done in a few days, leaving no other work for them to do.

The machines were one cause of the 'Captain Swing Riots' of 1829, when many were burnt by farm labourers angry at being done out of regular winter work. On Dartmoor, when there was little other seasonal work and it was necessary to keep the men busy, hedging and bank building was done. This involved moving some enormous rocks from the fields to build the numerous stone walls surrounding them.

South-east of Chapple Farm is a 17th-century cow house which appears to have been re-arranged in the 1900s, when a number of the windows and doors where blocked up. All have lintels made from single slabs of granite and the building incorporates some large roughly-squared blocks of granite ashlar.

Chapple was owned by the Vogwell family through most of the 17th century but after Richard Vogwell died in 1705, the farm passed to the Rowe family of Berrydown. In 1742, Andrew Rowe paid tithes as the owner of West Chapple and John Perryman for East Chapple. In 1754 John Rowe leased Chapple to James Knapman at an annual rent of £15.4s to be paid quarterly.

The Rowe family sold the freehold of the farm to William Brock in 1764 who, five years later, extended the tenancy agreement with James Knapman for a further five years at the slightly increased rent of £15.10s. The freehold of the property passed from father to son within the Brock family for 160 years.

William Brock	b.1696,	m. Elizabeth Endacott,	d.1782
William Brock jr	b.1757,	m. Elizabeth Moor 1795,	d.1826
William Brock minor	b.1804,	m. Susanna Gay 1830,	d.1862
William Dunning Brock	b.1831,	m. Charlotte Hill 1870,	d.1873
William Julian Brock	b.1870,	m. Emily Underhill,	d.1945

Farm fields at that time had names such as Tan House Meadow, Lower and Higher Broom Park, Long Byney, Higher Grattner, Great and Little Burrows, Great and Little Long Close, Great, Little and Middle Hellands and Broom Planet. [2]

In the 1880s, there were four families living at Chapple. John Cole and his wife Ann were tenants of the main farm with two labourers, William Decker and James Brock. William Northway married William Dunning Brock's widow Charlotte and they, together with their daughter Bessie and Charlotte's children, William and Flora, lived in another of the houses. John Osborne, a farm labourer with his wife, five children and two apprentices, Richard Hill and Henry Bond, lived in another. Finally, William Aggett, a thatcher, and his wife Jane occupied the fourth house. A fifth house in the hamlet was unoccupied at the time. Altogether, a total of 25 people were living at Chapple in 1881; today there are six.

Apprenticing children to farms in the Westcountry was once common and served as a practical way of dealing with the surplus of young children, bastards and orphans as well as 'hedge children'. They were the responsibility of the parish, so the parish apprenticed them to local farmers. Though they did not receive a wage, they received their clothing and food, and learnt a trade.

They would be indentured for anything up to 14 years or until they were 21 in most cases. Life was hard for these young children but the household lived as one family and all were treated alike. The farmer, as head of the household, was all-powerful and would have demanded as much from his own children as he did from his apprentices.

In fact, wives were no exception. The patriarchal right to 'discipline and punnish' a wife was not in question towards the end of the 18th century. A judge's verdict on a case in 1782 resolved that, if there was good cause, a husband could legally beat his wife so long as the stick was no thicker than his thumb. [3]

Examples of these apprentices go back hundreds of years and include, for example, Elizabeth Osborne aged eight, indentured to the Reverend Richard Skinner at the Parsonage in 1789. In 1819, Samuel Rendle then aged nine was indentured for 12 years to the Rowe family. In 1825 William Horsford, aged nine, was indentured at Batworthy for 12 years.

---

[2] Lower and Higher Broom Park refer to fields that had broom in or around them. Grattner as in Higher Grattner donates ploughed or cultivated land; Great and Little Long Close describe two small thin enclosed fields; Helland as in Great, Little and Middle Hellands is Cornish for 'old church site' and it is assumed that these fields must be close to the site of the ancient chapel on Moortown land after which Chapple Farm is named.

[3] See Lawrence Stone, *Road to Divorce*, p. 201

The system appears to have done little to reduce the birth rate among the poor of the village. The Turpin family contributed a large number of apprentices to the parish. In 1786 Elizabeth Turpin was indentured to Digory Lee at Greenaway and, three years later, her brother John was apprenticed to James Rowe at Scorhill. In 1804, Zachary Turpin aged seven was apprenticed at Scorhill for 14 years. It seems to have had no ill effects on Zachary as he stayed on in the village as a husbandman, married a local girl and produced five children of his own.

In 1924, William Julian Brock sold Chapple Farm to his sister and her husband, Herbert Thomas Vallance, though the family did not move there until 1931. Over the years there has been much coming and going in the hamlet: between 1900 and 1950 the following people were living there at one time or another:

James Lentern and his wife

William Hamilton

Aaron Sampson and his wife Mary Jane

James Webber

Richard Haggett

William and Hannah Lentern

Fred and Susan Webber

Richard (Dick) Hill and his wife Dinah Jane

John Mortimore

Tom and Flora Vallance and their daughter Dorothy

Herbert William (Bill) Vallance and his wife Kathleen (Kay) took over the farm in the 1950s. They typified the small upland farmer of the period and tried to be self-sufficient, buying in as little in the way of cake and other animal feed as possible. They kept a few attested South Devons for milking and some 15 head of young stock for rearing. The breeding was outwintered, the calves kept in. They had a flock of 30 greyfaced Dartmoor ewes and one or two Wessex sows; 100 head of poultry completed the stocking. Day-old pullets were bought in and reared free range and 20 or 30 were kept in batteries. In an article in the 'Farmer and Stock-Breeder' printed in 1958, they reckoned that in a good year their turnover could be as much as £2,500 but over the previous three years they averaged £1,500.

For cattle they received £471; sheep £224; eggs £300; poultry £41; cream £200; potatoes £108; oats £52; the hill cow subsidy £50; headage grant £17 10s and calf subsidy £35 for a net profit of £500.

Bill started selling clotted cream to a Torquay cafe owner who wrote to ask if he could provide a regular supply. When the restrictions on cream sales were lifted and the buyer was able to find supplies closer to home, Bill started selling by mail order to people all over the country. It was this ability of the small farmer to be flexible in what he produced, combined with the introduction of farm subsidies, that enabled them to survive. However, Bill said of subsidies that, in his opinion, "it should not be necessary to help everybody to help anybody".

The farm was sold in 1959 to Mr W. H. Stevens and his two sisters and at some time in the early 1960s, the thatch on the roof caught fire and was replaced with tiles. The Stevens's sold the property to Tommy Fox Pitt in 1965 who lived there with his wife, Marjorie , for 20 years. Tommy had recently retired from colonial service and farmed Chapple well into his eighties.

His life can best be summed up by extracts from his obituary - which he wrote ten years before he died - as well as by other scraps of information found amongst his papers by his grandson, George Lyon-Smith.

Commander Thomas Stanley Lane Fox-Pitt OBE was born on 27 November 1897. He went to Osborne at 12 and then on to Dartmouth in 1911, whence he was mobilised when war was declared in 1914. He served in HMS Lord Nelson in the bombardment of the Dardenelles forts when he was 15, and at the battle of Jutland in HMS Inflexible.

After the war, he left the Navy and spent some years studying architecture, agriculture and archeology until his father decided enough was enough and persuaded him to join the colonial service, which posted him to Northern Rhodesia. During his years in Africa he became increasingly distressed by the treatment of mine workers in the copper belt. Though his Colonial Office masters knew nothing of it, he became more and more left wing in his political beliefs and found Marx and his teachings closer to his heart than anything else he experienced in this country.

He married Marjory Florence Hope-Barton in 1930 and two years later their daughter, Caroline, was born, followed in 1935 by Ursula.

He returned to the Navy in 1939 at the outbreak of the Second World War and helped in the sinking of the Bismarck while serving on HMS Dorsetshire. Most of his war service was spent on convoy escort duty in the Atlantic and the Indian Ocean. He was awarded the Naval OBE for daringly retrieving valuable equipment from a partly-sunk U-boat.

After the war, he returned to his life in the colonial service in Northern Rhodesia and Baretsland and was promoted to Provincial Commissioner of the Eastern Province. Soon, however, he ran into conflict with his masters in the Colonial Office as a result of his support for freedom and justice for the black population. He committed himself to the cause of African independence and, according to George Lyon-Smith, become a member of the ANC.

As a result, he was declared a 'Prohibited Immigrant' and banned from returning to Zambia. He continued the struggle from his house in London, which became Kenneth Kaunda's HQ until Zambia and Malawi gained their independence in 1964. During that period he became Secretary of the Anti Slavery Society and, for a time, Secretary of the Fabian Society. He was awarded the Order of the Freedom of Zambia, which he claimed was his proudest moment.

In 1965, at the age of 68, he and Marjorie retired to Chapple Farm and over the next 20 years became much loved and admired by the local population. He kept South Devons, Exmoor horned sheep and turkeys that seem to have had the run of the place and were allowed to roost in the trees nearby.

Tommy had a habit of losing control of his tractor, which ran away with him on at least two occasions. He always assumed that the tractor could climb any slope but as he wouldn't have dreamt of spending money on new tyres, the machine constantly slid all over the place. On one occasion, it slid from the top to the bottom of one of his fields with a load of hay on the trailer behind.

Caroline Lyon-Smith bought West Chapple from her father in 1973 and converted it into more-or-less what it is today. The Lyon-Smith family used it as a holiday home initially, moving there permanently in 1980. Tommy died in 1985 and his funeral took place at Gidleigh Church on 21 October.

In 1986, David and Caroline and their family moved next-door to Chapple Farm. David's son, George, married Fiona Weir whose family lived at Parford, near Sandy Park outside Chagford. His daughter, Kate, married a barrister, Rawdon Crozier, and lives near Tavistock.

In 1987, David sold West Chapple to Douglas and Jenny Kyle, retired farmers from Buckinghamshire, who lived there for a couple of years before letting it to the Urmston family. In the end, the Kyles sold the house to Paul and Jill Nielson in 1991 who sold it to the present owners, David and Gabrielle Nickell, a year or two later.

On 30 March 1994, David Lyon Smith sold East Chapple, the Grade II-listed farm and farm buildings together with 43 acres of land and grazing rights on the moor, to Chris and Thalia Smallwood, and they continue to farm it enthusiastically. Thalia's parents, Bill and Patsy Morley, both well-known artists, live in a flat in part of the house.

Chris Smallwood qualified as a doctor at Birmingham Medical School in 1960 and in 1965, was elected a Fellow of the Royal College of Surgeons. He reached the peak of his career when he became Consultant Surgeon to the Home Office in 1974.

As far as medicine is concerned it seems that the sign of the cross and the power of faith were the best antiseptics in the year 1000 and little changed for 500 years. People had no knowledge of modern germ theory but they were very conscious of the contagious nature of diseases.

'Bald's Leechbook', a 10th-century manuscript [4] equivalent to a modern-day medicine book, lists remedies in order from head to toe, including the Viagra of the day - agrimony boiled in milk. A number of remedies in the book included ingredients with hallucinogenic qualities, which suggests that the treatments were designed as palliatives with little or no remedial effects. Trepanning and cautery with the use of only mild anaesthetic, and dependence on the use of leeches as a cure-all for most illness, were the norm.

Just up the hill from Chapple, on the way to Moortown, is a ruin of a chapel [5] from which, until very recently, three oak trees grew. It stands beside a brook known as Lower Wallands. The name derives from the Old English, 'walland' (la Wallen) meaning a walled-in space. A drama attaches to this building, as unfolded in documents in the Devon Record Office, as well as a translation by Alice Wells of the Register of Bishop Grandisson. It concerns the trial before the King's Justice, Thomas de Stouforde the elder of Chagford, of a clerk called Robert de Middelcote. . . [6]

> ". . . who on the Monday after the feast of the Annunciation in the second year of our Episcopate [28 March 1328] did use force against Agnes, the daughter of Roger the miller of Gidleigh Mill, in the chapel of the blessed Virgin Mary at Wallen (Capella Beate Marie Virginis apud la Wallen existentum) and against her wishes raped her, so violently that he killed the child in the womb of the said Agnes (Quendam puerum vivum in corpore ejusdem Agnetis existentem) and that on the Wednesday after the feast of St Mark the Evangelist, in the second year of the reign of Edward the King (27 April 1328) did steal from the house of Robert Rossel at Fonhalle (this is probably Venn manor house in Bishopsteignton) in the Hundred of Wonford and carried away silver and bread to the value of 4s 2d."

Robert de Middelcote fled the area, but was finally caught on the heath at Haldon Hill and accused of murder and highway robbery. He appealed to the bishop, declared himself innocent and claimed benefit of clergy. The bishop ordered that in all the churches in the deanery, it was to be announced that the case would be heard on 1 June 1328, in the cathedral. There is no record in the

---

[4] *Bald's Leechbook;* see Swanton, *Anglo Saxon Prose*, p. 259

[5] See photograph on page 99

[6] Reverend J. Rawson (Rector of Gidleigh), 'Story of an Ancient Chapel', 1920, and *Trans Dev Assoc,* vol.79 (1947).

Register of what transpired at the hearing; possibly his accusers were declared to be 'sons of perdition' or 'satellites of Satan', two favourite terms of opprobrium at that time and as a result the case was dismissed.

The Reverend Rawson believed that, as the Wallen chapel had been desecrated, it was never used again. For centuries, local people were terrified of going near it. Oak trees were planted in its ruins to ensure that, in time, nature would cause the building to collapse as it would of course have been sacrilege to have wilfully destroyed a holy place. This attitude is in sharp contrast to the large amount of money recently spent to cut down the trees in order to prevent further damage to the building. How times have changed!

On 14 May 1332, Alice de Moeles obtained a licence to have mass celebrated in her new chapel "atte Wallen" founded by Richard de Chageford, which was built in Throwleigh parish. There is some dispute as to exactly where that chapel was sited as no stone of it remains on Walland Hill, above the Teign on the boundaries of Throwleigh and Chagford parishes.

Situated on the banks of Forder Brook, which marks the boundary of the parishes of Gidleigh and Throwleigh, **SOUTH FORDER** is a Grade II listed farmhouse and carriage shed forming part of the attractive hamlet of Forder. The stream running through the grounds was originally called Afan Brook but over the years it became known as Forder after the ford which crossed it at this point.

The house is said to have been built in the 16th century, with later additions in the early 1700s and the final extension of a crosswing built in 1978. It was originally a 3-room-and-through-passage plan house facing south-east and is built of plastered granite stone rubble down a hillslope. The outside wall of a bread oven projects from the front towards the lower end of the hall and it seems likely that the farmhouse began life as a late medieval open hall house.

In 1683, the owner of nearby Forder Farm was William Vogwell, a rich and influential local landowner who, on his death, bequeathed North and South Forder for the upkeep of the Church and the poor house. In an Abstract of an Indenture dated 1767 confirming the 'Lease grant and farm lett', the trustees of the church settlement, Robert Martyn of Throwleigh, William Bennet and Henry Endacott of Gidleigh leased both North and South Forder to Thomas Gay of 'Gidley' for 21 years at an annual rent of £10.4s, to be paid quarterly.

In the 1788 Land Tax Assessment, James Brock is shown as tenant of both North and South

Forder and in the 1826 Assessment, Thomas Lee took over as tenant of both properties.

In 1881, South Forder was occupied by George Hill, a farm labourer born in Gidleigh in 1853, his Cornish wife Sarah and their three children, Bessie, James and George's stepson, George Hancock. James took over the tenancy of the house from his father for a few years and then in 1892 it was occupied by James Webber. Three years later, Amos Milford took over the tenancy and in 1911 it passed to Jim Pearce and his family.

Through the Vogwell bequest the house came to be held by the Church Lands Trust, whose trustees in the 1920s were some of the leading figures in the Parish.

The Rev J Rawson	Rector	William Hill	Ensworthy
Percy Norrington	Scorhill	Robert Dunning	Creaber
Aaron Sampson	Chapple	William Brock	Chapple

On 23 June 1921, South Forder and about 8 acres was sold for £300 to Thomas Hill the younger, a farmer from Throwleigh who lived there until June 1940 when he gave it to his brother-in-law Edward Wonnacott, a retired road-worker, through a Deed of Gift. Edward and his wife Mary, their daughter Louisa and son, Stanley, lived there for 15 years before selling the property to Joan Ewin for £950 in 1955. Joan's husband, Spencer Ewin, was a director of the John Player Tobacco Company and they used the house as a holiday home for many years.

In June 1959, Oliver Aggett - at the time the licensee of the Northmore Arms, or the New Inn, at Wonson - was paid £50 to release the Ewins from the 5 shilling tithe levied on the property (which seems a high price to pay for something that was abolished only a few years later). Joan Ewin died in 1977 and left the house to her husband. Their daughter, Beverly Abson, inherited the property when her father died and used it as a holiday home before selling it to the current owners, Mike and Val Date, in 1984. The property now consists of the house, garage, loose boxes, sand school and about 16 acres of land.

In a typical 'What goes around, comes around' story, Mike's father, a pharmacist living next to the Oxenham Arms in South Zeal where Mike was born, used to deliver the Sunday papers to South Forder in his Austin Seven in the 1930s. Mike and Val were told they had bought the property from under the nose of the politician, Norman Tebbitt, so at the time the locals liked to tease them by saying they had seen off the Tebbitts only to end up with the Dates.

Val Date recalls old Tommy Fox Pitt from Chapple Farm, then in his mid eighties and dressed in black cloak and boots, climbing on to his horse barking "Post Office!" and with that his mare would wander up the lane past South Forder to the post office at Throwleigh. Having finished his business, he would again climb on to his horse and shout "Home" and the mare would meander home again with the old gentleman doing nothing more than sit on its back.

In the yard beside the front door of the house is a famous four-foot-long 'pivot' stone which, at some time, formed the top hinge of the entrance gate to the property before the corner of the wall of the carriage house collapsed. [1]

It is thought unlikely that gate-hangings of this type have been made since 1600, which supports the belief that a cottage and yard were established here in the late 1500s, before the present house was built.

---

[1] *Worth's Dartmoor*, p. 359

NORTH FORDER is a Grade II listed Devon longhouse built of whitewashed granite stone rubble with large dressed quoins, a granite stack with its original granite ashlar chimney shaft and a thatched roof. It faces south-east and is built down a relatively steep hillslope. The inner room at the left is terraced so deeply into the hillslope that the eaves of the roof nearly touch the ground.

It probably began life as a late medieval open hall house with a shippon at the downhill end. Dating from the 1560s and altered very little over the years, it is a very attractive example of a Devon farmhouse. It is owned by the Aggett family who farm Forder from the main house, on the other side of the stream in Throwleigh parish.

North Forder was one of the properties bequeathed by William Vogwell to the Church on his death in 1683. In 1746 Thomas Gay paid tithes for it and in 1880 it was occupied by a farm labourer, born in South Tawton in 1820, called James Brock, his wife Ann and their two sons. Amos Milford occupied the property in 1895 and in the same year was appointed an overseer of the village together with William Endacott from Gidleigh Mill. Between 1911 and 1914 John Pearce and William Elston lived there, followed in 1920 by James Endacott. Five years later the tenancy was taken over by Robert Bevan.

Like South Forder, it was sold by the Church Lands Trust in 1921 to the Hill family. Oliver Aggett of Forder Farm then bought it from Ernest Hill when he decided to emigrate to Canada in the late 1920s. The Aggetts leased the house to Harry Hill for a number of years.

George Endacott, a retired water engineer (known in the village as Joe) leased it from Oliver in 1942 and has lived there ever since. He introduced the village to motorbikes when, in 1930, he acquired a belt-driven Connaught followed a few years later by a series of sports cars, including an early 'T' Type MG.

George recalls that Oliver Aggett and his wife, Lill, ran the Northmore Arms at Wonson for several years and took in lodgers from time to time, such as Miss Evans, a local school teacher. He also confesses that, as young boys, he and his friends used to chase after the baker's cart as it wound its way through the lanes. They held on to the rails at the side of the cart and, by sliding their hands under the canvas cover, were able to grab the warm inside out of one of the large 4lb loaves, leaving nothing more than the crust behind.

George is a member of the vast Endacott clan that seems to have taken over the whole of this part of Devon in the 19th century. His neice, Barbara Osborne, has done a great deal of work tracing the family history and points out that the family name is spelt variously Endacott, Endecott and Endycott.

The earliest spelling of the name appears to be 'Yendecote' and, according to a charter dated

1262, that was the name of a property owned by the family in the Manor of Itton at South Tawton. The affix 'cott' or 'cote' means homestead; 'yonder-cote' therefore meant the farthest homestead.

The Devon Lay Subsidy Rolls for 1327 mentions a Johannes de Yendecote being assessed a subsidy for land in South Tawton, and a Charter held by Exeter University dated 1448 shows the copyhold of a property conveyed to John Yendecote in Holcombe Paramour, in Winkleigh parish. The Chagford churchwarden's accounts of 1528 show a John Endacott purchasing 'Myddell Parke' which at the time contained a 'tynne worke'.

The first mention of the Endacott name in Gidleigh Parish records, however, is the marriage of a Jane Endacott to an attorney called Hole on 1 March 1689. It appears again on 25 June 1706, when Alexander and Thomazin Endacott christened their son Geoffrey at Gidleigh Church. Alexander, who lost his first wife, married a widow called Elizabeth Nosworthy in 1742.

Following this relatively slow start, the growth of the Endacott family in the area took off rapidly. It was as though they decided to colonise the entire world with their progeny: indeed, records show they left in great numbers for America, Canada and Australia. Of course, it was not unusual for families to be large in the mid-19th century but it was rare for so many to have survived so close to home.

According to Barbara Osborne, Sir Roper Lethbridge, who was elected president of the Devonshire Association in 1899 gave details in his presidential address of the Devon families who had settled in America and the colonies. Reference was made to a John Endacott of Chagford who sailed from Weymouth in the Abigail on 20 June 1628 and ended up as the first Governor of Massachusetts Bay.

Colonel Mansfield bought a field called 'Broadymead' from the Vallance family in 1945 and on it built a small bungalow which he named **BROADMEAD.** It lies a short distance from Chapple Farm on the lane to Coombe.

The Reverend William Keble Martin purchased the property from Mansfield soon after work on it was completed and he lived there, on and off, for over 20 years. He wrote and illustrated *The Concise British Flora in Colour* with its 1,486 perfect species illustrations, all of which were drawn direct from nature. It took Keble Martin 60 years of meticulous and devoted study, research, note-making and exquisite draughtsmanship to complete, and it has become a classic as a reference work of identification used by botanists and students.

Keble Martin was born in 1877 and during his schooldays at Marlborough was an enthusiastic lepidoperist and botanist, taking botany as a degree subject when he went up to Oxford. Students in the Botanic Gardens were accustomed to draw specimens as seen under the microscope and his habit of meticulous, detailed work is reflected in the exquisite illustrations to his books.

After his ordination, Keble Martin worked for 18 years as curate or vicar in industrial parishes in the north of England and in 1918 became Chaplain to the Forces in France. After the war, he moved to Devon where he was able to study different flora in various parishes. He was an active member of the two Botanical Exchange Clubs and the International Botanical Congress 1930. In 1928, he was elected a Fellow of the Linnean Society and edited a comprehensive 'Flora of Devon' for the Devon Association a year later.

He resigned his benefice in 1949 at what he described as the early age of 72, to devote his time to redrawing a number of the plates. He still continued to take temporary charge of occasional vacant parishes, however, usually spending between six and 12 months in each. Ultimately, he sold Broadmead and moved to Modbury where he died some years later. He is buried in Modbury churchyard.

This might be an appropriate place to mention, briefly, the trees and vegetation of the Moor. On Dartmoor there are only a few trees that can withstand the lack of good soil, the wind and driven rain. There are, however, two remarkable woods that have survived for hundreds of years. These are Wistman's Wood in the centre and Black Tor Beare in the north. The trees are remarkable, not for luxuriant growth but for their odd appearance and their extremely small size. Both are about 1,300 ft above sea level and contain mainly twisted and deformed miniature oaks, Quercus pedunculata, together with some mountain ash.

The vegetation on Dartmoor varies to a surprising degree but furze, Ulex europaeus, grows everywhere and from prehistoric times has been used for fuel, as it burns rapidly in contrast to the much slower-burning peat. Heather, Calluna vulgaris, is also widespread and in several colours, purple, rich crimson, dull lilac and even white. Heather can endure quite severe winters and, though it prefers drier soils, will grow on quite wet ground on the margins of some bogs.

Other common plants to be seen on the Moor are thyme, Thymus serpyllum, the whortleberry, Vaccinium myrtillus, reindeer moss, Cladonia sylvatica, cotton grass, Eriophorum angustifolium and not least, sphagnum moss.

Returning to Broadmead, the bungalow was bought by Lionel and Phi Edwards who set to work building a heather and gentian nursery on the property. Lionel was a retired Royal Marine Colonel who served from 1945 to 1972 and saw active service in Korea. They were extremely popular in the area and Lionel, a respected churchwarden, kept Louis Baycock on his toes. He died in 1996 and Phi the following year. Both are buried in Gidleigh churchyard where trees have been planted in their memory.

The copse beside the bungalow contains the ruins of the old smithy that was abandoned when the last incumbent, John Bond, moved to take over the Throwleigh Forge in the 1920s.

HAZLEWOOD, originally a wood-framed bungalow, was built by Lewis and Alice Binmore in 1926 on land owned by Chapple Farm. Alice was Gidge Webber's sister and after the house burnt down in the early 1950s, Gidge's son, Gideon, was responsible for rebuilding it.

Gidge Webber, his wife and a lodger called Percy Tucker took over the property from the Binmores. After his father died, Gideon sold the house and 4 acres to John and Anne Holman, who moved there in 1986 after selling the 160-acre Addiscott Farm in South Tawton, which they had bought in 1960.

John Holman was born in 1917 into a large South Zeal family. His father was the landlord of the "The Kings Arms" in South Zeal and his aunt, Mrs Lentern, was the landlady of The "Cawsand Beacon" which, you may recall, was frequented by John Skeaping at the outbreak of war. The Cawsand was sold a few years ago after the landlord lost his licence and was forced to close; it is no longer a public house. Nell Knapman, another of John's aunts, owned The Oxenham Arms so in those days, the family had the pub business well and truly sewn up in the village.

John recalls days when one of the banks in Okehampton sent out a man, once or twice a fortnight, to conduct any banking business that was required. The young children of the village would gather outside the Cawsand to fight for the coins they were able to persuade the men to throw for them.

Most of the public houses in the area were no more than cider houses in the early years, and the idea that you could be offered a full meal with wine and a choice of foreign beers would have been greeted with disbelief until quite recently.

Rough, locally-made cider was always the most popular drink and John said that his father regularly sent him to Jimmy Saunders at Spreyton Barton with their horse and cart, in order to collect two hogsheads of cider (130 gallons). They paid the farm 7d a gallon and sold it in the pub for 3d a pint. Most pubs kept five-gallon jars of whiskey and rum under the counter and apart from cider, they sold stout and draft ale. In winter, John remembers watching the farmers huddled round the fire in his father's pub clasping their pints of stout. They kept pokers in the hot embers of the fire to warm their ale.

There is a tale of a local farmer who had over-indulged on a rare visit to the pub. He returned home and, while staggering up the stairs late at night, heard his wife shout out, "Is that you, George?", to which he replied, "It b....y well better be!"

Anne Holman's father, William Jackson, served as an officer in the Royal Artillery during the First World War. He was a partner in the Westcountry firm of solicitors, Symes Robinson & Lee. Her great-great-grandfather, Charles Burnard, built Huccaby House which became home to the Burnard family for two generations. His son, Robert Burnard, was a close friend of the Reverend Sabine Baring-Gould and a founder member of the Dartmoor Preservation Association formed in 1883. He was one of the most famous Dartmoor characters of the early part of this century. Robert's grand-daughter, Lady Sayer, wife of Vice-Admiral Sir Guy Sayer, was a renowned conservationist, famous for her stalwart defence of the Moor and the lifestyle of the people who live on it.

Robert Burnard was the first person to propose a solution to the preservation of Dartmoor when he suggested the formation of a National Park. This was not created until 1950, 30 years after his death. He was a renowned and gifted amateur photographer, a Fellow of the Society of Antiquaries, President of the Devonshire Association and for many years, Secretary of the Dartmoor Preservation Association.

Anne Holman who died in May 2000 will be greatly missed by all in the village. She was District Commissioner for the Mid-Devon Hunt Pony Club, chairman of the Dartmoor Pony Society and more recently, secretary of the Gidleigh Parish Church Council.

BRIMSTONE DOWN is situated on the eastern side of the Teign on the road to Kestor. The house, like the settlement at Batworthy, is cut off from the rest of the village by the Teign and the steep valley through which it flows. Apart from the footbridge the only way to the house by road is over the Chagford bridge at Factory corner, a journey of twenty minutes or so. The house appears to have been built mainly in the 16th century of granite stone rubble and has 20th-century alterations. It formed part of the original Gidleigh estate for most of its early history and has spectacular views over the surrounding moor.

In 1826, the 26-acre property was owned by Dr Thomas Whipham and tenanted by Hugh Endacott. Fields on the farm were called Hole, Park Field, Little Brake and Great Brake. [1]

James Endacott (b.1803), the son of Theophilous and Elizabeth Endacott, married Mary Northcott in 1824 and took over the tenancy some time around 1835. In 1848, William and

Caroline Simmett appear to have lived there briefly but by 1850 the tenancy was in the hands of William and Ann Hutchings. In 1862, when the estate was put up for sale by auction, Brimstone was occupied by William Northcott who was paying £15 rent for the farm, or around 10/- per acre.

In 1866, William Endacott took over the tenancy. William (b.1837) was the fourth son of James and Mary Endacott. He was known as 'Brimpstone Will' and was married first to Jane Pedrick, with whom he had five children. After she died, he married Ellen Belworthy and produced a further six offspring. The Endacott family were a prolific family: one of William's brothers, Tom, had 14 children and another, James, had 12.

William Hutchings owned the property in 1921 and in 1949 it was acquired by Charles and Maude Bennet. Charles tragically drowned in the river below the farm the following year and his wife immediately sold the property to Colonel Vicary and his wife, Bridget.

In 1956 the farm was bought by Pamela Phillips who sold, two years later, to a dog breeder called Mary Darling. It was acquired by Michael and Carol Gaillard-Bundy in 1968 who fell in love with the place. They lived there for almost 16 years and when they sold to Frank and Helen Humphries in 1984, they rented Scorhill Farmhouse on the other side of the valley. A Mr Foster and his partner, Miss Fernandez, bought the house in 1987 and sold it to Andrew Watrous and Julia Swift, in 1991. They took on what was no more than a burnt-out ruin in 12 tangled acres of land, and set to work restoring it to its past glory.

KESTORWAY lies on the edge of the Moor on the road to Batworthy and Kestor. It was built in the 1930s by Colonel Vicary, who used it as a temporary base during the War when Scorhill House was occupied by All Hallows School. He sold it shortly before he died in 1975. In the early 1990s it was bought by Mr J. Laing of Teigncombe Farm for his gardener.

A planning application was made to pull down the bungalow and replace it with a much larger house. Gidleigh residents, however, objected strongly and made representation to the Dartmoor National Park and the West Devon Council on the grounds that such a change, to so prominently sited a house, would greatly affect the area. Though the application for a new house was granted, it was stipulated that it should be clad in granite to match the surroundings and the project was not pursued. The house is currently owned by Mr and Mrs Hammer.

---

[1] Brake, as in Little and Great Brake, means rough uncultivated land often where bracken or 'fern' grows.

BATWORTHY, situated on the south side of the Teign, was originally a small hamlet of three separate farms, Lower, Middle and Higher Batworthy. All that can be seen of the original hamlet now is Batworthy Farm itself, which is difficult to date with any degree of accuracy.

It is believed to have been built largely in the 16th century on the site of Lower Batworthy, but shows no sign of being a traditional Devon longhouse as one might expect from its outward appearance. The farm buildings followed later and finally, in the early 20th century, came a house called Batworthy-in-the-Moor, built next to the old farmhouse and on the site of the middle farm.

Over the years there have been more residents of the Batworthy hamlet than any other in the parish and the name has changed too. Years ago it was referred to as Battery or Bathery. 'Battery' in Devon is a form of elision common to most place names ending in 'worthy'. However, some years ago a new and rather straight-laced parson decided to force the parishioners of 'Bugworthy' to change the name of their village.

In 1781, John Coniam is shown to be the occupier of the lower and middle farms and in 1787 a William Hawkins occupied Higher Batworthy. In the 1826 Land Tax Assessment, it is owned and occupied by John Rowe junior and then in 1843 Lower and Middle Batworthy were tenanted by Henry Collins and Higher by John Ellis.

By 1842 John Rowe of Berrydown owned all the land at Batworthy, as well as Scorhill.

Batworthy then consisted of a total of 65 acres and was assessed a tythe of £3 per annum. The fields and pastures on the farm at that time had names such as Lower and Higher Bottom, Yonder, Long and Homer Grattner, Long-a-park and Comer Close. [1]

On 16 June 1865, John Rowe put Batworthy and Scorhill up for sale by auction and they were bought by the Reverend Richard Cornish. William Westcott, a farmer born in Moretonhampstead in 1809, retained the tenancy and farmed the property with his 70-year-old wife Ann, their sons George and Henry and grand-daughter Mary. On her 16th birthday, Mary left Batworthy to marry a gamekeeper called John Alexander Wait in Gidleigh Church.

In 1889, Francis Nonas Budd is shown on the list of electors as a tenant resident at Batworthy, together with James Garrish. Francis Budd collected over 6,400 ancient flint implements from fields around Batworthy, consisting of arrow heads, knives and scrapers most of which are in the Exeter Museum. They are thought to be the oldest objects found in the Parish (5000 BC)

As on most of the other farms in the parish, there was a regular turnover of tenants at Batworthy, including:

1895 - William and Miriam Perryman   1901 - George Dunning   1907 - Richard Lee

In 1902, Dr William Alexander Budd bought Batworthy and is thought to have been responsible for building Batworthy in the Moor.

1910 - Sydney Setter and Richard Lee	1941 - Reverend John Blencowe
1925 - James Perrott	1957 - Anthony Quentin Gamble
1930 - John and Blanche Mudge	1967 - Gordon Edward Hughes and
1935 - John Snell Turner and wife Nora	wife Elizabeth Jane

Gordon Hughes split the property and sold off individual houses over a period of time, including Batworthy Farm itself and 43 acres of land. This was bought by Eric and Rosemary Reynolds, who moved here from West Beer Farm at Cheriton Bishop on 17 August 1973. They decided to retire in 1992 and sold it to their daughter Mary Lou and her husband Chris Townshend. Chris and Mary Lou were married in Gidleigh Church in July 1991 and now have two children, Brennan 5 and Elinor Rose aged 2.

Batworthy-in-the-Moor burned down mysteriously in 1971 and was demolished. A modern house was built nearby on 12 acres, given the same name and occupied by Hughes until he sold it to Mrs M. D. Jennings on 30 July 1974. The house has changed hands regularly since:

1977 - John and Patricia Gibson	1990 - Clifford and Gill Lansley
1986 - Barry and Jennifer Burke	1993 - Tony and Jackie Mann

The Coach House behind the old farm originally formed part of the rambling Victorian building that burned down in 1970 and in September 1975 Eric Reynolds sold it as a holiday home with seven acres in September 1975 by Eric Reynolds, to Sir Alan Greengross from Notting Hill in London.

---

[1] Grattner, as in Long, Yonder and Homer Grattner, meant ploughed or cultivated field, Homer being the one closest to the farmhouse. Comer Close may have been named after an individual called Comer; however, in old English Comer meant valley so in some cases it referred to a small enclosed field in a valley.

Richard Hayter went into partnership with Eric and Rosemary Reynolds and bought Batworthy Cottage on 28 October 1974. It was sold to the Reverend Bully, vicar of Chagford, who lived there for a few years before selling to Sam and Abigail North. Sam and Abigail and their children, Esme and Digory, use it as a holiday home and visit Batworthy regularly.

Kenneth and Valerie Hill live in the 1950s Bungalow, and their daughter Serena Rouse, a forest ranger employed by the Dartmoor National Park, lives next door.

By the side of the approach road to the hamlet stands the Round Pound: apparently the remains of a large hut enclosure surrounded by a wall within which lie half-a-dozen small courts or pens. The Pound forms part of the remains of an Iron Age settlement, including hut circles and fields near Kestor, built around 400 BC.

The central hut in the enclosure is about 35ft in diameter and contained remnants of a small hearth on a raised floor at what must have been the superior end, or sleeping quarters of the hut. On the other side, the working quarter contained a small iron smelting furnace and forging pit which, when excavated, proved to be the first evidence of prehistoric metal working in Devon.

Outside the old wall of Batworthy Farm and in the river below is the tolmen or holed stone (tol maen), an immense block of granite with a hole, a yard wide and over two foot deep, cut through it. We are told that these tolmen served the Druids for purposes of purification and that a wrongdoer was lowered through the hole and into the water for lustration. Suspected criminals were told to crawl through these stone openings: if they were innocent the stone would remain stationary but if they were guilty of a crime the stone would crush them to death. The guilty were usually so terrified by the thought of what would happen to them that they confessed their crimes and sought penance from the Druids.

CHAPTER THREE

FARMING AND LAND USE

For centuries farming was the sole economic activity in Gidleigh. From the beginnings in the 11th century until the end of the 19th century, everyone was engaged in agriculture, the only source of livelihood unless wealth was brought in from outside. The changes in this long period were gradual. A man who had farmed in the Parish in 1650, or even 1550, and returned in 1850, would have recognised the pattern of life he found. The decisive shift occurred in the late 19th century, marked by the agricultural crises of the 1870s and 1880s. It is then that we witness the rapid turnover of tenancies and the increasing sale of land and houses recorded in the history of individual farms as owner and tenant alike grappled with worsening conditions. By the end of the 19th century the composition of the population had begun to change, accompanied by the start of efforts to safeguard the landscape and to record daily life. The rate of change has continued; the years since 1900 have seen a more varied society emerge, with most people no longer dependent on agriculture but aware that they live in a place shaped by its geography and history. The physical fabric is preserved as we look out of the window or drive down the lanes. How did this appearance emerge? The fields and hedgerows still have to be maintained and the landscape and the rhythm of the year reflect the natural world. The changes that have taken place in Gidleigh are of course only a part of a much wider story in which the former rural society has been replaced by the modern world. What follows is a description of the aspects that particularly shaped farming in Gidleigh and the surrounding area.

The settlement which had its origins around the year 1000 AD, covered "three furlongs" or some 100 acres by the middle of the 11th century, a clearing in what was otherwise uncultivated land and rough woodland. With "one plough", as recorded in the Domesday Book, enough for a few households, the population must have scratched a bare living from oats and a few cattle. Although the clearances expanded the pattern remained largely one of self-sufficiency for many years; families lived on what they produced. It was only the holders of estates that were engaged to any degree in a cash economy. Since land was the only source of wealth and livelihood, the question of boundaries became increasingly important as waste land was brought into cultivation during the colonization drive of the 12th and 13th centuries.

So far as Gidleigh was concerned there were two boundaries or land limits to be considered: that on the Moor side, and the lower part of the village, each with a distinct legal regime and range of activities. The effects of this division are still visible. If you stand on the slopes of the Moor and look back towards the farms you can see the division between the enclosed fields and woodland, reduced to individual possession, and the empty stretches of the Moor, the sown and the unsown, one of the classic divisions in human society. The division did not arrive inevitably, though the quality of the soil played a large part; the relationship between the lower slopes where people lived and the Moor was devised over an extended period, involving both the legal structure (who owned what) and farming practices.

When the manors were allocated at the Norman settlement the rulers relied largely on the existing system of land holding. In most instances this meant that the lord received an estate, as described in the Domesday Book, with a certain amount of enclosed land (indicated by the number of furlongs) the exact limits of which were not determined. The non-enclosed land was referred to as waste or common land. It was this undifferentiated land between one manor and another that had to be delimited in the course of the 12th and 13th centuries. Security and clarity of tenure were essential if the land was to be exploited.

In the case of Gidleigh, there was an extension outwards from the original settlement and the existing land was used more intensively as the population grew. New land was granted on condition that it was brought under cultivation and a farmstead established, in return for a lengthy tenancy. As the area of enclosed land increased the outer boundaries had to be settled. This involved determining the limit of the lord's estate vis á vis Chagford and Throwleigh on the one hand and as regards the Moor on the other. In the case of the boundary with the adjacent manors of Throwleigh and Chagford, the matter was settled by the 13th century, though we have few details. Gidleigh and Throwleigh had the same lord of the manor during this period which must have helped the process, and the population, though increasing, was sparse. The parish and manor boundaries were the same, the one reinforcing the other.

There was also the question of royal hunting rights which particularly affected Gidleigh and other villages bordering the Moor. The pattern of grazing cattle on the Moor seems to have been present from the beginning. While in the Saxon period Dartmoor had had an uncertain status as a royal chase, the forest laws were extended under the Normans to cover most of Devon. This meant that only the King and his followers were allowed to hunt the deer, under penalty of death for anyone else, and the development of land outside the enclosed fields was restricted. It was therefore a major change when

King John agreed in 1204 to the request made by the holders of small estates to allow all the land in Devon, other than Dartmoor and Exmoor, to be "disafforested", that is to say, freed from the royal hunting privileges so that new land (the "waste") could be enclosed and farmed. This act, one of the more favourable of John's reign, enacted 11 or 12 years before the Magna Carta, was a crucial event in shaping the history and landscape of the county.[1] The men of Devon paid 5,000 marks for this concession.

While the Charter of 1204 thus enabled the work of developing the land and taking in the waste to be pursued within the lower part of Gidleigh, it meant that the limits and status of Dartmoor itself had to be fixed more exactly. At the Norman Conquest the King himself had retained the Borough of Lydford (Edward the Confessor had held it previously) and the hunting ground of Dartmoor was treated as an extension of the royal manor. The Charter only disafforested the county "up to the bounds of the ancient regards of Dartmoor and Exmoor" and the men of Devon and their heirs were granted "the customs within the regards of those Moors as they were accustomed to have" in the time of Henry I (1100-1135) ("que...metas antiquorum regardorum de Dertemora et Exemora que regarda fuerunt tempore regis Henrici primi"). This derogation remained significant for Gidleigh, and indeed can be said to have shaped the character of the village.

In 1239 Henry III granted the manor and castle of Lydford and the Forest of Dartmoor to his brother, Richard, Earl of Poitou and Cornwall. There had already been disputes between the King's Forest officials and neighbouring landholders over respective rights. It was in this setting that in 1240 Henry III ordered the Sheriff of Devon to determine the boundary between the Earl of Cornwall's land and that of the neighbouring manors. William le Prouz, the lord of Gidleigh (and Steward to the Earl) was one of the four knights who represented these other landholders, an indication of his importance. A jury of twelve knights was accordingly summoned to accompany the Sheriff in determining the boundary line.[2] The route taken in the Perambulation along the Forest boundary includes features whose names are still familiar, such as Hound Tor ("Hundetorre") and, closer to Gidleigh, the Wallabrook ("Wallebroke").

The result, as shown in the map below, was to fix the boundary of the Forest in the centre and a circle of commons round the Forest in the border parishes. The land between the Forest and the

---

[1] S Rowe, *A Perambulation of Dartmoor*, gives the text of the 1204 Charter, p. 285 et seq. Rowe's book is a standard work on the early history and contains the main documents. C Gill (ed), *Dartmoor : A New Study*, gives a great deal of information, notably in the chapters on Saxon and early Medieval times p. 76, Farming p. 139, Exploitation p. 245 and the Forest Boundary p. 277.

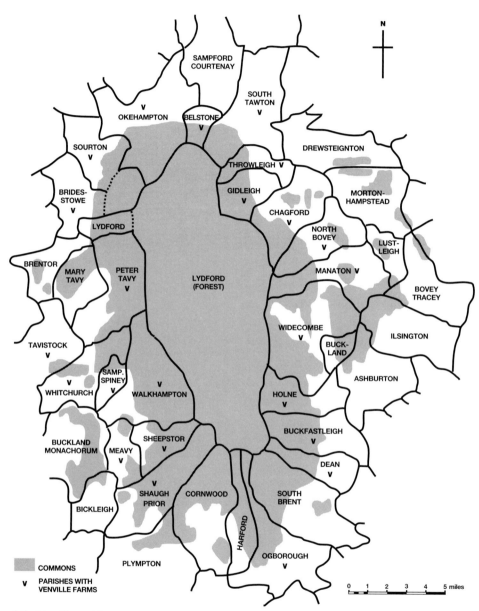

Dartmoor and the Venville parishes

enclosed fields became known as the "Commons of Devon" ("the whiche wast and Comyns lyeth from the Forest unto the Cornedyches, and hit ys callyd the Comyns of Devonshire"). Through its connection with the Forest, Lydford became the largest parish, as it remains. Gidleigh received its share in this process and much of the Parish consists of moorland to this day.

Gidleigh, like other parishes round the Moor, thus became involved with three distinct farming areas. There was, first, the area in the lower slopes where the fields were enclosed and the individual farmsteads were established in the 12th and 13th centuries. This was the centre of village and manor life and where land was ploughed and crops grown. Secondly there was the Gidleigh commons where cattle and sheep were grazed according to custom and which formed part of the manor or "vill". And thirdly there were the rights within the Forest in the centre of the Moor. All three areas were important to the livelihood of the Gidleigh farmers. Without them they could not manage to make a living. The parish boundaries, besides their importance for the Church, marked the division of the border commons and the limits of the estate. In the case of Gidleigh, estate and parish boundaries were established at much the same time in the 12th and 13th centuries, during the period of the Prouzs.

To take first the rights in the Forest or Chase of Dartmoor, these were progressively refined and defined. Already in 1297 we find an account being rendered to the Earl of Cornwall arranged under the headings of Lydford (the borough itself), the manor, and the Forest, the latter including venville rents, the amounts levied on the border farmers who pastured their cattle. In 1337 Edward III gave the manor of Lydford and the Forest of Dartmoor to his son, Edward, the Black Prince, who was created Duke of Cornwall.[3] After this date successive Princes of Wales held the land and exercised control. While custom was always significant, the exercise of the various rights was elaborated in increasing detail as a body of case law and practice emerged by the 16th century. In a document entitled

"Innstruccons from my Lorde Prynce to the Kyngs moost Honorable Counsell concerning my said Lord Pryncs Forrest of Dartmore in the Countye of Devonshire and in the mores and wasts of the same belongyn"

---

[2] Rowe, op cit., p 289. On the death of this Earl the Forest passed to his son Edmund. In 1300 Edmund died and the Forest reverted to the Crown.

[3] A Charter of 1337 created the Dukedom of Cornwall, with extensive estates of which Lydford and the Forest of Dartmoor formed part. The Duchy still has holdings in the Forest. When there is no heir apparent or if he is not yet of age the estate reverts to the Crown.

written around 1540 in the reign of Henry VIII, the rights of the different groups are set out with cumbersome precision. [4] The document has at the end an ingenious diagram explaining the system, with an appropriate reference to "the Vyndefelde men of Gydeley and Throwley" in the East quarter.

The first class consisted of those holding "ancient tenements", namely farms within the Forest itself. They had free rights to graze cattle, cut peat and the like but were required to perform services such as taking part in manor court juries and assisting in minding cattle drifts.

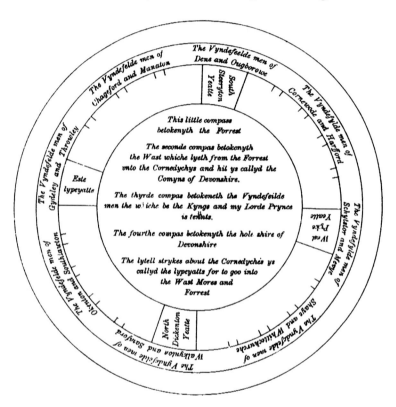

[4] The "Instruccons" are contained in Dartmoor Preservation Association, *The Rights of Common upon the Forest of Dartmoor and the Commons of Devon, Report of S Moore*, p. 164. This remains the most copious survey of the early history. The "lypeyatts" mentioned on the diagram were the leap gates or entrances (the equivalent to present day cattle grids) controlling the passage of cattle onto the Moor.

Next came the "venville tenants", the farmers from border parishes like Gidleigh, who were entitled to pasture their animals in the Forest by day but subject to "levant and couchant", which meant
they had to be removed at night unless they paid a small fee.

"Catell as they maye wynder upon these holdyngs come to the Kyngs Forrest by sonne and goo home by sonne."

In other words the cattle were kept on the farms in the winter but could be brought on the
Moor by day during the summer. The venville tenants could also take turf or peat ("turbary") and
stone "by hook or by crook" (i.e. not by quarrying), but were forbidden to take green oak or veni-
son. The men of Gidleigh were amongst those who enjoyed these venville rights, in return for which
the manor (or vill) paid venville rents to the Duchy.

The next class was that of the "strange men" (other Devonians living outside venville settlements) who were allowed to pasture their animals on the commons between the Forest border and
the "cornditches" (the ditch and wall between the Moor and the fields used for crops; a remnant of
this may still be seen along the road past Ensworthy towards South Zeal.) Lastly, came "the men of
Cornwall" who had similar rights initially but who were forgotten over the years. The Gidleigh
commons, like other parts of the Commons of Devon, were thus subject to use by persons from outside the Parish, one of the causes of friction over the years.

The animals grazing on the Moor (both the Forest and the commons) were rounded up and gath-
ered in pounds or "drifts" at regular intervals, usually three times a year. The owners were then required to
identify their cattle, sheep and horses, subject to a charge for their release levied by the Duchy of Cornwall.
A bill in the Exchequer of 1625 states that if cattle were not claimed after three days they were to be driven to Lydford Castle and, if not claimed within eight days, forfeited. Creaber Pound, situated below the
houses at Creaber, was the drift pound for the east quarter of Dartmoor. It was a wide area with walls on
two sides and iron gates (the remnants of the posts can still be seen either side of the road near Creaber
Cottage) and the drift was the responsibility of the local "moormen" as well as Duchy officials. Sorting out
which animals belonged to whom led to disputes. In the drift carried out in 1632 a black ox was put in
Creaber Pound and eventually sold; the owner then complained that the proper procedures had not been
followed. [5] Creaber Pound is also mentioned in a document of 1737 when it is reported:

---

[5] Crossing, *Echoes of an Ancient Forest,* p 105.

"W Bennet was struck several times by one, John Mallard whilst in Creaber Pound taking account of the cattle."

Rights on the Moor and the parish boundaries were accordingly jealously safeguarded, out of tradition and self-interest. This came to the fore in the late 18th and early 19th centuries when "newtakes" of former grazing land became extensive and threatened to reduce much of Dartmoor. There was a serious risk during the Regency period that the Forest would be divided up and sold off, so as to reduce customary grazing. Gidleigh was affected and sprung to the defence of the old rights and practices. The Duchy made a grant of 904 acres along the North Teign to a Mr Crawford in 1808. The enclosing walls of Teign (later known as Teignhead) Farm began to cross Gidleigh Commons. Seeing what was happening the Gidleigh commoners organised a perambulation of the Parish bounds and threw down the offending wall. Mr Crawford and the Duchy were most annoyed but decided to stand back. The wall (still known locally as "the Irishman's wall") was eventually rebuilt but so that only a small portion crossed Gidleigh Common. The Gidleigh commoners threatened further action but allowed it to stay. In rearranging the wall the original boundary stones got moved and the new stones have "DC" and "G" on them from this time (as was observed at the Beating of the Gidleigh Bounds in 1997). In view of the dispute, in 1843 the Tithe Commissioners launched an investigation at which the full story came out. A report was made by "James Jerwood of Southernhay in the City of Exeter, Esquire, Barrister at Law", in 1843 in which he states that

> *"Whereas divers disputes and doubts have arisen respecting the boundaries of the Parish of Gidley in the County of Devon and particularly respecting that portion of the boundary separating the Parish of Gidley aforesaid from the Parish of Lidford in the County of Devon"*

he had been appointed Assistant Commissioner for the purpose of "inquiring into, ascertaining and setting out the said boundaries." At the inquiry Mr Rogers, the agent of Mr Crawford, stated that:

> *"118 yards or perch of the wall had been erected. Then the Gidley people came out - a great number...I dare say 100 - this was in 1808. They pulled down a great part of the fence. I saw it done...We never rebuilt the fence torn down. We built another fence."*

In the light of report the Tithe Commissioners accepted the bounds as defined by the people of Gidleigh. The dividing line therefore crosses the northern part of the Teignhead newtake. [6]

The residents of Gidleigh continued to celebrate their enjoyment of the "Common Right" as the account of the Parish festivities in 1870 records. The practice of "Beating the Bounds" has a long history, the first recorded instance being in 1639. There was an interruption in the late 19th century before it was revived in 1906, and has been observed every seven years since, alternating with the surrounding parishes. The long walk, well attended and now more of a festive occasion than of economic significance, with races and a meal on the Moor, serves to bring people together and remind them of common links.

While cattle grazing was the main use of the Moor for Gidleigh farmers, it was not the only activity. John Hooker, writing at the end of the 16th century, declared that

"dartemore yieldeth iiij speciall commodities, pasture, corne tynne and turff cole" [7]

Although the right to take "turff cole" or peat has a long history, going back to a Charter of Henry III at least, peat cutting has now ended, incompatible with increased use of Dartmoor as a National Park and an area of environmental importance and natural beauty. The grazing rights have also been limited in order to protect the environment. Under the 1965 Commons Registration Act the rights were in effect frozen; those holding them were able to retain or apply for them, but others could not be added. [8] The number of animals allowed on the Moor is controlled by the Ministry

---

[6] The story is told in detail in E Stanbrook, *Dartmoor Forest Farms,* p. 11. Mr Rogers came from Ireland (as did Mr Crawford for whom he acted as Agent) where he had been in the militia quelling the disturbances that followed the 1798 uprising and a potato famine. He rented Gidleigh Barton between 1818 and 1822, when he moved back to Fernworthy. He settled down in Devon and some of his descendants live in Chagford. See also the account in Gill, op cit, p 250. The report in the Western Times of the 1870 celebrations is reproduced in the section on the Village Hall, Chapter Two above.

[7] Blake 'Hooker's Synopsis Chorographical of Devonshire', *Trans Dev Assoc,* vol 47, 1915, p. 334 at p. 345. S Gerrard, *Dartmoor,* sets out the age and composition of the peat based on analysis of the pollen residue, p 18.

[8] Two thirds of the Dartmoor National Park are registered as common land pursuant to the 1965 Act, the rights concerned being derived from venville rights in most instances. A Dartmoor Commoners Council was set up under the Dartmoor Commoners Act of 1985. The Council has 26 to 28 members, 16 of whom are elected, 2 appointed by the DNPA, 1 from the Duchy, 1 vet and 4 representing those with limited grazing rights.

of Agriculture, after consulting the Dartmoor Commoners' Association. The Association is divided, as in the past, according to the quarters of the Moor and Gidleigh is well represented.

A section of the Moor is occupied by the Army for troop exercises and firing practice, along with part of the area of other parishes. The residents of Gidleigh have been polled from time to time and found to be overwhelmingly in support of this practice. They may be influenced by the payment of a small sum to the Gidleigh members of the Commoners Association as compensation for the loss of grazing rights and which is used periodically for a supper and get together (Gidleigh folk only!) in the Village Hall.

While grazing on Dartmoor has been an integral element, the main focus of farming in Gidleigh was the enclosed land below the Moor, roughly 1,000 acres, about a third of the area of the Parish. This was developed from the initial settlement in a series of hamlets during the 12th and 13th centuries. The majority of farms were in existence by 1350. [9] In the 12th century, the main colonization period, the Prouzs, as lords of the manor, held the existing land and their interest, like that of those under them, was to expand the area under cultivation. It is difficult to imagine now that there was ever a time when much of the country was empty and had not been enclosed. The work of clearing the untamed land was largely the work of individual peasants and smallholders who received a charter from the lord of the manor granting them extensive rights in return for their efforts. Under so-called socage tenure, which was the most extensive (and later the copyhold of inheritance), they received a parcel of land at a small annual rent, perhaps with an obligation to attend the manor court at intervals, to grind corn at the lord's mill or supply a portion of their produce, and to pay a relief when the heir succeeded to the estate. On the waste land, which was the main instance in Gidleigh, the leases were at nominal rent, on condition that a farmhouse was built and new fields created out of moorland. By this combination of means a new class of farmers was established and a landscape created of small enclosed fields. Around the Moor the granite stones were dragged to the side to form the boundaries of the fields or used to build the houses. Fieldstone, lying on the surface or disturbed when ploughing, was the only stone available - granite quarrying did not get under way until the 18th century - and the clearing of the fields made much more available than had previously been the case. In Hoskin's words

---

[9] For the wider background see the chapter 'The Land' 'The Making of the Landscape' in Hoskins, Devon. p. 69. Gidleigh bears out his general approach.

"It is in these generations between 1150 and 1350 that the characteristic Devonian landscape was born: the lanes, the small irregular fields the great hedge banks, the isolated farmstead at the end of a track, and the little parish church…" [10]

The records from this period do not provide detailed evidence of the precise course followed in Gidleigh. The general pattern must have been on these lines however, which fit the history of the main farms so far as we can determine their development. None of the remains date from the 12th or 13th century so far as is known (though perhaps deondological research may show the timbers are older than has sometimes been assumed), but all are on sites where farming appears to have been in progress by 1350 if not earlier. In the case of the principal farms, the names of the occupants (derived in most instances from the name of the holding) are listed in early 14th century documents, notably the Assize Rolls of 1322 [11]

The location of the main settlements also supports the notion that the development was of the "wastes" towards the Moor. Batworthy, Berrydown, Scorhill, Creaber, Greenaway, Thule, Moortown and Ensworthy are all situated along the line between the Moor and the enclosed fields where such development is most likely to have taken place. Chapple Farm forms an exception, but it too must have been a farm settlement by the early 14th century when the chapel from which it got its name was built. That the remains of the buildings are not evidently from the early 14th century or before is not surprising. The number of buildings that survive is inherently limited, let alone six or seven centuries. The usual course, moreover, as Hoskins remarks, was to re-build or extend a house and there is plenty of evidence of that. In Gidleigh few entirely new houses if any were built after 1400 until the 16th or 17th century when more money appears to have been available. Rebuilding and adaptation of existing houses was the norm.

The Black Death of the 1340s halted the pace of land development for nearly 200 years while

---

[10] Hoskins, p. 92.

[11] The occupation by the Prouzs and their successors in the 12th century and after is dealt with in Chapter One. For the farm holdings the earliest written records are the following: Berrydown, Ralph de Beriden, Assize Roll 1322; Scorhill, John de Scoriawall, Assize Roll 1332; Creaber, doc. of 1238; Thule, Henry de la Thivele, 13th century; Moortown, John atte More, 1327; Ensworthy, John de Afensworthe, 1327: Greenaway, Ralph de Greneweyesfote, 13th century doc.; Chapple, Chapel there by 1328.

strengthening the position of the more independent minded smallholders; the accent was placed on enlarging existing farms and the temporary taking in of waste. The relatively large extent of waste available meant that "newtake" development remained an option for much longer than elsewhere. Buttern Farm appears to be an example of a late "newtake".

The rate of agricultural development was linked to the size of the population and the pressure that might exert. While there are few exact figures the evidence available enables some light to be shed on how matters progressed. The initial settlement of 1050 or so, with its "one plough" must have been small indeed, perhaps 20 to 40 people or so at most. The entire population of England at the time of the Domesday Book was only about one and a half million. By 1280 the enclosed land at Gidleigh had extended to 300 acres. When, in 1316, William Pruz was assessed at 72sh for land worth 2d an acre, the total must have been over 400 enclosed acres. That and the establishment of six or more farms by that time would bring the population to around 400. Since most of the inhabitants lived on what they grew there was an inherent limit on the size of the village. The Black Death in the 1340s reduced the population substantially; that of the entire country was reduced by a third or more. In the Subsidy Roll of 1525 35 men are listed. Adding wives and children leads to a figure of around 100. This total was fairly constant; the Subsidy Roll of 1641 lists 34 men. In 1801 the population was 125. The population between 1400 and 1800 is thus likely to have hovered at around 100 to 125 people, approximately what the amount of cultivated land could support.

The crops grown were corn, oats and barley, which provided food for the sheep and cattle as well as people. Hooker reports that corn (by which he means chiefly oats) was commonly grown on the sides of the Moor

> "and by reason of the harde wether and greate and contynuall stormes the harvest is verie late: And this one thinge is to be observed that all the yere through out commonly it rayneth or it is fowle wether in that more" [12]

Ploughing until the 18th century was done by oxen; horses were little used in farming before that. Packhorses were the main means of transport until the 19th century. There were no doubt pigs

---

[12] Blake, op cit, p. 345

and poultry in the farmyards and a rabbit warren in the chase at Gidleigh, along by the river. The mill established in medieval times was replaced or supplemented by the 18th century by horse mills in the individual farms, as at the Barton, Chapple and Moortown, where the remains may still be seen. Threshing was done by flail or winnowing. There was no industry at any time; there is no record or sign of tin mining activities within the Parish boundaries. [13]

Sheep wool was the main commercial crop. The Teign valley came to specialize in sheep at a fairly early date and there were cloth mills at Chagford bridge by 1250. [14] By 1400 wool was being sold extensively for weaving, either in the cottages or by the numerous small mills in the West country. Labour was cheap; it is estimated that in the middle period between 1596 and 1796 labourers' wages rose by only a half whereas the cost of living increased threefold. The extent to which labourers had recourse to kitchen gardens and small holdings (Gidleigh provides a number of examples) alleviated the situation but conditions must have been hard for most people.

Conditions may have improved in the first part of the 19th century, when the population of Gidleigh increased from 125 in 1801 to 182 in 1841, the highest recorded, part of a similar increase nation wide. The population of some of the main farms in the mid-19th century shows the pattern.

	1841	1851	1861	1871
FORDER	8	9	12	15
CHAPPLE	14	11	19	16
ENSWORTHY	31	26	13	17
MOORTOWN	13	11	9	7
THULE	9	9	8	9
TOTAL	85	76	67	67
PARISH TOTAL	182	166	134	154

[13] Tin mining in its heyday in the 14th to 16th centuries was a major industry, employing not just the miners themselves but a range of middle men and those who provided the capital. Persons from Gidleigh were probably engaged in these aspects. One of the John Rowes of Berrydown for example, took part in Stannary Court proceedings.

[14] T Whale, 'Some Remarks on the Bounds of the Forest of Dartmoor, with special references to the Parishes of Throwleigh, Chagford and Gidleigh', *Trans Dev Assoc,* vol 25, 1893, p. 510 at p. 523.

In 1861 725 acres were farmed, the average holding being 60 acres. [15] The cash crops remained wool, sheep, cattle and potatoes. The Chagford and Moretonhampstead area became well known for potato growing in the first half of the 19th century.

A broad decline set in as the century progressed. The 1850s saw the repeal of the Corn Laws which meant that agriculture was no longer protected from imports by tariffs and tonnage restrictions. With improved communications and refrigeration, imports rose: meat and wool from Australia and Argentina, grain from Canada, the United States and the Ukraine. There was a major agricultural depression in the 1870s. The price of farm land and farm rents stayed relatively high for a while, buoyed by the new money from industry. Even so the price of an acre fell nationally from £54 in 1875 to £19 in 1897. The price of lamb and beef collapsed. These developments were reflected in Gidleigh as elsewhere. The Whiphams, already in difficulties in the 1860s, began the series of mortgages in the 1870s which led eventually to the sale of the estate in 1920. As farm income dropped,

---

[15] The table below shows the average worked by 12 Heads of Households classified as farmers in the 1861 census.

FARM	ACREAGE	FARMER	AGE	PLACE OF BIRTH
Batworthy	50	Wm Westcott	46	Chagford
Brimstone	30	Wm Hutchins	35	Lydford
Barton	30	James Endicott	32	Gidleigh
Gidleigh Mill	56	John Endicott	56	Gidleigh
Chapple	70	Wm Brock	30	Gidleigh
Moortown	70	Wm Browning	38	Sampford Courtney
Little Ensworthy	49	George Leman	35	Throwleigh
Lower Ensworthy	30	Wm Mortimer	47	Gidleigh
Thule	90	John Newcombe	73	Throwleigh
Parsonage (Glebe)	20	Wm Hill	37	Throwleigh
Greenaway	60	Wm Sampson	63	Throwleigh
Berrydown	170	Wm Rowe	67	Gidleigh
	725			

The dwellings at Scorhill and South Creaber were occupied by agricultural labourers at this time; North Creaber was vacant. Buttern Farm had not yet been taken from the Moor. Source: R Rankin, *Gidleigh Parish, A Rough Guide*, p. 35.

rent arrears became common, leading to a rapid turnover in tenancies and evictions. In the 1870s and 1880s good land could be had for an annual rent of just 13s 6d an acre with few takers; on the poorer hill farms it became almost impossible to survive even with rents of only 10s. an acre or more sought by landlords. Both tenants and landlords were being squeezed.

One source of alleviation illustrated in Gidleigh was the sale or regrouping of farmland and the disposal of houses to newcomers. As children born in the area left for the towns or overseas, others came to take their place. This began with the Starks in the 1890s, to name a noted early example, and has continued. The farming community did not sit passively by. During both World Wars the Government called on farmers to "do their bit" and they responded. By 1941 the first tractor had appeared at Greenaway and others followed. The shire horses and cart horses went in the early 1950s. as John Jordan recalls. There are, however, probably more horses for riding in Gidleigh now than there were in the 19th century. Root crops, especially swedes, were grown successfully during the War but have since been uneconomic.

The main concentration has been on sheep and cattle raising. Already in the 19th century local farmers went to Scotland to buy Scotch Blackfaced sheep which have largely taken over from the Dartmoor Whiteface. The traditional breeds have held their own, however, and made something of a comeback in recent years; the Wells at Creaber concentrated on Dartmoor Greyfaced sheep and the Skiltons at Gidleigh Mill have been especially active here. Sheep and cattle from Gidleigh usually do well at Chagford and other shows.

Cattle remain a mainstay. South Devons were the main breed for both milk and beef but now only for the latter. Chris Townshend has a mixed herd of Galloways at Batworthy and John Jordan, a herd of suckler cows, South Devons on the inbye land and Black Galloways on the Moor. Ernie Bowden has South Devons, and at Buttern Farm Richard and Bob Hurdle have Friesian Hereford suckler cows. Chris Smallwood at Chapple has a small herd of pedigree South Devons and is producing some breeding bulls. (Chris took a cow to Downing Street in 1998, attracting national attention). David and Monica Alford produce table birds, hens, ducks, geese and turkeys.

Dartmoor ponies were once an important source of income. Many were sold as pit ponies, but the sale of ponies reared on the Moor now produces more news than money. However John and Diane Jordan and Crispin and Diana Alford have high quality Dartmoor ponies recognised internationally.

The climate in Gidleigh is relatively mild and the rainfall plentiful: 53 to 55 inches a year on average, according to Chris Hamlet of Combe in Throwleigh, who takes measurements for the

Meteorological Service. Grass is now the main crop and grows well. There are, however, mineral deficiencies, particularly cobalt. These are tackled by dosing the animals with slow release boluses, mineral licks and the application of trace elements (after testing has been done) or the use of calcified seaweed. John Jordan and Chris Smallwood are comparing the last two methods.

The number of working farms has decreasd sharply over the years, from a dozen in the 19th century to less than half that today. Although some fields have been taken out of cultivation with the conversion of farms to private houses, the acreage being farmed has remained broadly on the same scale through a consolidation of holdings. Besides various agricultural support schemes, funds have been made available in recent years to preserve the environment, notably the Environmentally Sensitive Area Scheme for Dartmoor. Several farms and holdings in Gidleigh are now in this scheme and Gidleigh Common was the first common on the Moor to become an ESA.

There is a 250 acre forestry plantation on the left of the road leading up to Berrydown from Gidleigh Lodge, stretching almost to the river. The trees are pines and conifers, with more traditional growth along the river. Few now remember the shape of the hill up to Gidleigh Tor before the trees were planted in the 1950s. Further up the road on the right is the site of the former Berrydown Nursery, a four acre property that specialised in heath plants and trees. The house built there in 1997 is no longer tied to agricultural use. The Park Authority has a scheme to supply a variety of tree seedlings for those wishing to plant trees in areas of fields or along hedgerows, and use has been made of this in Gidleigh. The Woodland Trust has a wood either side of the river down by the bridge, on the Gidleigh-Chagford boundary. A pattern of commercial and environmental uses is thus coming into existence, bolstered by 'nature reserves' in individual fields, the role of the National Park and agricultural policies.

Last but not least, the walls and hedgerows have over the past ten years been recognised as worthy of preservation. Work on these is labour intensive and the number of people supported by agriculture has dwindled to a handful. Funds provided through the Countryside Stewardship Scheme and the Dartmoor ESA help in the maintenance of these distinctive features of the district.

These pages give some idea of how farming in Gidleigh has evolved since its beginnings nearly a thousand years ago to reach the landscape visible today. A list of some of the field names is given below.

FIELD NAMES

The fields changed hands over the years as the farm boundaries were redrawn with changes of ownership and cannot be allocated to farms in a simple way. The most complete and recent listing is contained in the 1843 Tithe Assessment, part of a national exercise at the time. The following are some of the names from this and other sources for the main farms.

BATWORTHY: Lower and Higher Bottom, Yonder, Long and Homer Grattner, Long-a-park, Comer Close

BERRYDOWN: Shuta Park (Shuta is Celtic for orchard), Middle and Lower Grattner (Grattner or Gratton means ploughed field), Bowey, Great Neat Down, Sheellands

BRIMSTONE DOWN: Hole, Park Field, Little and Great Brake

CHAPPLE: Tan House Meadow, Lower and Higher Broom Park, Long Byney, Higher Grattner, Great and Little Burrows, Great and Little Long Close, Little and Middle Hellands, Broom Plane

ENSWORTHY: Honeypool, Thorne Park, North Down, Lower Gratton, Higher and Lower Cleave, Garden Park, North Meadow,

GIDLEIGH BARTON: Yellands ("Old Lands", a reference to the early clearing), Homer Sweet Lakes, Little Long-a-park, Higher and Back Orchard, Broadmeads.

GREENAWAY: North and South Wales, North and South Ireland, Cherry Park, Great Meadow, Middle Close, Mousey Field, Rixey Meadow (Names like Wales and Ireland meant that they were some way from the house).

MOORTOWN: Long Ley, Square Close, Burrows, Brake's Park, Croft, Higher Wallands, Twenty Acres (which was in fact only one acre in size).

NORTH CREABER: Pit Meadow, Cleave, Witthay, Higher and Lower Water Park, Brake, Long Close

SCORHILL: Reeve Close, Backsey, Berry Park, Cutland, Water Park, Smiley Park.

SOUTH CREABER: Rush Close, Journey, Post Close, Higher and Lower Parson's Hay (a reference to glebe land), Hurdle Plot, Yonder Brake (Brake meant rough land, often with bracken or fern).

THULE: Long Close, Grist Park, Croft, Great Broom

APPENDIX ONE

RECTORS OF GIDLEIGH

DATE	NAME	PATRON
Before and after 1066	Godwin the Priest	Robert, Earl of Mortain (after 1066)
1238	Richard. Chaplain. *Found dead in the highway.*	William Prouz
1259	Michael de la Leghe. Subdeacon. *Absolved by Bishop Branscombe of involvement in forgery and dealing in property and benefices.*	William Prouz
1276	Elyas de la Walle. Priest	William Prouz
1278	Roger de Kynesmandune. Chaplain	Sir William Prouz
1284	Walter Pruz. Subdeacon	Sir William Prouz
1324	Roger Hocke. Accolyte. *Received dispensation to study theology at Oxford. It was during his absence in 1328 that Robert de Middelcote, the Priest at Chapple, attacked the Miller's daughter.*	Alice de Moeles
1332	Walter Bot. Licence of non-residence for a year *Had been Rector of Lundy Island.*	Alice de Moeles
1347	Thomas Piper. Priest. *Resigned the same year.*	Alice Daumerle
1348	Walter de Hertilande. Priest	Alice Daumerle
1349	John de Horewood. Priest	The Bishop
1368	Richard Chaggeforde. Priest. *Licensed in 1332 to celebrate mass in the chapel of "Our Lady atte Wallen".*	Sir John Daumerle
1391	John Elys. Chaplain	Sir John Daumerle.
(Not recorded)	John Clerk. *Resigned in 1434 and allowed an income of 4 marks quarterly from the Church at Gidleigh.*	Sir John Daumerle

DATE	NAME	PATRON
1434	Stephen Wydebrook. *Presented illegally by the previous Rector and a commission was held.*	Richard Coade
1437	Roger Yunge	Richard Coade
1439	Nicholas Eggesbury. *Dismissed for neglect of services.*	Richard Coade
1454	Richard Luky	Walter Coade
1475	John Payne. *Had held the Chantry at Sticklepath and exchanged it with Richard Luky. Major building of the Church around 1450-1475.*	Walter Coade
1516	John Farwell	Richard Coade.
1549	Richard Discomb	Walter Coade.
1580	John Mather	The Crown.
(Not recorded)	William Downe	
1631	Humphrey Gaye, B.A. Wadham College, Oxford. *Made Terrier of Gidleigh. Married by Mayor of Okehampton during Commonwealth.*	Henry Battishall
1683	Edward Seddon. *Also held living at Throwleigh.*	Bartholemew Gidley
1711	Richard Wills. B.A., Exeter College, Oxford	Bartholemew Gidley
1712	William Bedford	Bartholemew Gidley
1726	James Amyatt. M.A., Wadham College, Oxford *Also held the living at Throwleigh.*	Bartholemew Gidley
1735	Christopher Moorhouse	Bartholemew Gidley
1752	John Besley. B.A., Trinity College	Bartholemew Gidley
1756	Richard Skinner. B.A., Balliol College,1751	Bartholemew Gidley
1791	William Southmead B.A.,Balliol College. *Lived in London.*	Henry Rattray
1833	John Atkins	Rev Thomas Whipham
1834	John Hodgson	Rev Thomas Whipham
1836	Arthur Whipham. M.A., Trinity College Rector of Hatherleigh 1865-68, Rector of Belstone 1877-1882	Rev Thomas Whipham
1862	Owen Owen	Rev Arthur Whipham
1891	William Fox	Rev Arthur Whipham
1893	Henry Rickett	Alfred Guy Whipham

DATE	NAME	PATRON
1896	Montagu Burnett	Alfred Guy Whipham
1900	Douglas McLaren	Alfred Guy Whipham
1903	Francis Anderson	Alfred Guy Whipham
1905	J.R. de Haviland	Alfred Guy Whipham
1909	C.L. Capel-Cure	Alfred Guy Whipham
1912	W.R. Mesney. *Formerly Archdeacon of Sarawak*	Alfred Guy Whipham
1914	J. Rawson	Alfred Guy Whipham
1927	Charles Trounsell	Charles McIlwraith
1954	John Scott	Col A. Vicary
1968	John White	Col A Vicary
1970	Louis Coulson. *Benefice with Throwleigh in 1972*	The Bishop of Exeter
1979	William Bulley. *Benefice with Chagford in 1979*	The Bishop of Exeter
1984	Louis Baycock	The Bishop of Exeter

APPENDIX TWO

THE LETTERS PATENT OF HENRY VIII

In 1516 Henry VIII issued "Letters Patent" confirming a Charter under which Martin, Duke and Earl of Cornwall and Mortain, granted the manor of Gidleigh to his nephew, Giles de Gydleigh, and confirmed the rights of the farmers of Gidleigh to graze cattle on the Moor (so-called "venville rights"). The authenticity of this document has long been doubted - an 18th century commentator wrote that it was "certainly an infamous forgery" [1] - but there have also been those prepared to give it some standing. While parts of the story may now be beyond our reach, it merits examination to see what it says and what can be clarified.

The story begins with Thomas Westcote who, in his manuscript *View of Devonshire,* compiled by 1630, introduced it as follows:

> "I shall by some be thought to lead you a Pixy path by telling you an old tale (and yet perchance new to you) of one Martin Duke and Erle of Cornwall, who granted to his nephew Giles de Gydleghe the manor of Gydleigh. Of the truth of which donation albeit some make doubt and question and some utterly denye. Yet I cannot forbear to spare you that I have seen such a possible instrument, the original very fayr but partly unlegable with a very authentic and large seal included in a box for the more security, the impression a triple towered castle. It was exemplyfied under the great seal of England in the 8th of Henry the eight. The tenor thus:-" [2]

When Westcote's manuscript was published in 1845 the editors, Dr Oliver and Mr Pitman Jones,

---

[1] G Boase and W Courtney, *Bibliotheca Cornubiensis,* vol I, which records that a J Anstis had written above the Charter "The following is certainly an infamous forgery."

[2] Westcote, *View of Devonshire,* 1845 edition, p. 433

omitted the document because of doubts about its authenticity. The original manuscript, including the Letters Patent, is now in the British Library. Various copies of the Letters Patent were made, including one which was in the possession of Alfred Whipham. [3]

The document is in Latin. An English translation is given below.

"Henry by the grace of God, King of England, France and Lord of Ireland to all to whom these present letters may come Greetings. We have viewed a certain charter of Martin. Duke and Count ("Ducis et Comites") of Cornwall, Mortain and Lord of Leghatforde (Lydford) made to Giles de Gidleigh ("Egidio de Gidleigh"), his nephew, and under the seal of the said Martin as it is said sealed worded as follows. Be it known to those present and to come that we Martin Duke and Count of Cornwall, Mortain and Lord of Leghatforde have given, granted and by this our present charter of special favour have confirmed to Giles de Gidleigh ("Gydleigh") our nephew for his homage and good service all that our manor castle and Lordship and the whole tithing together with our park of Gidleigh ("totum illud manerium castrum et Dominium nostrum ac rotum decenium cum uno parco de Gydleigh") parcel of our manor of Leghatforde, together with all our natives and their families as well procreated as to be procreated, 19 ferlings of land of Cornwall according to the measure there being attached to the same manor of Gidleigh together with their appurtenances and also with tenements, rents, profits, reversions and services and with one water mill with right of grinding as well as free for conventionary (tenants), together with waters, roads, paths, fisheries, ponds, turbaries and also with theitr homages, wardships, marriages and reliefs of Odo Theuyll from the lands and tenements in Theule, of Guy Anysworthye, of Rolf Chapell from lands and tenements at Chapell, of Arnulf Suchford from lands and tenements in Suthforde, of Wolfram Berydon from lands and tenements in Berydon, of Austin Crebaire from lands and tenements in Crebeare, of Osmund (?) Grenewaye from lands and tenements in Grenewaye, of Sampson More from Lands and tenements in More which they hold of us by the service of gloves and also toll and team, infangthef (?) and outfangthef, attachments, corrections of vagabonds, estrays, wapentake exactions and assize of bread and beer together with all pleas to be held there, courts and suits of court with view of frankenpledge and all rights fines and amercements of court there belonging and with all customs, liberties and advantages of old times, therewiith accustomed and in accordance with the custom

[3] The West Country Studies Library in Exeter has several 17th century copies of Westcote's manuscript, including the Letters Patent, and an English translation (possibly made in the 19th century) of the Letters.

of our manor of Leghatforde and also with the advowson of the church of Gidleigh and all things what-soever to the same manor belonging in wet or dry. Furthermore we have given and granted and by our present charter of our special favour we have confirmed to the said Giles de Gidleigh his heirs and as-signs together with all the tenements as well as free as of conventionary (tenants) free ingress and egress in and all our pastures, commons and waste of Fyndefelde and Dertemore with all kinds of beasts of burden there in all the aforesaid perambulations, moors and forests as entirely and fully and in all the aforesaid as freely and with all the customs and advantages as we the said Martin and our predecessors have had and now have the same in our possession and afterwards in future our heirs and assigns and our successors may have there To have and to hold all these premises together with all these parts as is foresaid to the aforesaid Giles de Gydlegh his heirs and assigns freely, peaceably in their entirety, ab-solutely, by heirship for ever of us our heirs and assgns or our successors Rendering therefore yearly to us the aforesaid Martin our heirs and assigns or to our successors he and his heirs one red rose at the feast of the birth of St John Baptist in place (discharge) of all services, reliefs suits of court and other secular demands and tallages, and over and above paying to us our heirs and assigns or our successors thirteen pence at the feast of St Michael in September and also serving to ourselves our heirs and assigns or our successors suit at our court twice a year at Leghatforde and not elsewhere throughout his tithing of Gydlegh, and with him two men personally to appear there to wit at the lawful court next after the month of September and the other at the next lawful court in the month of May if these be summoned without presenting anything. Should they fall into mercy after a summons served amends. And saving (?) to ourselves our heirs and assigns or our successors tallage and..... ("quidamne decanu"?) from Gydlegh aforesaid to our manor of Leghatforde and not elsewhere if demanded Yet so that neither we the aforesaid Martin nor our heirs nor our assigns nor yet our successors the Duke and Count of Cornwall and Mortain and Lord of Leghatforde nor any one else by us or in our name shall have any right or claim in all the aforesaid premises in Gydlegh aforesaid together with the advowson of the church of Gydlegh aforesaid and the common pasture of Fyndefelde and Dertemore after all manner of beasts of burden there and pasturage without payment to ourselves, our heirs and assigns or our successors there made or to be made nor that we should be able to demand or claim or assert for ourselves (such pay-ment) in any part thereof nor shall we do in future, but by these presents we are to be for ever excluded from every action of right of title or claim in respect of all the aforesaid premises together with the afore-said advowson of the church of Gydlegh and the common pasture of Fyndefelde and Dertemore aforesaid And we the aforesaid Martin and our heirs and successors Duke and Earl of Cornwall and Mortain

and Lord of Leghatforde bind ourselves our heirs and assigns to warrant acquit and defend all the afore-said premises together with the advowson of the church of Gydlegh aforesaid and the common pasture on Fyndefelde and Dertemore together with all other rights advantages and customs and other privileges thereto belonging as aforesaid in Gydlegh, Fyndefelde and Dertemore to the aforesaid Giles de Gydlegh his heirs and assigns without account rendered to the aforesaid Martin our heirs or assigns, against all men and all women as well living as dead for ever by testimony whereof we have appended our im-pressed seal to the preceding charter in the presence of Hubert Duke of Exeter, Albert Duke of Devonshire, Baldwin Earl of Albemarle, Guy de Treverbyn and many others at Leghatforde 16 of the Calends of May in the 5th year of our creation And hereof we give notice to all therein interested. In testimony whereof we have caused these Letters Patent to be drawn up, witness myself at Westminster the 5th day of November in the 8th year of our reign.
Tunstall
In the Exchequer of our Lord the King at Lostwithiel Michelmas term in the 9th year of King Henry VIII before the auditors there."

The questions that arise are treated in turn below. Consideration of the document has been hindered in the past because the different aspects have not been distinguished.

1. The authenticity of the Charter as a document of the 12th century.
Letters Patent were issued to confirm earlier titles or arrangements and were not themselves nor-mally used to grant title. The document declares that "We" (the King) have viewed the Charter and concludes, after setting out the text, that "In testimony whereof" the King has ordered the Letters to be drawn up and officially witnessed them.

So far as the authenticity of the initial Charter itself is concerned, the evidence is overwhelm-ing that it cannot have been written in the 12th century. The Earldom of Mortain ended in 1199 when John, the last to hold the title, became King. By the reference to the Earl of Mortain the Charter purports therefore on the face of it to have been made before 1199 at the latest. Accepting that for the moment, the question is: when in the 12th century and which Earl made the grant?

The witnesses include contemporaries or near contemporaries of King John who held the Earldom between 1189 and 1199. One witness was Hubert de Burgo, afterwards Chamberlain to King John, and another, Odo de Treverbyn, was included in the list of the Perambulation of the Forest in 1240. Thus we arrive at a possible date of the original Charter, witnessed on "16 of the Calends of May in the fifth year of our creation." Since John was made Earl of Mortain in 1189 this brings us to 1194 as the date or possible date of the Charter. The date of 1156 has also been advanced. [4]

The difficulties with the authenticity of the text as a 12th century grant are multiple.

i) The Charter is in the name of Martin, Duke and Earl (or Count) of Cornwall and Mortain. In 1194 the Earl of Mortain was John. The possibility that he might sometimes have used the name of Martin is not supported by any evidence. The Charter he issued when as Count of Mortain he granted certain immunities to free tenants in Dartmoor forest begins "Johannes Comes Moreton" The deforesting Charter of 1204 is likewise in the name of John. In 1156, to take the other date proposed, the Earl of Mortain was named William. At no time, it appears, was there ever an Earl of Mortain named Martin.

ii) It is odd that although the Charter purports to grant the manor to Giles de Gydleghe ("Egidio de Gydleghe"), he is already called "de Gydleghe". How can this be? The gift of the small manor of Gidleigh furthermore seems hardly on the scale that a nephew of the Count of Mortain (and possible future King) might expect. John made another nephew Duke of Gloucester; although he later put him to death after a dispute; we may perhaps charitably conclude that it is the thought that counts. And who among John's sisters was Giles's mother?

iii) The holders of land and tenements who are listed at Thule, Ensworthy, Chapple, Forder, Berrydown, Creaber, Greenaway and Moortown are unlikely to have been in occupation as early as 1156 or 1194 or, if they were, to have held their land on the conditions specified in the Charter. The terms used to describe their tenure "which they hold of us by the service of gloves", attendance at the manor court, together with the advowson of Gidleigh Church and the rendering which Giles is called upon to make each year of "one red rose at the feast of the birth of St John Baptist", are all legal conditions from a much later period. These are practices that date from the 13th or 14th century.

The weight of evidence in the document itself that it cannot date from as early as the 12th century is thus substantial and can be regarded as conclusive.

2. Were the Letters Patent issued at the instigation of Bartholemew Gidley?

---

[4] 1194 was the date advanced by the Rev Rawson in correspondence with the Rev Reichel who had referred to the Charter in an article (*Trans Dev Assoc,* vol 44, 1912, p. 349). Hughes ('Gidleigh', *Trans Dev Assoc,* vol 79, 1947, p. 92) advanced the date of 1156 as a tentative possibility.

The argument has been advanced that the Letters Patent have their origin in the efforts of Bartholemew Gidley, perhaps to show a long lineage and descent from Giles de Gydleghe. This was argued by Mrs B Cresswell in *Notes on Devon Churches, The Fabric and Features of Interest in the Churches of the Deanery of Okehampton*, written in 1921. Against this, however, is the fact that there is no evidence that Bartholemew Gidley ever made any such claims. He is described in contemporary documents (including the purchase deeds of the manor of Gidleigh) as coming from Winkleigh and he is buried in Winkleigh Church.

There is also the question of the dates. Westcote included the Letters Patent in his manuscript which was finished in 1630 and he himself died shortly thereafter. The last purchaser of Gidleigh that he mentions is Henry Battishill, who bought the estate in 1628. Bartholemew Gidley was still a student at Exeter College, Oxford in 1632 and did not buy the estate at Gidleigh until 1638. Since for Westcote it is already "an old tale", any link with Bartholemew Gidley is hard to establish.

Mrs Cresswell says that the arms of the seal were those of Bartholemew. However he did not receive those until 1666, by which time Westcote (born 1567) had long died. The arms as described by Westcote are those of a triple towered castle. Gidley's arms are different and the seal is probably that of Lostwithiel, which has a triple towered castle on its coat of arms. The Letters were issued at Lostwithiel where the Duchy of Cornwall had its Palace or administrative headquarters and where the seal appears to have been added.

There is accordingly no substantiated link with Bartholemew Gidley.

3. Were the Letters Patent issued in 1516, and if so why?

Since the original document no longer exists it is not possible to examine the parchment and determine its age by scientific tests. The description in Westcote gives some details, however, and we have the full text. It was quite customary to request Letters Patent in the 16th century; indeed they were often required when there was a change of ownership or a new overlord took possession. Of the two seals, one was probably that of Lostwithiel and the other the great seal of England. Whatever the authenticity of the claimed Charter, it would be a bold man who forged the great seal of England in the eighth year of Henry VIII's reign. Certainly a hanging offence. The case for believing that the Letters themselves were issued in 1516 is prima facie strong. This fits in with Westcote's text and the language used.

The question why they were issued at that time is harder to answer and can probably never be categorically determined. There are a number of elements however that suggest how it might have come about.

First, at that date the Duchy of Cornwall was in the hands of the King. When the monarch has no male heir or the heir has not come of age, the practice is for the reigning monarch to exercise authority over the Duchy, of which Lydford and the Forest of Dartmoor form part. In 1516 Henry VIII had no heir, and indeed it was on this ground that he later divorced his Queen, Catharine of Aragon. She, as it happened, had been granted a third of the revenues of the Duchy in her marriage settlement. Since the Tudors were notoriously short of money and keen to shake up the administration, there is evidence that the running of the Duchy received more attention at this time. [5]

With that general background it is significant that the document lays stress on rights and obligations in three areas: Fyndefelde, Dartmoor and the manor of Lydford. "Fyndefelde" is a reference to venville lands. These lay outside the Forest in border parishes such as Gidleigh and gave the farmers there rights within the Forest; the commons on the Moor (such as Gidleigh common) were also subject to the Duchy's control. Westcote has a chapter on "certain Tenants of the Forest called Fenfield-men" and describes their rights. [6] The other two areas singled out, Lydford and the royal Forest, were part of the Duchy lands and virtually synonymous by the early 16th century; they had the same boundaries, and the privileges that could be exercised within the Forest were expressed in terms of rights permitted within the manor of Lydford and subject to the jurisdiction of its court.

The other main aspect dealt with in the Letters Patent is that of the rights and duties of the tenants of the farms vis à vis Giles de Gydleghe as the lord of the manor of Gidleigh, and Giles's position as regards the Earl of Mortain and the services he was to perform in return for the grant.

We do not know what particular event caused the Letters to be drawn up and applied for. There is no special circumstance so far as is known relating to the Coades, who were in possession of Gidleigh at the time, which might have lead to the document. In the 16th century there was, however, an effort to systematise elements of medieval custom and it is during this period that the rights and privileges on Dartmoor came to be described with more elaboration. Since the opportunities to expand cultivation through exploiting waste land had been largely exhausted by this time, attention turned to determining existing rights and ensuring these were safeguarded.

While there were perhaps underlying factors that lead to the document being drawn up as a way

---

[5] Dartmoor Preservation Association, *The Rights of Common upon the Forest of Dartmoor and the Commons of Devon* contains much information on the early period.

[6] Westcote, p. 84.

of specifying rights, so that the position was established for all concerned, there remains the question of Giles de Gydleghe. Where does he come from? There is no mention of him before the Letters Patent. There is no satisfactory answer to this question. The Coades would of course have been aware that their title was derived by marriage and have had in their possession the deeds regulating the various marriage settlements. Such matters were given great attention and the Coades would have had the main papers relating to the marriages with the Moeles in 1323 and the Damarells in 1347, and known of the Prouzs before that. Westcote himself writes of a Robert le Pruz who, he says, married Johanne, heir of Giles de Gydleghe ; this le Pruz or his father was steward to Reginald Earl of Cornwall. [7] Between the documents and memories, the idea of this distant if not mythical ur-ancestor might have gained credence.

When seeking in the early 16th century to assert rights within Dartmoor and to safeguard their own position, the holders of land at Berrydown and the other farms, the venville tenants, might therefore have been confronted at Lydford by a demand from the King's men for proof of their rights or a threat to them. They would have had no legal document to hand setting out their customary rights on the Moor. Thus they might have been told something on the lines of "If you want to have your rights on the Moor recognised you will have to produce some proof of ancient title. And to get that confirmed you will need to obtain Letters Patent in your favour and accept the King's jurisdiction in the matter." This was very much how the emerging Tudor administration operated.

Local factors may also have played a part. Lists of manors enjoying venville rights were drawn up periodically by the Duchy. Since Gidleigh and Throwleigh had the same lord for much of the medieval period the two might have been regarded by the royal officials as one unit for venville purposes. In the account issued in 1505-1506, Gidleigh is not mentioned by name but only Throwleigh, which is recorded as paying 2s 6d as venville rent. At one stage Ensworthy appears to have been singled out for special mention (a similar development occurred in the case of Jurston at Chagford). Possibly the Gidleigh farmers felt therefore that they were being edged out and needed to reinforce their own claim There might have been a dispute over the share of the rent to be paid (it was paid by the vill collectively in most cases, not by individual farmers) or the extent of grazing rights, or over the boundary of Gidleigh common. It may be noted, however, that in the diagram attached to the "Instruccons for my Lord Prince" relating to Dartmoor, issued around 1540, the "men of Gydeley" are specifically mentioned,

---

[7] Westcote, p 403 and 431. Westcote writes that *"The daughter of Giles de Gidlegh brought it (Gidleigh) to the clarous family of Pruz, and so termed Dominus de Gidlegh; from him to Coad; and now by purchase to Batteshull,"* (p 403)

as well as those of Throwleigh.(The diagram is reproduced in Chapter Three.) In short, while Gidleigh is not mentioned in the 1505 accounts, the Letters Patent were issued in 1516 and Gidleigh was subsequently referred to. It is not possible to prove a cause and effect relationship but this at least was the sequence. Thus the Gidleigh farmers did eventually receive a degree of recognition of their status.

There may accordingly have been various grounds why the Gidleigh landowners were anxious to assert their rights. They might have feared that if they did nothing they might suffer serious loss. The King might claim rights in Gidleigh itself or its common. There is also the question of the "19 ferlings of land of Cornwall" (presumably a reference to land belonging to the Duchy, not the county) which is mentioned in the Charter as being attached to the manor of Gidleigh before the royal duchy was established. In these circumstances the holders of land in Gidleigh would have had a motive in demonstrating a title that dated from before 1337 when the Crown assumed control of Lydford and the Forest. Hence the search for the mysterious Giles de Gydleghe and a grantor, the Count of Mortain, from before the royal takeover. In that way the Gidleigh owners could escape too close an embrace by the Duchy and its royal master and show an independent basis from that of Throwleigh.

In considering the matter and their options the local farmers would certainly have felt that right and custom was on their side. Had they not been told by their grandfathers, who in turn had been told by their ancestors, that the men of Gidleigh had always grazed their cattle on the Moor? The Charter of 1204, granted by King John, permitted the deforestation of Devon (i.e. that the waste land could be used for farming) with the exception of Dartmoor and Exeter, where royal privileges were retained. It was nevertheless expressly stated in the Charter that the men of Devon and their heirs were granted "the customs within the regards of these Moors as they were accustomed to have" in the time of Henry I (1100-1135). The issue for the men of Gidleigh was thus how this was to be demonstrated or, which came to much the same thing, how it could be shown that they had rights which dated from before the transfer of the Duchy to the Black Prince in 1337. Hence the recourse to the Earl of Mortain. Accepting the lordship of the Count of Mortain did not entail any burden in practice since there no longer was such a person. Any dangers there might be on that score were covered in the document by a statement that the Count expressly bound himself and his successors not to interfere with rights on the venville lands. Such a restriction could also be applied therefore to the royal officials or to those to whom the King had granted a lease of the Forest.

A further consideration - very much the kind of notion that would have been present in the minds of the draftsmen who drew up the document - is the doctrine in English law of "time immemorial". It was given a precise legal meaning in a statute of Edward I and references to the doctrine are to be found in the proceedings to determine venville rights. [8] Anyone who could prove they had enjoyed a right continuously since the accession of Richard I had a prescriptive right to it. On these two legal bases therefore - the Royal Charter of 1204 preserving customary rights on Dartmoor and enjoyment since "time immemorial" - the men of Gidleigh had in fact good grounds for their claim in the 16th century.

That said, they still had to prove it of course. To make the account credible recourse had to be made to contemporaries of the 12th century Count and hence the detailed references to the occupiers of the farms (the claimants in effect). All the farms ("lands and tenements")mentioned were in existence by 1350 or earlier and certainly by 1516. The names used in the document were not those of the occupants in 1516 and resemble those in use in the first half of the 14th century, as recorded in Assize Rolls, but more as adaptations of such names than those actually to be found there. The acknowledgement that Giles and his heirs are to make to the Earl of Mortain each year, namely the submission of "one red rose at the feast of the birth of St John Baptist", together with the payment of 13 pence, is in fact the same as that used in 1329 when Alice de Moelys (the former Alice Prouz) granted a number of manors, including Gidleigh and Throwleigh, to William de Moelys. [9] ("Rendering therefor yearly one rose at the feast of the nativity of St John the Baptist in discharge of all service...").The reference to rendering a rose was not unusual in the 14th century but may be significant here. The transfer in 1329 included the advowson of Gidleigh Church which is also referred to in the purported Charter.

Overall the wording of the Charter reflects the practices of the first half of the 14th century and those current before 1337 at any event.The consistency of the document in that respect is such that the draftsman must certainly have been aware of what he was doing.

When the document is boiled down - regarded as a whodunit, who stood to gain, what was the motive? - the practical meaning is relatively straightforward.

(i) The holders of Berrydown, Creaber and the other farms sought to demonstrate that they had had rights on the commons and within the Forest from an early date. Since they are all named (including Forder) the result is confirmation that the whole manor (or vill) enjoyed venville rights. It

---

[8] Thus in an Inquisition held in 1382 the jurors found that *"the fines villarum ought to be paid by the tenants of divers vills next to the Forest of Dartmoor, from the time whereof memory is not, to the Lord the King..."* Cited in *Worth's Dartmoor*, p. 342.

[9] *Devon Fleet of Fines,* vol II, no 1199, p. 251

was necessary to include all the farms in order to establish that the whole vill was engaged.

(ii) They had these rights as regards both the lord of the manor and the Duchy of Cornwall.

(iii) In order to achieve this they had recourse (or perhaps there really was such a person) to Giles de Gydleigh, and to the Count of Mortain, neither of whom was in existence so that the obligations Giles was called upon to perform vis à vis the Count did not have any consequences.

This is what the result, quite subtly achieved, comes down to.

While the story is never likely to be clear in all its details, the general direction emerges. Since it involved what was in part obscure, and possibly deliberately so, the authors were perhaps never keen to spell the matter out further and relied briefly on the Letters Patent once these had been obtained. Thus it had become an "old story" by the time Westcote wrote in 1630 and a matter of which "some make doubt and question and some utterly denye," while Westcote himself simply recorded what he has seen. The impression he gives in his book is that of a man who wished to record what he had witnessed and it is unlikely that he would claim to have seen the document and its two seals unless he had actually done so. By the 17th century in any event the extent of legal rights, even those on the Moor, had moved on and titles were more clearly established than had appeared in the early years of Henry VIII, when something like our present system was emerging uncertainly from the rigidities and customs of earlier times.

In summary of the Letters Patent and the Charter, the position may be put as follows:

1. The weight of evidence that the Charter could not have been granted as early as the 12th century, such as in 1194 or 1156, is overwhelming and may be regarded as conclusive. The language and terms employed are drawn from usage in the first half of the 14th century.

2. The efforts to link the document with Bartholemew Gidley cannot be substantiated and do not fit the dates.

3. It seems probable that the Letters Patent themselves were issued in 1516. This concurs with the account given by Westcote and the content of the document and the royal seal. Exactly why the Letters were issued at that time we do not know for sure but the most likely explanation is that they were part of an effort by the men of Gidleigh to maintain their venville rights on the commons and within the Forest of Dartmoor. The reference to the grant by the Earl of Mortain to Giles de Gidleigh was the means to achieve that end.

BIBLIOGRAPHY

N Alcock, 'Devonshire Farm-houses, Part II', *Transactions of the Devonshire Association [Trans Dev Assoc]*, vol 101, (1969) p. 83

A Ainsworth, *West Country Larder,* (Peninsula, 1990)

J Amery and R Worth, 'Gidleigh Castle', *Trans Dev Assoc,* vol 57, (1925), p. 267

N de Baumgarten, 'Genealogies et marriages occidentaux des ruruikides russes du X au XII siecles', *Orientalia Christiana,* vol IX, no 35, (1927, Rome)

S Baring Gould, *Devon,* (Methuen 2nd ed. 1911), and *A Book of Dartmoor,* (Methuen, 1900)

P Beacham (ed), *Devon Building,* (Devon Books, 1990)

Billings, *Directory of Devon,* (1857), p. 102

Blake, 'Hooker's Synopsis Choreographical of Devonshire', *Trans Dev Assoc,* vol 47, (1915), p. 334

S Blaylock, *Gidleigh Castle: A Survey of the Standing Remains, 1991-1992,* (Exeter Museum Archaeological Field Unit, 1992)

G Boase and W Courtney, *Bibliotheca Cornubiensis,* vol I, (Longman Green, 1874)

W Brown, *Lydford Journey*

J Butler, *Dartmoor Atlas of Archaeology,* Vol Two: The North, (Devon Books, 1991)

B Cherry and N Pevsner, *The Buildings of England: Devon,* (Penguin, 1989)

M Cook (ed), *The Diocese of Exeter in 1821,* (Devon and Cornwall Records Society, 1960)

L Costello, 'The Bradford Pool Case', *Trans Dev Assoc,* vol 113, (1981), p. 59

L Court, *Some Devon Saints and Shrines,* (Morgan and Scott, 1921)

B Cresswell, *Notes on Devon Churches. The Fabric and Features of Interest in the Churches of the Deanery of Okehampton,* (1921)

W Crossing, *Echoes of an Ancient Forest,* Forest (reprint, 1994)

H Croxford, *A Walkabout Guide to Gidleigh,* (1988)

Dartmoor National Park Authority, *A Guide to the Archaeology of Dartmoor,* (Devon Books, 1996)

Dartmoor National Park Authority, *The Archaeology of Dartmoor from the Air,* (Devon Books, 1985)

Dartmoor Preservation Association, *The Rights of Common upon the Forest of Dartmoor and the Commons of Devon,* report of S Moore, (Plymouth, 1890)

L Deacon, *Hardy's Sweetest Image,* (Salisbury Poetry Circle, 1963)

L Deacon, *Tryphena and Thomas Hardy,* (Toucan, 1962)

'Holy Enterprises: Victorian Folk Religion at Chagford', *Devon & Cornwall Notes & Queries,* (Special Issue, 1996), p. 183

Devon County Council Planning Dept, *Devon's Traditional Buildings*

Reichel, Prideaux & Tapley-Soper (eds.) *Devon Fleet of Fines, vol. II, 1272-1369,* (Devon and Cornwall Records Society, 1939)

E Duffy, *The Stripping of the Altars,* (Yale, 1992)

G Dunstan (ed), *The Register of Edmund Lacy, Bishop of Exeter, 1420-1455.* (Devon and Cornwall Records Society, 1963)

E Gaskell, *Devonshire Worthies,* (Queenhithe, 1907)

S Gerrard, *Dartmoor,* (Batsford/English Heritage, 1997)

C Gill (ed), *Dartmoor : A New Study,* (David and Charles, 1970)

Todd Gray (ed), *Devon Documents,* (Devon & Cornwall Notes & Queries, 1996)

M Hardy, *A Short and Only Slightly Inaccurate Account of the History of Gidleigh and Gidleigh Castle,* (1996)

W Harrison, *Description of England,* (1580)

E Hemery, *High Dartmoor,* (Hale, 1983)

R Hingeston-Randolph (ed), *Episcopal Register of Bishop Bronescombe,* (Bell, 1889)

W Hoskins, *2000 years in Exeter,* (Phillimore, 1960)

W Hoskins, *Devon,* (David and Charles, 1972)

G Hughes, 'Gidleigh', *Trans Dev Assoc,* vol 79 (1947), p. 91

W Keble Martin, *Concise British Flora in Colour, and Flora of Devon,* (Ebury, 3rd ed. 1974)

H Loyn (ed), *Doomsday Book Studies,* (Alecto, 1987)

Lysons, *Magna Britannia,* (Cadell, 1832), vol 6

Manhood, *Treatise on the Laws of the Forest,* (1615)

W Marshall, *The Rural Economy of the West of England,* (1796)

C Moorehead, *Freya Stark,* (Penguin, 1985)

F Osborne, *The Churchwardens' Accounts of St Michael's Church, Chagford, 1480-1600,* (1979)

J Page, *An Exploration of Dartmoor,* (Seeley, 4th ed, 1895)

A Parreaux, *Daily Life in England in the Reign of George III*

Pole, *Collections towards a Description of the County of Devon,* (1791)

Polwhele, *History of Devonshire,* (1793), (reprinted Kohler & Coombes, 1977)

P Randall-Page, *Sculpture and Drawings* (1977-1992)

R Rankin, *Gidleigh Parish, A Rough Guide,* (2000)

M Ravenhill and M Rowe (ed), *Early Devon Maps,* (Devon Books, 2000)

J Rawson, 'Story of an Ancient Chapel', *Devon & Cornwall Notes & Queries,* (1920), p. 129 and 'The Earls of Mortain', *Devon & Cornwall Notes & Queries,* (1921), p. 1

O Reichel, 'The Hundred of South Tawton in Early Times', *Trans Dev Assoc,* vol 44, (1912), p. 343 and 'Extracts from the Pipe Rolls of Henry II relating to Devon', *Trans Dev Assoc,* vol 29, 1897, p. 453

Risdon, *Choreographical Description or Survey of the County of Devon,* (1811). (Reprinted Porcupine, 1970)

S Rowe, *A Perambulation of Dartmoor,* 3rd ed, (Devon Books, 1985)

A Sealby, *Dinah the Dartmoor Pony,* (Black, 1935)

R Sellman, *Aspects of Devon History,* (Devon Books, 1962)

J Skeaping, *Drawn from Life,* (Collins, 1977)

P Stafford, *Queen Emma and Queen Edith,* (Blackwell, 1997)

E Stanbrook, *Dartmoor Forest Farms,* (Devon Books, 1994)

M Stanbrook, *Old Dartmoor Schools Remembered,* (Quay, 1991)

R Stanes, *The Old Farm : A History of Farming Life in the West Country,* (Devon Books, 1990)

L Stone, *Road to Divorce,* (Oxford, 1990)

M Stoyle, *Locality and Loyalty,* (Univ of Exeter Press, 1994)

H Summerson (ed), 'Crown Pleas of the Devon Eyre of 1238', *Devon & Cornwall Notes & Queries,* (1985)

Swanton, *Anglo Saxon Prose.* (Everyman, 1996)

Thorns (ed), *Domesday Book : Devon,* (Phillimore, 1985)

T Tusser, *Five Hundred Points of Good Husbandry,* (1580)

G Vancouver, *General View of Agriculture of Devon,* (1801). (David & Charles, 1969)

E Varwell, *Throwleigh,* (S Lee, 1938)

Page (ed.) *Victoria History of Devon,* Part 2, (Constable, 1906).

I Walker, *Harold: the Last Anglo-Saxon King,* (Sutton, 1997)

E Waugh, *Diaries* (ed M Davie), (Penguin, 1979)

T Westcote, *A View of Devonshire in MDCXXX* ed. Rev G Oliver and Pitman Jones, (Exeter, 1845)

T Whale, 'Some Remarks on the Bounds of the Forest of Dartmoor, with special references to the Parishes of Throwleigh, Chagford and Gidleigh', *Trans Dev Assoc,* vol 25, 1893, p. 510 and *Trans Dev Assoc,* vol 33, (1901), p. 393

P Whiteaway, *The Tale of Berrydown*

W White, *History, Gazeteer and Directory of Devonshire, 1850.* (Reprinted Kelley, 1968)

A Williams, *The English and the Norman Conquest,* (Boydell, 1995)

S Winholt, *Devon*

S Woods, *Dartmoor Stone,* (Devon Books, 1988)

G Worgan, *Agriculture of Cornwall,* (1809)

R Handsford Worth, *Worth's Dartmoor* (David and Charles, 1981)

INDEX

Abrahall   137

Aggett   18, 24-5, 41, 48-9, 54, 66, 89, *102,* 142, 148, 150

Alford   75, *101,* 115, 127-131, 134, 137, 175

All Hallows School   59-61, 63, 83, 156

Almond   73, 76

Ash, Aysh   13, 45, 88, 113, 119, 132

Aveton Gifford   11

Barford   84

Barnett   84-5

Battishill   12, 30, 180, 188, 190

Batworthy   7, 57, 66, 80, *99, 102,* 142, 155-9, 175, 177

Baycock   29, 111-2, 154, 181

Bayley   38, 56

Bazley   25

Beating the Bounds   59, *103,* 168-9

Beddow   26

Beer, Bere   46, 113

Bell   39

Belstone   116, 119

Belworthy   111, 156

Bennet, Bennett   77, 88, 108, 147, 156, 167

Bentham   49, 123

Bentinck   75, 78, 113

Benwell   63-4

Berrydown   12, 15, 17, 24, 57-9, 61, 64, 79-85, 171, 173, 175-7, 184, 187, 190, 192

Berrydown Cottage   85

Berrydown Nursery   83-4, 176

Bexson   90

Bideford   1, 28, 122

Birch   42

Bishop   102

Blackaton   13-4

Black Death   12, 172

Blaylock   29

Bond   41, 142, 154

Bourne   64

Bovey Tracey   31, 115

Bowden   18, 44, 46-8, 113, 175

Bradford Pool   14-6, 43, 56

Bragg   73-4, 113

Brett Young   113

Brimblecombe   41, 82, 111, 119, 123

Brimstone Down   19, 62, 155-6, 175, 177

Broadmead   152-4

Brock   18, 32, 53, 57, 114, 132, 141-3, 147-8, 150, 175

Bromell   46, 48-50, *102,* 123

Bronescombe   26, 179

Budd   157-8

Burnard   30, 155

Buttern   7, 59, *91, 94,* 122, 134-7, 175

Callis   117

Canute   6

Castle Farm   39, 41, *98,* 130

Chagford   9, 13, 15, 17, 25, 29, 37, 43, 46, 48-9, 51, 56, 60, 62, 64, 73, 75, 78-9, 81, 83-4, 87, 113, 115, 121-3, 145-6, 155, 159, 162, 169, 173-6

Chapple   12, 24-5, 35, *99,* 115, 117, 132, 137-147, 152, 154, 171, 175, 177, 184, 187

Cheriton Bishop   158

Cherryford 64

Chudleigh 42

Civil War 13, 14

Cleminson 32, 54, 69, 72

Coade 11-2, 30, 180, 189, 190

Coldstone 42, 46

Condé Nast 38

Cook 27, 68

Cornish 53, 57, 157

Cornwall, Duchy of, Earl of 11, 59, 163, 165-7, 183, 187,191, 193

Costello 14, 43

Crawford 31, 168-9

Creaber 7, 12, 15, 35, 43, 56, 82, 90, 132, 148, 167, 171, 174-5, 177, 184, 187, 192. North Creaber 45, 64-9, *96*, 113. South Creaber 69-76, 89

Creaber Cottage 47, 77-9

Crediton 22, 111

Cresswell 31, 188

Croxford 27

Cullen 58, 62, 112

Damarell, Daumerle, D'Aumale 11, 30, 179, 190

Dartmoor Commoners 25, 58, 85, 162, 165, 168-170, 176

Dartmoor National Park Authority 7, 19, 25, 64, 75, 155-6, 159, 170, 176

Dartmoor Preservation Association 155, 166-7, 189

Dartmouth 28, 122

Dasher *101*, 128-30

Date 53, 123, 148-9

Domesday Book 8, 9, 161-2, 172

Donkeys Corner 123

Downe 80, 107

Drewe 78

Drewsteignton 14, 29, 112, 122

Dunning, Denning, Dunning Morris 13, 18, 32, 70, 72, 76, 89, 127, 148, 158

Dunstan 26-7

Edith (AEdgytha) 8-9, 22-3, 32

Edwards 119, 153-4

Endacott, Eudecott, Endicott, Endycott 18-9, 25, 32, 37, 41-2, 45-6, 48, 53, 57, 61, 66-8, 72, 82-3, *96, 102,* 111-3, 116, 119, 122-3, 127, 141, 147, 150, 155-6, 175

Ensworthy, Avenesworth, Afenysworth 12, 17, 59, 83, 115, 127, 130-4, 148, 167, 171, 173, 175, 177, 184, 187, 190

Ensworthy Cottage 122

Exeter 1, 8, 9, 16-7, 22, 28, 46, 47, 52-3, 77, 87, 152, 157

Fernworthy 60, 73, 74, 76, 122, 169

Field names 45, 57, 68, 72, 79, 88-9, 111, 113-4, 119, 133, 141-2, 155, 157, 177

Finch 24

Fisher 137

Ford 60-1, 132

Forder 12, 17, 19, 25, 27, 48, 124, 131, 173, 184, 187, 192, North Forder 17, 117, 150-2, South Forder 17, 117, 147-9

Forestry Plantation 38, 176

Fox-Pitt 26, *95*, 144-5, 148-9

Gaillard-Bundy 24, 62, 156

Gallimore 76

Gatcombe 11

Gay, Gaye 57, 107, 141, 147, 150

Gerrard 7, 169

Gidleigh Castle, Barton and Castle House 11, 16-7, 19, 28-34, 43, 46, 54-5, 68-9, 72, 82, *92, 93,* 126, 130, 169, 173, 175, 177

Gidleigh Comon ESA 176

Gidleigh Cottage 39-41, *106*, 130

Gidleigh Lodge 47-50, 130, 176

Gidleigh Mill 15, 19, 41, 43-7, 68, 150, 174

Gidleigh Park 18, 25, 33-8, 41,42, 47, 51, 76, 82-3

Gidleigh Pound 30

Gidleigh Tor 38, 122

Gidley, Bartholemew (and family) 14-8, 25, 30-2, 43, 57, 70, 82, 108, 110, 180, 187-8, 193

Gidley King 17-8

Giles de Gydleghe 10, 181-191

Gill 9, 121, 163, 169
Glebe Farm 27, 68, 107-113, 126, 142
Godwin the Priest 9, 22, 26, 27
Godwine, Earl 8, 23
Gould, Baring 36, 135, 155
Grandisson 146
Gray, Todd 35, 109
Greenaway 12, 19, 25-6, 70, 85-90, 112, 143, 171, 174-5, 177, 184, 187
Grumley-Grennan 113
Gytha, Gydda 8, 9, 22-3, 32

Hamilton Smith 31, 33
Hamlet 175-6
Hammer 156
Hannaford 1, 122
Hardy, M,S 30, 32
Hardy, Thos 50
Harold, King 8, 32
Harvey 42-3, 112
Hatherleigh 30, 31, 109
Hawkes 132
Hayter-Hames 73, 76
Hazlewood 134, 154-5
Henderson 17, 37-8
Henry VIII 10, 23, 183-6, 188, 189, 193
Hill 18, 25, 41, 50-2, 54, 59, 66, 69, *102*, 111-2, 115-6, 119, 122, 127-130, 133-4, 141-3, 148, 150, 159, 174
Hingston 123-6
Hittisleigh 29, 112
Hollander 47-48
Holman 46, 51, 54, 72, 112, 116, 130, 135, 154-5
Holwill 30
Holy Trinity Church, Gidleigh 12, 13, 17, 22-9, 44, 58, 80, *92, 99,* 107, 123, 130, 152, 154-5, 157-8, 185-7, 192
Church Lands Trust 28-9, 148, 150
Rectors 26-7, 54-5, 179-181
Hooker 109, 169, 172
Hooper 39
Hoskins 10, 19, 170-1
Holy street 18, 35

Hughes 38, 123, 158, 187
Hurdle 137, 175
Hutchins 75, 156, 174

Jackson 116-7, 115
Jordan 90, 119-120, 122, 175-6
Jurston 122, 190
Jury 29

Keble Martin 152-3
Kelly's Directory 19
Kestor 7, 60, 113, 155, 159
Kestorway 62, 156
Kingsland 48, 63, 89, 102
Kingsteignton 18, 31
Knapman 13, 16, 46, 66, 118, 141, 154
Kyle 145

Leaman 47, 111, 114-5, 133-4
Lee 42, 88, 143, 147, 158
Leedom 64
Leman 174
Lentern 59, 64, 115, 134, 143, 154
Little Berrydown 84-5
Little Ensworthy 19, *100,* 127-131, 174
Loram 83
Lostwithiel 119, 186, 188
Lower Ensworthy 174
Lower Park 59, 63-4
Loyn 9
Lustleigh 11
Lydford 11, 80, 115, 163, 165, 167-8, 174, 184-6, 189, 191
Lyon Smith 75, 123, 144-5
Lysons 10

MacIver 90, 123
Madgwick 62, 72
Manaton 74, 112
Mann 63, 158
Manwood 66
Mariners Way 25, 28, *105,* 122

Martyn	117, 147
May	81, 84
Mayne	37, 47-8, 68-9, 134
McIlwraith	18, 32, 36-7, 39, 42, 47, 50, *102*, 181
Mid-Devon Hunt	56, 58, 73-6, 155
Mill End	47
Milton	32, 54, 72, 84
Moeles	11, 30, 147, 179, 190, 192
Moortown	12, 70, 83, 90, 117-122, 127, 142, 146, 171, 173-5, 184, 187
Moore	42, 55-6, 77, 84, 111, 141
Moretonhampstead	17, 73, 87, 90, 122, 134, 157, 174
Mortain, Earl of	9-10, 179, 183-4, 186, 191, 193
Mortimore	41, 46, 63, *97*, 143, 174
Murchington	64, 69, 72, 82, 117,
Murray	131
Nailor	*102*
Nash	35, 53, 61
Newcombe	28, 53, 111, 113, 119
Newton	32
Newton Abbot	31, 58
Nickell	145
Nielsen	145
Norrington	58, 62-3, 148
North Cadbury	11
Northcott	46, 53, 113, 132, 155-6
Northmore	44-5, 63, 76, 89, 135, 148, 150
Norton	24
Okehampton	17, 29, 32, 36, 43, 45-6, 56, 60, 69, 73, 109, 121, 132-3, 154
Old Rectory, The	27, 32, 51, 54-6
Osborne	13, 30, 39, 41, 57, *98*, 111, 142, 150, 152
Packard	72, 77
Page	25, 41
Parr	75
Pennington	24
Perrott	158
Perryman	141, 158
Pevsner	10, 23
Pole	10
Polwhele	10, 136
Poor Law, Parish Overseers	28, 70-2, 89, 112, 134, 142, 148
Postbridge	73-4
Princetown	73
Prinsep	38, 82
Prouz, Pruz, Prouse	10-1, 18, 26, 29-30, 163, 165, 170-2, 179, 190
Providence	41, 42, 46, 68, 83, 112
Pybus	113
Rankin	19, 64, 174
Rattray	16, 180
Rawson	11, 54, 123, 146-7, 181, 187
Reichel	8, 12, 188
Rice	42, 83
Risdon, Ryesdon	10, 13, 88, 132
Roberton	84
Rogers	31, 168-9
Round Pound	7, 60, 159
Rowe, Roo	13, 16-7, 55-6, 61, 64, 78-81, 84, 113, 116, 124, 141, 142-3, 157, 163, 165, 173-4
Rowe-Leete	55-6, 62, 76
Sampson	18, 26, 28, 53, 66, 88-9, 112, 114, 143, 148, 174
Sampford Courtney	13, 132, 174
Scorhill	7, 12, 15, 24, 56, 62-3, 80, 83, 143, 148, 156-8
Scorhill Circle	7, 56, 60, *101*
Scott	13, 46, 53-5, 122, 181
Sellman	28
Shovel Down	7
Sillem	72-3, 89-90
Skeaping	47, 77-9, 154
Skeats	43, 46, 52
Skewes	107, 112
Skilton	47, 53, 174
Smallwood	53, 145-6, 175
Southard, Southward	31-2
South Zeal	46, 48, 51, 73, 76, 89, 113, 122, 148, 154, 167
Sparks	50

Spreyton   29, 51, 72, 112, 154
Spiller   41, 73, 76
Squire   64
Stafford   8
Stanbrook   31, 169
Stanbury   18
Stanes   88, 109, 121
Stark   57, 175
Sticklepath   39, 77
Stoyle   14
Summerson   26
Swanton   146
Swift   156

Tavistock   82
Tawton   8, 9, 152, 154
Teign, Teignhead Farm   156, 168-9
Teign, River   16, 34-6, 38, 147, 155, 159
Terry   83, 134
Thorn   9
Throwleigh   9, 11, 13, 18, 21, 25, 27, 29, 32, 42,
                        45-6, 48, 52, 65, 72, 75, 83, 107,
                        109-111, 113-4, 117, 119, 122, 147-9, 154
Thule, Thewyll, Thowle, Thuele   12, 70, 89, 109, 113-5, 119,
                        134, 171, 173, 174, 184, 187
Tincombe, Tencombe   13, 56, 117
Tithes, Tithe Commission 27-8, 48-9, 60, 168-9
Townsend   158, 175
Trounsell   54, 181
Turpin   41, 66, 143

Underhill   53-4, 118-9, 127, 131
United States   31, 37, 42, 129, 152, 174
Urmston   41, 145

Vallance   18, 61, 102, 115, 134, 143, 152
Vancouver   121
Van der Steen   43, 66, 68, 134
Varwell   21, 113
Venville rights   64-5, 70, 132, 164-7, 170,
                        183, 185, 189-190, 192-3

Venn   32
Vicary   52, 58-63, 134, 155-6, 181
Village Hall   2, 18, 25, 35-6, 48, 50-4, 90, 102, 130, 169, 171
Vogwell   13, 24-5, 70, 117, 141, 147, 150

Walker   8, 9, 115-6
Wallabrook   8, 16, 104, 163
Warren Inn   74, 78, 89, 113
Watern Coombe   14, 16
Watrous   156
Waugh   37
Way Cottage   32, 42-3, 106, 130
Webber   18, 54, 59-62, 91, 94, 97, 112, 122,
                        123, 127, 134-5, 137, 139, 143, 148, 154
Weir   145
Wells   1, 43, 73, 76-7, 83, 146
West   85
Westcote, Thos   10, 13, 183, 187, 189, 190, 193
Westcott   53, 66, 157, 175
Whale   12, 173
Whateley   123
Whipham   18, 24, 31, 35-6, 52, 76, 123, 174, 180-1, 184
White   35, 90, 118, 122
Whiteaway   81, 84
Whiteleagh   11
Widecombe   11, 74
Widworthy   11
Winkleigh   14, 30, 152
Wilkinson   83-4
Williams   8
Winbolt   37
Wonnacott   148
Wonson   16, 25, 45-6, 48, 76, 135, 148, 150
Woodland Trust   176
Woollcombe   85
Worgan   120
Worth   65, 69, 149
Wyllie   26